1983

A CONSTITUTIONAL HISTORY OF THE UNITED STATES

OTHER BOOKS
BY FORREST McDONALD

Alexander Hamilton: A Biography

The Presidency of Thomas Jefferson

The Phaeton Ride: The Crisis of American Success

The Presidency of George Washington

*The Last Best Hope: A History of the United States
(with Thomas P. Govan and Leslie E. Decker)*

*The Boys Were Men: The American Navy in the
Age of Fighting Sail*

Enough Wise Men: The Story of Our Constitution

Confederation and Constitution, 1781–1789

*The Torch Is Passed: The United States in the
Twentieth Century*

*E Pluribus Unum: The Formation of the
American Republic 1776–1790*

Empire and Nation

Insull

We the People: The Economic Origins of the Constitution

*Let There Be Light: The Electric Utility
Industry in Wisconsin*

A CONSTITUTIONAL HISTORY OF THE UNITED STATES

FORREST McDONALD

THE UNIVERSITY OF ALABAMA

WITH THE ASSISTANCE OF
Ellen S. McDonald

A GROLIER COMPANY

FRANKLIN WATTS
NEW YORK   LONDON   TORONTO   SYDNEY

Special thanks to
ALICE ANN BOSWELL, BETH KELLUM,
RUSTY LOFTIN, HAL TURNER,
and ROY WEST.

Franklin Watts
730 Fifth Avenue
New York, New York 10019

Library of Congress Cataloging in Publication Data

McDonald, Forrest.
    A constitutional history of the United States.

    Bibliography: p.
    Includes index.
    1. United States—Constitutional history.
2. Trade regulation—United States—History.
I. McDonald, Ellen Shapiro. II. Title.
KF4541.M35   342.73′029   81-11620
ISBN 0-531-05420-9   347.30229   AACR2

CONTENTS

PREFACE   3

1 WE THE PEOPLE...   9

    Evolution of the Compact Theory   10
    The First Written Constitutions   17
    Inadequacies of the Early Constitutions   22
    The Philadelphia Convention   26
    The Political Philosophy of the Constitution   31

**2 EARLY CONSTITUTIONAL ISSUES AND
THEIR RESOLUTIONS, 1789–1807**   35

    Filling in the Constitution   36
    Constitutional Issues Settled by Means Other   42
      Than Adjudication
    Judicial Determination of Constitutional Issues   48
    The Marbury Case and the Attack on the Courts   55
    Who Determines Constitutionality?   60

3 THE CONSTITUTION AND THE NEW ECONOMIC ORDER   **65**

The Economic Transformation   66
The National Government as Promoter of   69
Economic Development
The Commerce and Contract Clauses Under the   74
Marshall Court
Economic Issues and the Taney Court   83
The Direction of Constitutional Law Concerning   89
the Economy

4 FEDERAL–STATE RELATIONS   **93**

Defiance of Federal Authority to 1816   94
State Challenges to the Marshall Court, 1816–1832   100
The Nullification Controversy   106
States' Rights, Slavery, and the Taney Court   109
The *Booth* Cases   117

5 CIVIL WAR, RECONSTRUCTION, AND THE FREEDMAN   **121**

The Constitutional Nature of the War   122
Constitutional Issues of the War   125
Reconstruction: Political   131
Reconstruction: The Court   136
Civil War and Reconstruction: The Constitutional   145
Outcome

6 THE CONSTITUTION IN THE AGE OF INDUSTRIALIZATION   **147**

In the Matter of Race   150
Economic Regulation: The States   155
Economic Regulation: The Federal Government   160
The Expansion of Federal Regulation   165

**7 FOUNDATIONS OF A CONSTITUTIONAL
REVOLUTION: 1910–1937**   **175**

Economic Regulation   179
Foreign Affairs   185
In the Matter of Civil Liberties   189
The Challenge of the New Deal   193

**8 CONSTITUTIONAL REVOLUTION:
1937–1957**   **201**

The New Deal Court   202
The Mushrooming of Government   206
The Problem of Civil Liberties   210
Negro Rights Reconsidered   217
The Bricker Amendment   224

9 BREAKDOWN   **229**

Of the People   230
Of the Legislative Branch   234
Of the Executive Branch   237
Of the Judiciary   241
Of the Federal System   246
   and the Separation of Powers

**THE CONSTITUTION OF THE UNITED
STATES**   **255**

**JUSTICES OF THE UNITED STATES
SUPREME COURT**   **279**

GLOSSARY OF TERMS   **283**

TABLE OF CASES   **289**

INDEX   **297**

A
CONSTITUTIONAL
HISTORY
OF
THE
UNITED
STATES

PREFACE

*T*his work is designed primarily to be used in an undergraduate survey course of American constitutional history. It is as comprehensive and as accurate as I could make it within the framework of that design; it is by no means, however, as full, as technical, or as detailed as the large tomes—such as those of McLaughlin, Hockett, Swisher, and Kelly and Harbison—that were used over the years when constitutional history was a bread-and-butter course in graduate departments of political science and history.

There are two main reasons for the decision to approach the subject in this way. The first is that, as every scholar in the field is aware, there has been a "knowledge explosion" in this area of study in recent years. Virtually every old generalization has been overturned or at least subjected to many qualifications; any effort to incorporate all the new knowledge in the old format would require a volume so large and detailed as to be unreadable. On the other hand, there is, I believe, a need for a short interpretive work that offers new generalizations to explain as much of the new material as possible. This I have attempted to write.

The second reason is related to the first. It is a sad fact of life in contemporary America that reading is neither the favorite activity nor the most common skill among college students. It is pointless to write a book or assign it to students if they are unwilling or unable to read it. This book is written to be read—which, in my experience, requires brevity as well as simplicity both conceptually and in terms of vocabulary. I have tested it in manuscript form with my own undergraduates; for every word that gave them trouble, I found a more common one, and for every concept that proved difficult for them, I rewrote until they found the idea clear and readily comprehensible. In addition, a glossary of terms is included at the end of the text.

If a supplement to this book should be desired, the most useful supplement, in my judgment, is a short casebook; I have found Stanley I. Kutler's *The Supreme Court and the Constitution: Readings in American Constitutional History* (New York: Norton, 1977) to be highly serviceable. Beyond that, five or six books or articles are recommended at the end of each chapter. No effort has been made to compile a definitive bibliography or to include highly technical works. Rather, the first criterion has been readability tempered by reliability; and several works have been suggested because they are stimulating, present fresh points of view, and so on. Thus, for instance, Julius Goebel's monumental study of the origins of the Supreme Court to 1801—an extremely learned book, which no undergraduate would voluntarily attempt to read and which few could understand if they did—has not been recommended. Walter Berns' fresh, penetrating, and provocative study of the First Amendment, on the other hand, has been.

A word about the focus and organization of the book is in order. The subject is the history of the Constitution, which I understand to mean (a) the makeup of the complex and fluid system of government in America and (b) the law that governs that system of government. The focus is thus by no means exclusively upon the history of the Supreme Court's decisions. Indeed, for the better part of the first century of American history under the Constitution, the Supreme Court made no claim to being the sole or final arbiter of what the Constitution meant. That fact has dictated the somewhat unusual plan of organization I have followed. The first chapter extends from the colonial period through the establishment of the Constitution, with an emphasis upon the evolution of constitutional theory. The second, extending from 1789 to 1807, is concerned with the crucial question, who determines constitutionality—the answer to which, despite *Marbury* v. *Madison*, was a plural one. Chapters 3 and 4, instead of following the conventional pattern of dealing first with the Marshall Court and then with the Taney Court, cover the period up to the 1850s from two different perspectives. Chapter 3 deals with the constitutional questions relating to the nation's economic development and transformation during those years; Chapter 4 covers the same years and is concerned with federal–state relations. The subsequent chapters cover single time-blocs—but, again, despite the growing power of the Court after the Civil War, I have periodized not by courts but in accordance with my interpretation of general constitutional developments.

Finally, a personal note may be useful. I am generally regarded as a "conservative" historian; and though I have no quarrel with the classification, I have found that it often leads to confusion, among conservatives and non-conservatives alike, for "conservatism" means many things to many people. In any event, I have not set out to write a conservative interpretation of constitutional history. I have, however, written with a point of view. I agree with William Gladstone, the great British statesman, that the United States Constitution is "the most wonderful work ever struck off at any given time by the brain and purpose of man." I share Jefferson's belief that it is the right and duty of all branches of the federal government and of the states as well—and not just of the federal judiciary—to guard the Constitution against encroachments. Yet I also share Hamilton's belief in "loose construction" and the proposition that an independent federal judiciary is indispensable to the preservation of the system. I have no objection to "judicial activism" if that activism is governed by the letter and spirit of the Constitution.

Within the framework of that set of values and attitudes, I have striven to be objective. Thus no reader should be surprised to find I have treated sympathetically, though not uncritically, a wide range of constitutional positions—those of both Hamilton and John C. Calhoun, of both John Marshall and Roger Brooke Taney, of both the late nineteenth-century Court and the New Deal Court. Nor should anyone be surprised to find that I am less than sympathetic to the tendencies of recent Supreme Court decisions.

Forrest McDonald

The time may ere long arrive when the minds of men will be prepared to make an offer to recover the Constitution, but the many cannot now be brought to make a stand for its preservation.

Alexander Hamilton

1
WE
THE
PEOPLE...

*D*uring the early years of the American Republic it was said that the United States had a government of laws, not of men. In the Old World, government had been arbitrary: Within broad limits, the ruler did as he pleased, and it was unthinkable that anyone should attempt to tell a king or queen what he or she could or could not do. In England, from which Americans derived most of their ideas about proper government, the exercise of power was limited by tradition as embodied in the common law and an unwritten, "mixed" constitution. But, from the American point of view, those safeguards proved inadequate to protect them from arbitrary rule. They sought further protection within the framework of the British Empire, and, that failing, they declared themselves independent from Britain. Upon doing so, they determined that their own governments should be bound by law, as set down in written constitutions.

That decision had profound implications: It made possible the development in America of the freest system of government that had ever been devised. But the decision was not reached suddenly, and it was not easy to implement. It raised a question that was not easily answered: If government is to be controlled by law, who determines what that law shall be? Working out the answers to this and a host of related questions was a long and difficult process.

EVOLUTION OF THE COMPACT THEORY

The Declaration of Independence, though having no legal or constitutional status of its own, lays down the fundamental principles on which government in America would be established. The document is ambiguous on a number of subjects, but on two vital points—the legitimate function of government and the legitimate source of governmental power—it is clear. The proper *function* of government is to protect the natural rights of man, which derive from God and can neither be given away nor taken away but can be, and in the absence of government are likely to be, transgressed by unprincipled individuals or groups. The legitimate *source* of government authority is the consent of the governed as expressed in a written or implicit compact between the rulers and the ruled. If any government systematically violates the rights it is instituted to protect or repeatedly violates the terms of the compact, it is the right and duty of the people to abolish it and to create a new government on whatever basis—monarchical, aristocratic, democratic, or mixed—"seems most likely to effect their safety and happiness."

These were radical new principles, and in embracing them Americans not only departed from their own colonial experience but instituted a *novus ordo seculum*, a new order for the ages. It is true that temporary governments had been created by compact. In 1620 the adult males on board the *Mayflower*, lying off the New England coast outside the domain of either the Virginia Company of London (under whose auspices they had sailed) or the government of England, found themselves without any recognized authority. Accordingly, they signed an agreement whereby they "solemnly and mutually in the Presence of God and one another, covenant and combine ourselves together into a civil Body Politic." The Plymouth Colony was governed by the Mayflower Compact for the next seventy-one years. Meanwhile, colonists established at least three other governments by similar compacts—those of Providence, Connecticut, and New Haven. But none of these governments was based upon natural-rights theory, none was permanent, and none was recognized under English law. That of Plymouth was effectively repealed by making it part of the colony of Massachusetts Bay, those of Providence and Connecticut were made legitimate only by royal charters, and that of New Haven was absorbed into the charter government of Connecticut.

The only source of colonial government that was recognized as legitimate in America was the Crown of England—not the people, not settlers contracting among themselves, not Crown and settlers compacting mutually, but the Crown alone. Two of the thirteen colonies, Connecticut and Rhode Island, were corporations chartered by the Crown. Three of them, Pennsylvania, Delaware, and Maryland, were "proprietary" colonies in which the Crown had, in effect, granted royal authority to individuals, William Penn and Charles Calvert. The governments of all the other colonies had begun, directly or derivatively, with either corporate charters or proprietary grants, which were subsequently annulled. Thenceforth, these "royal colonies" were ruled by the Crown through appointed governors and judges and legislatures (in part locally elected) authorized by the Crown.

And not only was the Crown the *source* of all legitimate authority, it more or less established the *forms* of the colonial governments as well. The government of each colony mirrored, in a general sort of way, that of the parent government in England. Each had a governor corresponding to, and in most colonies appointed by, the English monarch; each had either a governor's council or an upper house of the legislature, usually appointed in England and corresponding to the hereditary House of Lords; each had an elected lower house of the legislature whose members were, as in the mother country, chosen by voters with certain minimal amounts of property from the ranks of people who had higher property qualifications. Finally, each colony had a variety of courts whose makeup, jurisdictions, and authority were so complex as almost to defy description.

How, then, did Americans come by 1776 to accept a theory of government that differed so strikingly from their historical experience? The answer lies in the events of the decade and a half before independence. To put it simply, the British government was determined to adopt a number of new policies and measures which many colonists regarded as unacceptable. Lacking any authoritative institutional means of registering their protests—no written constitution to point to, no Supreme Court to appeal to—the disaffected colonists groped for arguments to justify their opposition. Those arguments were developed randomly at first, proceeding by fits and starts, but they gradually took on a pattern and steadily became more radical. By the time they came into full focus and reached a climax in 1776, they had assumed a form that almost precluded the establishment, or preservation, of stable government.

The first step in the argument was taken in 1761, when the Massachusetts lawyer James Otis employed the principles of natural law in the celebrated *Writs of Assistance* case. The idea of natural law was an ancient one. Its premise was that "right reason," or the "immediate and intuitive apprehension of moral and spiritual values"—in other words, knowledge of what is right and just and of what is wrong and unjust—was placed by God in all men; and no legislative enactment or royal order could change what is right and what is wrong. In the eighteenth century the idea of natural law was popularized as the basis of a "science" of government and international law, most notably by the work of the great Swiss theorist Emmerich de Vattel (1758). But Otis gave natural law a new application, using it as a ground for striking down an Act of Parliament. Under British law, customs officials could obtain writs of assistance granting general authority to search anywhere for smuggled goods—unlike search warrants, which must describe what is being looked for, where it is to be sought, and why it is expected to be found there—but those writs expired six months after the death of the king during whose reign they were issued. When British customs officials in Boston routinely sought new writs of assistance after the death of George II, Otis, as counsel for a local merchant, argued that they were "unconstitutional" because their blanket authority was contrary to natural justice and therefore was against God's will. "Should an Act of Parliament be against any of His natural laws," Otis contended, "their declaration would be contrary to eternal truth, equity, and justice, and consequently void." The argument was persuasive, but Chief Justice Thomas Hutchinson deferred a decision until he could find out more about the law in England; and, though Otis lost the case, the idea of appealing to natural law as a means of contesting acts of Parliament was rapidly picked up by lawyers in the other colonies.

The next two steps in the development of the American argument came in response to the Stamp Act, which was passed by Parliament in March 1765 and immediately set off loud protests in the colonies. The main challenge to the act, written by the Philadelphia lawyer John Dickinson and adopted in the resolutions of the Stamp Act Congress (October 1765), was the "rights of Englishmen" argument. The colonists, as faithful subjects, were entitled "to all the inherent rights and liberties" of natural-born subjects in Great Britain; one of those rights was that they could not be taxed except with their consent, granted "personally or by their representatives"; and as their local circumstances prevented them from being represented in Parliament, they could not be taxed except by their own colonial legislatures. A related argument, advanced by Patrick Henry in the Virginia Resolves the same year, added the claim that Virginia was immune to parliamentary taxes by the terms of its orginal royal charter.

Parliament repealed the Stamp Act in 1766, but at the same time it passed the Declaratory Act. Rejecting colonial efforts to limit its power by appeals to natural law, to rights of Englishmen, or to charter provisions, Parliament declared that it had "full power and authority to make laws and statutes of sufficient force and validity to bind the colonies and people of America, subjects of the crown of Great Britain, in all cases whatsoever." A year later, as if to add emphasis to this declaration, Parliament passed the Townshend Duties, taxing American importations of paper, glass, paint, lead, and tea.

In the face of that unqualified declaration, amounting almost to an ultimatum, few Americans were disposed to challenge the new taxes. Then John Dickinson came up with yet another argument, one that was powerfully persuasive. In an unsigned series of newspaper articles entitled *Letters from a Farmer in Pennsylvania*—which were republished and read throughout America and in much of Britain as well—Dickinson worked his way around the Declaratory Act with what may be called the constitutional argument. Drawing on his vast and deep knowledge of English law and history, Dickinson demonstrated that Parliament's powers were limited by the unwritten but traditional English constitution and showed—to the satisfaction of American readers—that the Townshend Duties clearly violated that constitution. And, as most Americans knew by now, even if they knew nothing else of English law, the celebrated English jurist Sir Edward Coke had long ago ruled (in *Dr. Bonham's* case, 1606) that whenever Parliament passed an act contrary to the traditional constitution "the common law will control it, and judge such an act to be void."

Unfortunately for Americans seeking a legitimate way to resist parliamentary legislation, that view was obsolete in England. The modern view there was in keeping with what would come to be called positive law: That the law in England was whatever Parliament said it was, even if it was contrary to the "constitution," the common law, and tradition. As Sir William Blackstone had put it in the first volume of his then recently published (1765) *Commentaries on the Laws of England*—a masterful treatise that was read by almost every American lawyer and many who were not lawyers—"if the parliament will positively enact a thing to be done which is unreasonable, I know of no power in the ordinary forms of the constitution, that is vested with authority to control it." Parliament could, in short, require of all persons subject to its authority anything that was not "naturally impossible."

There was only one place the American position could be taken from there if it was to remain within "the ordinary forms of the constitution" or, indeed, within the framework of any conception of law. The pivotal question arising from Blackstone's pronouncement was whether Parliament's authority extended to the colonies. Thus far, the colonies had conceded that it did in some cases (notably the power to regulate trade among the various parts of the empire) but not in others (notably the powers to control the internal affairs of the colonies and to tax them). Englishmen had generally belittled the American claims, and Blackstone had demolished them. Accordingly, in the late 1760s and early 1770s increasing numbers of Americans began to deny that Parliament had any authority over the colonies. Perhaps the best-known statement of that position was made by John Adams in 1773. The royalist governor of Massachusetts, Thomas Hutchinson, had said that he knew "of no line that can be drawn between the supreme authority of Parliament and the total independence of the colonies." Adams replied that if there were no such line the colonies must be independent, for otherwise they would be slaves of Parliament.

But the implications of denying the authority of Parliament were not, as yet, so drastic: Americans still professed (and most of them strongly felt) loyalty toward the king. That they could do so was mystifying to Englishmen, for government in the mother country had become one of "Crown *in* Parliament," whereby the Crown, the Lords, and the Commons functioned together under the leadership of the king's ministers. In other words, the American notion that the three traditional branches were, or should be, entirely separate—derived from the writings of the Frenchman Montesquieu and the man who most influenced Montesquieu's thinking on the subject, the English Tory Viscount Bolingbroke—was as obsolete as the belief that the authority of Parliament was limited by the constitution. In any event, Americans now took the position that Parliament and the various colonial legislatures were co-equal bodies, all of which owed allegiance to a common Crown.

The logical implication of that position, in turn, was clear. If the colonists sought a legal means of resisting Parliament's unconstitutional efforts to legislate for them, their proper recourse was to appeal to the Crown for help. Thomas Jefferson developed this argument in his influential pamphlet *Summary View of the Rights of British America* (1774). The First Continental Congress followed through by sending a petition to the Crown asking for a redress of grievances. The Crown, of course, would have no part of it; indeed, George III had already dispatched royal troops to suppress the American resistance.

It was then that colonists turned to a nonlegal argument, the doctrine of natural rights. The theory of natural rights most familiar to Americans was the version formulated by the Englishman John Locke in his *Two Treatises of Civil Government*, which had been used to justify the deposing of King James II in England's Glorious Revolution of 1688. In some distant past, Locke maintained, man had existed in a "state of nature" without government and in that state had had God-given rights to life, liberty, and property. But, because men are sinful creatures, some violated the rights of others, and none could be secure. For their mutual protection, men came together and formed governments, whose sole function was to defend individuals in the enjoyment of their natural rights. As long as government rested upon consent and performed its function, it was legitimate and must be obeyed. If it ceased to do so, it ceased to be legitimate and the obligation to obey it ended. Those who had lived under it could and must abolish it and try again by creating a new government that seemed more likely to do its job.

Once the natural-rights theory became widely accepted— which it did with a rush after the publication of Thomas Paine's powerful propaganda tract *Common Sense*—the days of British authority in America were numbered. Six months later the United States was born. The argument, and sometimes even the language, of the Declaration of Independence was that of John Locke's Second Treatise.

THE FIRST WRITTEN CONSTITUTIONS

Americans learned one vital lesson from their experiences between 1760 and 1776. It was not enough, in seeking to safeguard their liberties, to trust to an unwritten constitution. The fundamental law or "higher law" could be relied upon only if it was set down in writing for all to see. The task of drafting written constitutions, however, proved to be considerably more difficult than most Americans had imagined. Moreover, the difficulties were compounded in three important ways by the Declaration of Independence itself.

The first difficulty was inherent in the founding of a nation on the principles of natural rights. That is, if the compact theory of the origin and purpose of legitimate government was sound, civil disobedience and even rebellion were justified whenever, in the judgment of people affected by particular laws, government trespassed on natural rights. This was no mere abstraction: It was a formidable practical barrier to the establishment of stable constitutional government. Every one of the colonies/states, in practice, regularly violated the natural rights of some of its inhabitants and not only because all but one legally sanctioned human slavery. Freedom of conscience, for instance, was among the most self-evident of natural rights, and yet most of the colonies/states discriminated by law against various dissenting religious groups. Under natural-rights doctrine, the dissenters would have been justified in disobeying the law or in rebelling against government if the law were not changed; and, in fact, there were at least three armed uprisings against state authority during the first five years after the American Revolution. If every group with a complaint responded by rebelling, the result would be chaos and anarchy— a return to the perils of a state of nature.

Jefferson, in writing the Declaration, guarded against such a radical interpretation of the doctrine, but in so doing he created another barrier to stable government. It was wrong, he wrote, to abolish governments "for light and transient causes." Rebellion was justified only when a government followed a persistent course, over a long period of time, that made unmistakably clear its intention to reduce the people under absolute tyranny. Most of the Declaration, in fact, is a recitation of charges against George III, aimed at proving that he had just such a design. In other words, Americans were taught, in the very document that proclaimed their independence, that their separation from the mother country came about because of the abuse of executive power. They would not soon learn to trust executive authority again; and yet, a government without executive power is no government at all.

The Declaration's third contribution to the problem was a bit more involved. Independence was the joint action of thirteen separate political societies, and thus had about it an inherent ambiguity. It left open the question whether one country or thirteen came about as a result of the break. The Continental Congress had referred to the "United Colonies" and then to the "United States," but that did not clarify the question, for the words involved a contradiction in terms. If the colonies/states were "united," they were one; but if they were one, it made no sense to refer to them in the plural. The Declaration itself begins by referring to the Americans as "one people" but then comes down squarely on the side of plurality. It consistently refers to the United States as "they," not "it," and uses the verb "are," not "is"; and it concludes "that these United Colonies are, and of Right ought to be Free and Independent States."

The problems created by these three features of the Declaration—the embracing of the natural-rights theory, the discrediting of executive power, and the choice of a plural-nation, rather than a single-nation, interpretation of independence—handicapped the establishment of effective constitutional government from the beginning. The first national constitution, the Articles of Confederation (drafted 1777, ratified 1781), was a "league of friendship" established by multilateral treaty; each state expressly preserved its "sovereignty, freedom and independence." The Articles provided not for an executive branch but for a unicameral Congress in which each state had one vote. Congress was entrusted with the conduct of the war and with carrying on foreign relations, but it was given no power to pass laws binding upon individuals. (For that reason, the Confederation had no ordinary civilian courts.) The states also reserved the exclusive power to tax. For revenues, Congress was dependent upon requisitions apportioned among the states, the quotas being based upon the value of lands. Amendments to the Articles required the approval of the legislatures of all thirteen states.

Because the individual states retained sovereignty—defined as the supreme law-making power—the state constitutions, not the Articles of Confederation, determined the kind of government under which Americans would live. The two states that had corporate charters, Connecticut and Rhode Island, decided to continue to operate under them after independence. The other eleven adopted written constitutions during the revolutionary period.

In form, these early state constitutions were "republican"—a term everyone used though there was confusion as to its meaning. Some thought it meant any government in which there was no hereditary monarchy or aristocracy; others thought it meant government in which the ultimate source of authority was "the people." The clearest expression of the commitment to republicanism in the state constitutions was the emasculation of the executive branch. Most governors were elected for one year at a time, most were chosen by the legislatures themselves, and most had only formal and ceremonial functions. Two states did vest their governors with a little power. In New York the governor had a three-year term and was given a legislative veto and power to make various administrative appointments, but neither power could be exercised without the approval of a cumbersome council. Massachusetts' governor was elected for one year but was given a veto (which could be overridden by a two-thirds majority of both houses of the legislature) and some appointive power. On the other extreme, Pennsylvania had no governor but a thirteen-member executive council that was subordinate to the legislature.

For the most part, the new constitutions lodged virtually all power in the lower house of the legislature. Georgia and Pennsylvania had no upper house at all. Each of the others had a bicameral legislature, but only in New York and Maryland was the upper house constituted in a substantially different way and given independent powers that enabled it to check the will of the lower house. In those two states senators were chosen for long periods, and only men meeting high property qualifications were eligible to serve. Elsewhere, the upper house was thoroughly dependent on, or subordinate to, the lower.

In terms of political theory, then, the new constitutions went beyond mere republicanism and established radical representative democracy. That is, they essentially abandoned the concept of "mixed government," which had theoretically formed the basis of both the English and the colonial systems, for they preserved the monarchical and aristocratic branches only formally, if at all, and lodged substantive power in the popularly elected house of the legislature, the democratic branch of government. It should be added that the electorate was limited: women, children, and slaves, who constituted perhaps four-fifths of the population, had no voice in the political process, and probably a fifth of the free adult males were deprived of the vote by property qualifications. Two additional features further prevented the legislatures from directly reflecting the will of "the people." One was that property qualifications for officeholders were generally higher, and sometimes far higher, than for voters, with the result that only about two-fifths of the free adult males were eligible to serve in the lower houses of the legislatures. The other was that representation was based not upon population but upon place, with the result that individual votes did not carry the same weight. As a rule, the larger cities and towns were underrepresented in relation to their populations; frontier areas were overrepresented in New England and underrepresented in the South. In short, the lower houses of assembly represented the people in a historical and geographical sense, though not necessarily in a statistical sense. But, for all their limitations, the state constitutions provided for a larger measure of popular participation in government than could be found nearly any place else on earth.

Radical as they were in terms of political theory, however, the constitutions were as a practical matter designed to accomplish a conservative goal—to preserve the power structure that existed once royal officials, proprietary officials, and Loyalists were expelled. New groups did, more or less by accident, come to power after 1776 in New York and Pennsylvania; but elsewhere the constitutions lodged the preponderance of power in the upper and middling ranks of men.

One final aspect of the early efforts at constitution making requires notice. It was not at all clear, at first, who, if anyone, had a legitimate right to declare what the fundamental law should be. Of the eight constitutions established in 1776, six were drafted by extralegal legislative bodies and simply declared to be in effect; two that year and one the next were drafted by bodies especially elected for the purpose, but they were never submitted to anyone for ratification, either. Proclamation of a constitution by legislative order was scarcely a satisfactory procedure, for what one legislative body could enact another could repeal. To cope with this problem, some early constitution makers appended to their constitutions a list of principles that, they declared, no government could properly violate. The first such declaration was the Virginia Bill of Rights, written by George Mason and used as the preamble to the Virginia Constitution in June 1776. A number of other states followed Virginia's example, some refining and adding to the list of rights. But that did not solve the problem, for none of the constitutions made these rights legally binding upon government, and, in fact, state legislatures often violated them.

Not until 1780 was a genuinely satisfactory solution worked out. The Massachusetts Constitution of that year was the first to be written by a body chosen solely for the purpose and then ratified by what locals regarded as the ultimate source of authority, the towns. That procedure made of the constitution a fundamental law, superior to the legislature it created and therefore not subject to legislative alteration. Significantly, too, it was under the Massachusetts Constitution that a judge first declared a bill of rights to have the force of law—in the case of *Quock Walker* v. *Nathaniel Jennison* (1783), holding, in effect, that, as the bill of rights of the state constitution declared that all men were created equal, slavery was unconstitutional. The Massachusetts procedure was followed, with variations, in the establishment of all subsequent state constitutions.

INADEQUACIES OF THE EARLY CONSTITUTIONS

These early constitutional arrangements proved inadequate for their announced purposes. The United States won its independence despite, rather than because of, the efforts of the Confederation Congress. After 1783, when the British recognized American independence in the Treaty of Paris, Congress became even less effectual. Many men elected by state legislatures to seats in Congress thought it not worth their while to attend, and so, more than half the time, Congress lacked a quorum and could do no business. The emissaries it sent to Europe were able men, but they could accomplish little because European diplomats could never be sure whom or what they were dealing with. The foreign creditors of the United States—the government of France and private bankers in Holland who had lent money to support the cause of independence—could not count on repayments from a Congress with no source of revenues except the voluntary contributions of states, which came in trickles.

International problems arose from a variety of sources, and Congress was powerless to deal with them. Off the Barbary Coast of North Africa, pirates plundered American shipping. Spain, whose American empire included Florida and the territory west of the Mississippi River, harassed American frontiersmen by closing navigation of the river and inciting Indians against them. In the northwest, the British retained several military posts on American soil in violation of the peace treaty. Britain also enacted restrictions that hampered American trade. In sum, the United States was treated as an unwelcome newcomer in the family of nations and lacked the governmental means to do anything about it.

From time to time, frustrated members of Congress urged that the Articles be amended to make them more nearly adequate; but a combination of indifference, fear of central authority, and concern for the special interests of particular states usually defeated such proposals. Three proposed amendments did clear Congress and were sent to the states for ratification. One of these, which would have given Congress a limited power to regulate international commerce for a period of fifteen years, met a lukewarm response and was approved by only a few states. Two others, designed to give Congress an independent source of revenue, came closer to acceptance. An amendment sent out in 1781 would have authorized Congress to collect a duty on imports; it was quickly ratified by every state except Rhode Island, but Rhode Island refused to budge, Virginia revoked its ratification, and that ended that. In 1783 Congress tried again with a revised revenue amendment, which remained pending for four years. On its fate depended the fate of the Confederation.

Meanwhile, Congress did what it could—and, considering that it had neither power nor money, that was not insignificant. It laid the foundations for administrative machinery and a diplomatic corps, both of which would ultimately be effective. It set up a three-man Treasury Board, which brought the public debt into some semblance of order by sorting out the tens of thousands of claims of citizens who had furnished money, goods, or services to help pay for the war. Most important, Congress acquired from the states clear title to the land north of the Ohio River, provided for its survey, and established a system of government for the territory. The last was accomplished through the celebrated Northwest Ordinance of 1787, whose main significance (apart from prohibiting slavery in the area) was that it provided for settlers a progressively increasing measure of self-government as the population increased and admission to statehood when the population reached sixty thousand.

If Congress had inadequate power, the states had an excess—and sorely abused it. During the war the unbridled state legislatures recklessly suppressed the legal rights of hordes of people suspected, or accused, of being loyal to Britain; they passed bills of attainder, declaring long lists of people guilty of treason without trial; they confiscated private property wantonly. Nor did lawless government end with the coming of peace. The legislatures overturned private contracts, reneged on public debts, openly violated treaty obligations, enacted fraudulent systems of public finance, and censured courts when they dared interfere to protect private rights. On top of all that, they levied taxes twenty to a hundred times as high as in the colonial period. On the whole, Americans were less secure in their lives, liberty, and property than they had been under royal authority. Thomas Jefferson, fearing that events would take such a turn if the legislatures were given unchecked power, had warned that "173 despots would surely be as oppressive as one"; and he added, "An *elective despotism* was not the government we fought for." Now Samuel Adams' protégé, Elbridge Gerry, put it bluntly: "The evils we experience arise from an excess of democracy."

But the states, too, made some solid achievements, or at least some of them did. The governments of New York and Pennsylvania were energetic, prudently administered, and effective. Massachusetts, as indicated, abolished slavery; three states took steps that would lead to abolition; and all states prohibited the slave trade, at least temporarily. Virginia and Maryland repealed their laws requiring the payment of taxes for the support of a religious establishment, and the latter admitted Catholics to full political rights. Several states revised their land laws, making it easier for common people to become property holders. North Carolina and Georgia were booming despite corrupt and almost comically inept governments. Indeed, apart from New England and South Carolina, prosperity and economic growth prevailed throughout the country, though there was a brief recession in 1786–87.

For all the shortcomings of Congress and the state govern- ments, then, things were far from bad enough to set off a general wave of discontent and desire for constitutional change. But there was enough discontent in some places and enough dissension in others so that a few farsighted leaders could seize the chance, when a chain of circumstances created the opportunity during the winter of 1786–87, and bring about a grand convention to revise the Articles of Confederation and "consider the exigencies of the Union."

The movement for a convention had, in fact, been set in motion before the occasion was ripe. Early in 1786 the legislature of Virginia was discussing an agreement that had been worked out with Maryland in regard to navigation on the Potomac, when some- one suggested the convening of a commercial convention that would include delegates from Pennsylvania, Delaware, Maryland, and Virginia. That proposal smacked of the development of a regional confederation to replace the national one—the idea of regional confederations had gained some adherents—and James Madison, then an ardent nationalist, countered with a proposal for a national commercial convention. Madison's motion was adopted and Virginia sent out the call. Seven states sent delegates to the resulting Annapolis Convention in September. The delegates there, under the leadership of Madison, Alexander Hamilton, and John Dickinson, adopted Hamilton's resolution declaring that their assignment was hopeless and recommending instead the calling of a national constitutional convention.

At first the recommendation was widely ignored, but then two dramatic events occurred. In January 1787 the New York legis- lature voted to reject the 1783 revenue amendment, which the other twelve states had ratified; and every member of Congress recognized that the death knell of the Confederation had been sounded. Almost simultaneously, Congress learned of Shays' Rebellion, an armed uprising against the government of Massachusetts. In actuality, that "rebellion" was a protest against excessive taxation and was easily quashed, but reports of it that spread elsewhere described it as a widespread, well-organized, and heavily armed effort to redivide all the nation's property by force. Terrified, Congress promptly voted to urge the sending of delegates to the proposed convention. Some states had already agreed to do so, and now all the others except Rhode Island followed suit.

THE PHILADELPHIA CONVENTION

The Constitutional Convention met in Philadelphia on May 28, 1787, and completed its work on September 17. Though the convention followed the rule of Congress that each state's delegation had one vote, the delegations varied in size, from New Hampshire's two to Pennsylvania's eight. Fifty-five men attended the proceedings at one time or another; thirty-nine signed the finished document. The delegates were able, practical men of the world whose combined experience in law, trade, farming, war, and politics was enormous and whose knowledge of history and political theory was astonishing. A few of the delegates were men of mediocre talents, but most were extremely able, and upwards of a dozen were truly awesome. Taken as a whole, they were as brilliant an assembly of statesmen as ever met in America, and perhaps in the world.

The work of the convention took place in four broad phases. In the first, which lasted just under two months, the delegates agreed to propose an entirely new constitution instead of amendments to the Articles. Rejecting, as the basis for debate, a plan offered by William Paterson of New Jersey and following instead one offered by Governor Edmund Randolph of Virginia, they argued, negotiated, traded, and compromised until they reached general agreement on the outlines of the proposed new government. On July 26 they took a ten-day recess and turned their resolutions over to a five-man committee of detail, whose work in drawing up a rough draft of a constitution formed the second phase. During the third phase, August 6 to September 10, flesh and blood were added to the constitutional skeleton: It was determined which branches of which governments should have what powers and what powers should be denied. The final phase was the work of a five-man committee on style, which wrote the finished product.

The document finally agreed upon was a constitution in two senses of the term. First there is the physical sense: It describes and defines how government in America shall be *constituted*, what its parts shall be and how each shall function in relation to the others. In that sense, the word is used in much the same way as when we say a person has a "strong constitution" or a "weak constitution." Then there is the legal sense of the term: The Constitution is law, but it is law of a very special kind. Blackstone defined law as "a rule of civil conduct prescribed by the supreme power in the state, commanding what is right and prohibiting what is wrong." The Constitution meets that definition of law, except that its commands and prohibitions apply not to private individuals, not to the citizenry, not to the people, but to government. It is, in other words, law that governs government. Because each of these concepts is central to the American system of government, it will be well to analyze briefly what the Constitutional Convention decided upon, and how it did so, in regard to each.

As for the Constitution in the physical sense, the document provides for a national government consisting of three branches, legislative (Article I), executive (Article II), and judicial (Article III). Deciding on the makeup of the legislative branch was difficult; the delegations were almost evenly divided between those who insisted upon preserving the one-state/one-vote rule of the Articles and those who wanted representation to be in proportion to population. The disagreement was settled with a compromise. Congress would have two houses instead of one, a Senate in which states preserved equal votes (two apiece) and a House of Representatives in which the number of seats apportioned to each state was based upon its population, as determined by a census to be taken every ten years. Senators were to be elected by the state legislatures for six-year terms on a staggered basis, one-third of the terms expiring every two years. Representatives were to be elected for two-year terms by the qualified voters in districts. (The states set the qualifications, the only restriction being that the qualifications must be the same as those for the lower house of the state legislature.) The passage of laws required a majority vote of both houses, but because the two represented different constituencies, they were also given different powers. The Senate, as the agent of the still partially sovereign state governments, was given a share of executive authority: Presidential appointments and treaties required the approval of two-thirds of the senators. The House of Representatives, as the representative of the people, had no voice in executive affairs but had the sole power of initiating tax laws.

The constitution of the executive branch was the subject of even more disagreement in the convention than was that of the legislative. General fear of executive power had rooted quickly and deeply, and though most members had come to appreciate its necessity, most also remained uneasy about it. Indeed, but for the existence of George Washington, whom everyone trusted and knew would be the first chief executive, the office of president probably would not have been established. Even with Washington around—he presided over the convention—the problem was a thorny one. Benjamin Franklin and a few others proposed a plural executive, preferably of three men, as the safest kind. Most wanted a single executive but could think of no acceptable way of electing one. Having Congress elect the president would be a convenient way, but that would make the executive branch dependent upon the legislative. Having him chosen by popular election might have been desirable theoretically, but communication was so slow and erratic that that was impracticable. Finally, the awkward electoral-college system was hit upon. In each state, the voters or the legislatures, as the legislatures should decide, would choose a number of electors equal to the number of senators and representatives to which the state was entitled. (This feature gave the states, as states, a larger voice in electing the president than it gave to people as voters; and it gave the less populous states a relatively larger vote than the more populous.) The electors would meet in their own states and vote for two candidates, one of whom must be a resident of a different state. Whoever got the most votes, if a majority, became president, and whoever got the second most, if a majority, became vice president. In the absence of a majority, the House would elect the president and the Senate would elect the vice president.

Even after going to such elaborate lengths to ensure that only the best were chosen, the convention was reluctant to give the president specified powers. Indeed, many powers traditionally inherent in the executive—such as the powers to declare war and peace, control the military, coin money, negotiate with foreign governments, and appoint administrative officials—were either vested in Congress or shared between the president and Congress. Otherwise, and in contrast to its careful enumeration of powers of Congress, the convention sketched the powers and duties of the office only in general terms, leaving it for the first president to fill in the details. The delegates hedged their bets in other ways as well. By their apportionment of electoral votes, they made the president the representative partly of the states, partly of the people; they set his term at four years, midway between those of senators and representatives; they gave him power to veto legislation but provided that Congress could override the veto with a three-fourths majority in both houses; and they provided for his removal from office if, upon impeachment by the House and trial by the Senate, he was found guilty of "high crimes and misdemeanors."

No less difficult was the problem of the makeup and authority of the judicial branch. Everyone agreed that there must be a court system, but fears and feelings as to how it should be constituted and what jurisdiction it should have proved to be insurmountable. In the end, the convention passed the buck: It provided for a Supreme Court, consisting of a chief justice and such other justices as Congress should decide, and for such "inferior tribunals" (which could include state courts) as Congress should determine. The Supreme Court was given original jurisdiction in a few specified kinds of cases; its appellate jurisdiction, if any, was left to Congress. In sum, the constitution of the judiciary was for practical purposes assigned to Congress.

As for the Constitution as law, the most obvious feature is the supreme-law clause in Article VI: "This Constitution, and the Laws of the United States which shall be made in Pursuance thereof; and all Treaties made, or which shall be made, under the Authority of the United States, shall be the supreme Law of the Land; and the Judges in every State shall be bound thereby, any Thing in the Constitution or Laws of any State to the Contrary notwithstanding." But there are more specific commands and prohibitions as well, the most important being in Article I, sections 8, 9, and 10. Section 8 itemizes the powers of Congress, Section 9 lists things Congress is forbidden to do, and Section 10 lists things the state governments are forbidden to do. Article IV lays down certain rules governing relations among the states and between the states and the national government, and it requires the United States to guarantee to each state "a Republican Form of Government."

Finally, the Constitution answers, through the process provided for ratification, the question of the ultimate source of authority in America—the "supreme power," in Blackstone's phrase, that gives the law to government. That source, that power, resided in the people, but not in the people as a whole; rather, it resided in them as people of the several states. In 1787 the people were so divided because of the plural terms in which independence had been declared and because, having created or accepted the creation of separate state constitutions, they were bound by prior contracts. They could create more local or more general governments but only by agreeing to relocate power previously lodged in the individual state governments. To do that was, in its very nature, to make fundamental changes in the state constitutions, and therefore something that could be done only by the people of each state acting for themselves.

It was for that reason—and also for the shrewd political reason that it would make ratification easier—that the Constitutional Convention specified the adoption procedure it did. The rules for amending the Articles, requiring approval by all thirteen legislatures, were entirely ignored. Instead, the Constitution was sent to Congress, with a request that it be passed along to the state legislatures and thereafter submitted to popularly elected special conventions in each state "for their Assent and Ratification." If the conventions of nine states should ratify, the Constitution would become binding on those nine states, and they could proceed to organize a government. Whether any other states subsequently joined the reconstituted union was up to them, individually.

THE POLITICAL PHILOSOPHY OF THE CONSTITUTION

The Constitution was in fact quickly approved. The conventions of three states ratified before the end of 1787, two more did so in January 1788, and by the time New Hampshire voted its approval in June, the ninth state had been obtained. Virginia and New York ratified during the next month. This is not to suggest that there was no resistance. Pennsylvania ratified only after some trickery by Federalists, as supporters of the Constitution misleadingly called themselves; a majority of the delegates in Massachusetts, New Hampshire, New York, and Virginia probably opposed ratification when their conventions began; North Carolina refused to ratify in 1788 and did not change its position until November 1789; Rhode Island held out until May of 1790. Even so, it was a remarkably quick victory for the Federalists.

Along the way, the Constitution was thoroughly analyzed, debated, discussed, and explained in newspaper articles, pamphlets, and the ratifying conventions. The most celebrated defense of the Constitution was a series of eighty-five essays, signed "Publius" and collectively known as *The Federalist*, which were written by

Hamilton, Madison, and John Jay. From these various analyses, from the Constitution itself, and from our knowledge of the history of the times, it is possible to obtain a reasonably clear understanding of the political and legal philosophy on which America's fundamental law was based.

In part, the genius of the system lay in its solution to a problem created by the break from England. In the Bolingbroke-Montesquieu description of the English constitution, which Americans generally, if mistakenly, accepted, government was restrained by the principle of the separation of powers, each branch of government having ways to block or retard the actions of the others. The principle theoretically made sense in the English system, for each branch represented people whose status was inherited—kings, lords, and commoners. In the United States, however, there was no hereditary status except that of slaves, and therefore the model was inappropriate; and yet Americans were virtually unanimous in believing that government without a separation of powers led inevitably to tyranny, even if all officers were elected by the people.

The Constitution's solution lay in the adoption of two new principles which Americans had worked out, namely federalism and a mixed system whereby the branches of government were separate but their functions overlapped. In accordance with the first, power was distributed along a vertical axis, being divided among national, state, and local governments. In addition, to check against the potential tyranny of majority rule, the Constitution separated the people from government in two ways. It provided that some officials be chosen directly, others indirectly: members of the House directly by the voters in districts, senators by legislatures elected directly by the voters, the president by electors elected by the voters or the legislatures, and judges by the president with the approval of the Senate. There was also a time barrier: House members served two-year terms, the president four, senators six, and judges for life or good behavior. By these means, though all power came from the people, there was no way the people or any group of people could express their will directly and immediately.

A second aspect of the genius of the system stemmed from the fact that the division and definition of power on the horizontal axis was neither inflexibly fixed nor precise. The executive and legislative branches, though separate, each had a foot in the door of the other, and the same was true of the different levels of government; many powers were ambiguously stated; the court structure was only outlined, leaving it to Congress to change it and even to incorporate the state courts as part of it. This very fact—that power was ill-defined and free to shift in response to the same kinds of political struggles that had given the Constitution birth—made the system viable. It could live through wars and revolutions and the most profound economic, social, and technological changes the world had ever seen, and be amended more than twenty times, and still its essence would remain the same.

QUESTIONS
FOR DISCUSSION

1. What did James Otis mean by "unconstitutional"? Could he successfully argue his case before the Supreme Court today?

2. What is positive law? Can you think of ways around Blackstone's notion of parliamentary supremacy? What checks are there on the United States Congress today?

3. What did the Founding Fathers see as the function of government? Is today's view different?

4. What are "rights"? Where do "rights" come from?

5. What is the difference between a republic and a democracy? Was the Constitution designed to promote the development of a democracy? How would the Founding Fathers feel about our concepts of democracy?

6. Is the Constitution still an effective means of governing governments?

RECOMMENDED
READINGS

BERNARD BAILYN, *The Ideological Origins of the American Revolution* (Cambridge: Harvard University Press, 1967).

PAUL CONKIN, *Self-Evident Truths* (Bloomington: Indiana University Press, 1974).

MERRILL JENSEN, *The Founding of a Nation: A History of the American Revolution, 1763–1776* (New York: Oxford University Press, 1968).

FORREST MCDONALD, *E Pluribus Unum* (Indianapolis, Ind.: Liberty Press, 1979).

CLINTON ROSSITER, *1787: The Grand Convention* (New York: Macmillan, 1966).

GARRY WILLS, *Inventing America* (Garden City, N.Y.: Doubleday, 1978).

2
EARLY CONSTITUTIONAL ISSUES AND THEIR RESOLUTIONS, 1789–1807

Just as Americans learned, after 1776, that writing satisfactory constitutions was more difficult than they had supposed, they learned, after 1789, that working out the details of constitutional government was more complex than they had expected. Despite its excellence, the Constitution proved to have defects. It required twelve amendments during the first decade and a half; it had blanks that could be filled only by Congress; and it had contradictions and ambiguities that needed to be worked out by compromise, experience, and precedent. It left open two crucial questions: Who determines when government is acting unconstitutionally, and what is the remedy? And, finally, it failed to anticipate a most significant development, the emergence of political parties. For all these reasons, it was not until 1807 that the constitutional system had firmly jelled.

FILLING IN THE CONSTITUTION

The First Congress of the United States (March 1789 to March 1791) enacted so much fundamental law that it almost amounted to a second constitutional convention. Everything it did, of course, from adopting rules of procedure to the way it handled petitions from the public, was likely to set a precedent, an example that future congresses would be reluctant to break; but there was more to it than that. Congressional measures in four broad areas—the bill of rights and the acts creating the judicial system, the executive departments, and the financial system—became lasting features of American government. The first was added to the Constitution in the form of amendments. The others were merely laws, subject to future alteration or repeal; but for practical purposes they, too, more or less became part of the Constitution.

The question of a bill of rights had been raised in the Constitutional Convention, but there was general agreement that it was unnecessary. As was said then and again in *Federalist* Number 84, it made no sense to create a national government by listing the powers it could exercise and then to cloud the issue by listing powers it could not exercise. That argument was flawed, however, for Article I, Section 9 had already prohibited the national government from doing a variety of things. Besides, anti-Federalists had stirred up a great deal of agitation for a bill of rights, and Federalists came to realize that amendments would, at the least, increase popular support for the Constitution.

James Madison took the lead. Studying the proposals that had been made formally or informally in the ratifying conventions, he eliminated duplicates and found eighty recommended amendments. Nine states had requested restrictions on the taxing power, a prohibition against congressional interference in the time and place for holding elections, and a declaration that all powers not delegated to the federal government should be reserved to the states. Seven states requested a guarantee of trial by jury in civil cases; six called for an increase in the number of representatives, protection of religious freedom, and a prohibition of standing armies in peacetime. Five wanted prohibitions against quartering troops in private homes and unreasonable searches and seizures and insisted upon state control of the militia, the right of the people to bear arms, and the rights of freedom of speech and of the press. Four requested guarantees of due process of law, speedy and public trials, the rights of assembly and petition, limits on the power of the federal judiciary, and bans on monopolies, unconstitutional treaties, excessive bail, and the holding of appointive federal offices by members of Congress.

Dismissing the least practical and least popular, Madison reduced the remainder to nineteen proposed amendments and introduced them into the House in May 1789. Debates were held, off and on, until August 24. Madison's proposal that the amendments be woven into the text of the Constitution, rather than tacked on at the end, was defeated; but, except for being consolidated into seventeen amendments, they passed the House much as he had introduced them. On September 2, the Senate took up the proposals and immediately made a fundamental change. In the form in which the amendments had passed the House, they would have applied to the states as well as the national government; hence, for example, states would be prohibited from restraining freedom of speech. The Senate removed the applicability to the states; hence, for example, states remained free to tax all citizens for the support of established churches, as Connecticut did until 1816 and Massachusetts did until 1833.* Otherwise, the Senate generally concurred with the House, though it and a joint House-Senate committee that met on September 25 consolidated the amendments further, leaving only twelve amendments to be sent to the states for approval. The first two, which concerned the number and salaries of congressmen, were never ratified. The

---

*The Supreme Court confirmed that the Bill of Rights did not apply to the states in *Barron* v. *Baltimore*, 7 Peters 243 (1833). As will be discussed in Chapter 9, the Court in recent years has ruled that the Fourteenth Amendment extends some of the rights of the first eight to cover the states.

other ten, known as the Bill of Rights, were approved by the necessary three-quarters of the states and became part of the Constitution on December 15, 1791.

The second great constitutional task, the creation of the federal judiciary, was largely the work of Senator Oliver Ellsworth of Connecticut. The undertaking was extremely complex, involving the settlement of problems on three different levels—procedural, ideological, and jurisdictional. The procedural problems alone were awesome. Anglo-Saxon jurisprudence, from which American law and legal procedures were derived, was itself a maze, involving common law, equity, and statutory law as well as a bewildering assortment of special and local variations. American law was Anglo-Saxon law compounded by a factor of thirteen: As the federal courts were to learn, there was no national common law because each state had its own version. To solve the problem, Ellsworth questioned lawyers among his fellow senators, and when their combined knowledge was not enough, he incorporated Connecticut practice into the bill for the national judiciary or invented a commonsense procedure of his own.

The ideological barriers were less easily surmounted. Broadly speaking, there were two extreme schools of thought in regard to the way the court system should be organized. Extreme nationalists wanted to create a full network of federal courts, give them all the power the Constitution could be stretched to allow, and reduce the power of the state courts as much as possible. Extreme advocates of "states' rights" wanted to confine the Supreme Court to the narrow original jurisdiction prescribed by the Constitution and to deposit as much of the judicial power as possible in the existing state courts. Ellsworth's bill split the difference. Besides a six-member Supreme Court, there would be one district court for each state. The district courts would be national, but the judges had to be residents of the state for which they were appointed. That ensured the following of traditional local procedures except when different procedures were specifically spelled out by act of Congress and thus imposed little that was unfamiliar upon local lawyers. In addition, Ellsworth's bill provided for circuit courts, consisting of two traveling members of the Supreme Court and the district judge in the state in which trials were held, the main function of the district judge being to make sure that trials followed local procedures. Finally, state courts were made part of the system by giving them concurrent jurisdiction with federal courts; appeal to the Supreme Court was provided for when the constitutionality of a state court ruling was challenged.

The problem of jurisdiction arose from the ambiguity of the Constitution. Article III, Section 2 states that the judicial power shall extend to all cases involving the Constitution, national laws, and treaties, and to a few special kinds of cases. That part of the section is clear; the ambiguous part is in the following paragraph:

> In all cases affecting Ambassadors, other public Ministers and Consuls, and those in which a State shall be a Party, the Supreme Court shall have original Jurisdiction. In all the other Cases before mentioned, the Supreme Court shall have appellate Jurisdiction . . . with such Exceptions . . . as the Congress shall make.

The paragraph can be read in two very different ways. One way is this: "In all the other cases," the Supreme Court will have jurisdiction, on appeal from a lower court, unless the Congress deprives it of jurisdiction. The other way is this: The Supreme Court will have jurisdiction in both kinds of cases, and its jurisdiction in the second kind will be appellate unless Congress makes it original. Ellsworth's bill took the latter position and gave the Supreme Court original jurisdiction in certain cases in which jurisdiction would otherwise have been appellate.

In September the bill was passed by both houses of Congress, was signed by President Washington, and became law as the Judiciary Act of 1789. The act would, over the years, be modified in its details and the number of courts would be expanded, but the basic structure of the system would remain the same.

The third great task of the First Congress, the creation of the executive departments, involved an unforeseen constitutional issue. Early in the discussion of the subject, someone routinely moved that the secretaries of state, treasury, and war be appointed by the president with the Senate's approval and be removable by the president. The appointment procedure was the one called for by the Constitution, but the only constitutional provision for removal was by impeachment. Representative William Loughton Smith of South Carolina insisted that, though the power to appoint implied the power to remove, the two powers must be in the same hands; and he quoted *Federalist* Number 77 (written by Hamilton), which said that senatorial approval would be necessary for removal. The implications of that interpretation were large. Had it prevailed, the executive departments could have evolved into semipermanent ministries, independent of the president—or, as in the British parliamentary system, responsible to the legislative as well as the executive. Opponents of Smith's motion, led by Madison, had no satisfactory answer to his argument; in fact, his interpretation was logically sound. Even so, Madison and his supporters refused to abide by a strict construction of the Constitution and voted the motion down. Presidents would have sole power to remove all appointive officers except judges.

That settled, Congress proceeded, in separate acts, to create the departments of state, war, and treasury. As these were the same departments established by the Confederation Congress, there was little disagreement until discussion centered on the makeup of the Treasury Department: Many wanted a three-man treasury board rather than a single secretary, for fear that a single secretary might become, as in Britain, a "prime minister." A compromise was reached. The Treasury Department would, like the others, be headed by one man, but the secretary would not handle the public funds (that being entrusted to a treasurer, an auditor, and a comptroller). For extra safety, it was provided that the secretary of the treasury would be responsible to Congress as well as the president; he was required to report to either branch "respecting all matters referred to him or which shall pertain to his office." That provision, in fact, opened the door for the development of a prime ministership, for it enabled Alexander Hamilton—who became the first secretary and saw himself in that role—to draft and, in effect, to introduce legislation. That was a power denied even to the president, at least as Washington read the Constitution.

It was Hamilton who devised the legislative program that comprised the fourth major task, the creation of a national financial system. Both the Congress and the states had taken on huge public debts to finance the revolutionary war, and neither had made much headway toward repaying them. The subject aroused strong feelings, partly because the taxes necessary to pay the debts would be enormous, partly because certificates of public debt (early forms of government bonds) had declined in value to fifteen or twenty cents on the dollar, and a large percentage of them had, at those prices, been bought by speculators from the soldiers and suppliers who had originally earned them. Popular sentiment for paying the public debts at a reduced rate, or on a basis that would compensate the original holders, was therefore widespread. Indeed, the inclusion of specific provisions for managing the public debts in the Constitution might well have prevented ratification. Instead, the Constitution merely stated that the debts would be "as valid" under the Constitution as they had been under the Confederation.

Hamilton's proposals, submitted at the request of the House and passed in two separate acts, were an ingenious plan for using the public debts as the basis of the nation's monetary system. By the terms of the first act the debts were not to be repaid but "funded." That is, the primary revenues of the government were pledged as a permanent fund to make regular interest payments, but the government was left free to repay the principal soon, late, or never, as it pleased. The most controversial part of the measure, a provision for the assumption by the national government of responsibility for state debts, almost defeated the bill, but it was passed by a narrow margin and the act was signed into law on August 4, 1790. The second step in Hamilton's plan called for the incorporation of a national bank whose assets, against which it would issue notes that passed as money, would be mainly certificates of the public debt rather than gold or silver. The act establishing the Bank of the United States was signed on February 24, 1791. Monetized debt—that is, paper money issued against the security of government bonds—would remain the principal basis of the currency of the United States through most of its history. (Since 1914 federal reserve notes, the main modern form of paper money in America, have been based upon corporate debts as well as government debts.)

CONSTITUTIONAL ISSUES SETTLED BY MEANS OTHER THAN ADJUDICATION

The controversy over the establishment of the Bank of the United States raised the first great debate over the proper interpretation of the Constitution. It also raised a more fundamental question, namely, which branch or branches of government determine how the Constitution is to be interpreted? Congress had disregarded the Constitution when it gave the president sole power of removal, but that action had gone unchallenged. The action of Congress in passing a bill to charter a national bank was another matter, for James Madison, in arguing against the constitutionality of the bill when it was in the House, declared that the Constitutional Convention had considered a motion to give Congress power to charter corporations and had voted it down. That statement was widely publicized and thus someone had to take it into account.

George Washington had no doubt as to who that someone should be. The president is the only officer of government who is constitutionally required to take an oath to "preserve, protect, and defend the Constitution of the United States," all others being required only to "support" it. Washington read the requirement literally and viewed the veto power as his means of defending the Constitution against congressional encroachment. But there was a problem. Washington was neither a lawyer nor a constitutional theorist, and the question whether Congress had power to grant a corporate charter was far from simple. Where, constitutionally, was he to look for advice? Washington found the answer to that question in a literal reading of the document: The president is specifically empowered to require the written opinions of his department heads. As it happened, two of his department heads, Hamilton and Secretary of State Jefferson, were lawyers, and though Attorney General Edmund Randolph was technically not head of a department, his office was authorized to give legal advice to the president. Accordingly, Washington asked all three men for written opinions.

Jefferson's opinion against the constitutionality of the bank (which was essentially the same as Randolph's) became the classical statement of the "strict construction" or states' rights interpretation of the Constitution. The guide to proper construction of the Constitution, Jefferson said, was the Tenth Amendment, then in process of ratification, which declared that "all powers not delegated to the United States, by the Constitution, nor prohibited by it to the states, are reserved to the states, or to the people." Nowhere in the Constitution, he pointed out, was Congress delegated power to create a bank or any other corporation. Nor could the power be reasonably inferred from any of the powers actually delegated. It was not granted by the general-welfare clause ("Congress shall have Power to lay and collect Taxes . . . to . . . provide for the . . . general Welfare"), for that was not a grant of power but a limitation on the taxing power, requiring that it must be used for the good of the whole country rather than for that of individual parts. The only other possible source from which the power to charter a bank could be inferred was the clause authorizing Congress to pass all laws "necessary and proper" for carrying into effect the specified powers. "Necessary," Jefferson declared, does not mean "convenient"; the clause restricts Congress to those means without which it would be absolutely impossible to carry out its constitutional duties.

Hamilton's opinion in favor of the constitutionality of the bank became the classic statement of the doctrine of "loose construction" of the Constitution. As for the power to create corporations as a means of carrying out legitimate ends of government, he said, that was inherent in sovereignty. States, for instance, could

set up corporate bodies to govern cities even though their constitutions did not specifically authorize them to do so, for the gov-
ernance of cities was one of their proper functions. Congress could
not do so because city government was not within the scope of
its functions; but as Hamilton reminded Washington, Congress
had passed and Washington had approved two earlier acts of
incorporation, those providing for the government of the Northwest
and Southwest territories. As for the necessary-and-proper clause,
Hamilton said it must be interpreted loosely; to follow Jefferson's
idea would paralyze government, for it could rarely be proved that
any measure was absolutely necessary. Then Hamilton formulated what would become the standard rule of interpretation: "If
the *end* be clearly comprehended within any of the specified powers, and if the measure have an obvious relation to that *end*, and
is not forbidden by any particular provision of the Constitution—
it may safely be deemed to come within the compass of the national authority."

Hamilton's argument satisfied Washington and he signed the
bill, but the procedure had been less than satisfactory. Two years
later, he tried a different way of obtaining reliable advice on constitutional matters. His department heads were deadlocked over
the proper way to cope with the doings of the French minister to
the United States, Edmond Genet, and Washington sent a series
of questions to the Supreme Court for its opinion. After lengthy
discussion, the Court declined to answer the questions, on the
ground that its constitutional function was to hear and judge cases
and it therefore could not properly give extrajudicial advisory
opinions. That answer, or refusal to answer, was an important
constitutional decision, setting a precedent of strict separation.

The Washington administration resolved two other important
constitutional questions more as matters of convenience than on
any other basis. The Constitution authorized the president to make
treaties "by and with the Advice and Consent of the Senate."
During Washington's first year in office, when he and Secretary
of War Henry Knox were negotiating some Indian treaties, they

went into the Senate chambers for "advice and consent." A great deal of embarrassment resulted. Washington had prepared seven questions; Vice President John Adams read them to the Senate and asked, after each one, "Do you advise and consent?" On point after point the senators, conceiving of themselves as a deliberative body, were disposed to debate and ended up postponing the question. Washington, accustomed to dealing with advisors as subordinates, became visibly angry and, after another confrontation a few days later, determined never to seek the Senate's formal advice again. Thenceforth, the senatorial "advice" part of the Constitution was dead.

The other decision resulted in the formation of the cabinet. The Constitution had not authorized a cabinet but, as indicated, empowered the president only to require written opinions from his department heads. Some anti-Federalists had criticized the document for making no provision for an official advisory council, and Washington himself was uncomfortable without one. At first he thought that there was nothing he could do about it. But by 1792 his department heads (especially Hamilton and Jefferson) had become so mutually antagonistic that, in an effort to restore harmony, he instructed the three secretaries and the attorney general to begin meeting together to discuss the full range of executive matters and make formal recommendations to him. In the midst of the French crisis of 1793 he made increasing use of the device for a different reason—he badly needed the advice. Washington did not, however, personally attend the meetings; that was a later development.

One more important constitutional issue, resolved by Washington on his own, arose as a by-product of the emergence of political parties. Parties were generally regarded as fatal to popular governments, for they were, by definition, groups of people who put their own interests and desires ahead of the interests and desires of society as a whole. The authors of the Constitution, to the extent that they took parties into account at all, thought that one advantage of the system they were creating was that it would make the development of national parties almost impossible. Although James Madison, among others, so believed, it was Madison himself, working in collaboration with Jefferson, who was most effective in bringing the first party into existence. The two Virginians began their labors toward that end in 1791, after having become convinced that Hamilton's financial policies and influence in government were dangerous to American liberty. Calling themselves Republicans to avoid the negative label anti-Federalists, they nonetheless found most of their support, at first, from former opponents of the Constitution. Gradually, however, they gained more followers, and as they did, their Federalist opponents began to harden into a party themselves. This was especially true after the outbreak of the wars of the French Revolution. Americans were bitterly divided on that issue, Republicans ardently favoring revolutionary France and opposing France's principal enemy, Great Britain. Washington, who despised the very idea of parties, tried to steer a neutral course when France and Britain went to war, but that only convinced Republicans that the administration was pro-British.

Party division came into sharp focus in 1795 with the controversy over Jay's Treaty with Great Britain. Chief Justice John Jay had been sent as a special minister to Britain in 1794, when it appeared that British belligerence would provoke the United States into a war. Jay negotiated a treaty that avoided war and won the United States some commercial advantages, but Republicans denounced the treaty as a sell-out. They fought vigorously to prevent its ratification, but the Senate approved it by the barest allowable margin, twenty votes to ten.

That set the stage for a constitutional confrontation. In March 1796 the House was debating legislation to appropriate the money necessary to implement Jay's treaty when Republican Representative Edward Livingston of New York proposed a resolution demanding that the House be given all the correspondence, instructions, and other papers connected with Jay's mission. After heated debate, the resolution was passed and sent to the president.

Washington responded with a thundering refusal. The papers, he said, were none of the House's business and were not "relative to any purpose under the cognizance of the House of Representatives, except that of an impeachment; which the resolution has not expressed." Then he proceeded to lecture the congressmen on the Constitution. Secrecy was sometimes necessary in the conduct of foreign relations, he said, and though the use of "national security" as an excuse for secrecy could be dangerous, the Constitution checked the danger by making the Senate privy to such matters, but not the House. As for the House's claim that the power to initiate appropriation bills gave it the right to withhold approval of treaties, Washington made two telling points. One was that the House had been routinely carrying treaties into effect for seven years and no member had ever asserted a right to do otherwise. The other was that, as the official journal of the Constitutional Convention showed, the proposal that treaties would not become effective unless ratified by a law had been overwhelmingly rejected. The House responded to the refusal by passing a resolution declaring that it did have the right to see the papers; but it was clear that there was no way to pry them from George Washington. The matter was closed.

The problems created by the rise of political parties, however, had only begun. One of these problems necessitated a constitutional amendment. The Constitution provided that presidential electors vote for two persons and that the front-runner become president and the runner-up vice president. In 1796 both parties ran presidential candidates, with the bizarre result that the Federalist John Adams was elected president and the Republican presidential candidate, Jefferson, was elected vice president. Four years later a more awkward result ensued: The Republican candidates for president and vice president, Jefferson and Aaron Burr, ended up in a tie for the lead, which threw the selection of the president into the House. Shortly thereafter, the Constitution was altered by the Twelfth Amendment, which specifies that electors vote separately for president and vice president.

JUDICIAL DETERMINATION OF CONSTITUTIONAL ISSUES

As these various constitutional issues were being resolved by the executive and legislative branches, the judicial branch was laying the foundations for the position that the courts, and ultimately the Supreme Court, had final authority to determine questions of constitutionality. The idea of "judicial review" of the constitutionality of legislative enactments had been around for a long time, but it had been discredited in eighteenth-century England and, before the 1790s, won little acceptance in America. On a few occasions American lawyers had argued for the principle, but with limited success. In the case of *Rutgers* v. *Waddington* (1784), for instance, Hamilton urged the Mayor's Court of New York City to declare an act of the legislature void because it violated the state constitution, but the presiding judge ruled that the court did not have that power. If the legislature "think fit positively to enact a law," he said, "there is no power which can controul them." Two years later, in the case of *Trevett* v. *Weeden*, a Rhode Island court did declare a state law unconstitutional, only to be strongly censured by the legislature.

And yet it was taken for granted by many lawyers that the Supreme Court would have the power of judicial review under the Constitution. In the Virginia ratifying convention, for example, both John Marshall and Patrick Henry so indicated, though Marshall favored and Henry opposed ratification. Oliver Ellsworth in Connecticut's ratifying convention, William R. Davie in North Carolina's, and Charles Pinckney in South Carolina's concurred. Hamilton gave the classic defense of the doctrine in *Federalist* Number 78: In their very nature, courts must interpret what the law means, and if one law conflicts with another, they must decide which is to prevail. If the Constitution, as fundamental law, is in conflict with a statute, the courts have no option but to decide in favor of the Constitution.

It was in the federal circuit courts, not the Supreme Court, that judicial review was exercised most frequently in the beginning.

The first instance came in 1792, in the case of *Champion and Dickason* v. *Casey*, when the Circuit Court for the District of Rhode Island declared unconstitutional a state law giving a debtor a three-year extension in the time allowed for settling with his creditors. The court ruled that the law impaired the obligations of contracts and was thus prohibited by Article I, Section 10. In at least three more instances, in Massachusetts in 1794, Pennsylvania in 1795, and Vermont in 1799, circuit courts declared other state laws unconstitutional, apparently without eliciting any protests that they had no authority to do so.

But it was one thing to declare state laws unconstitutional and quite another to challenge an act of Congress. The supreme-law clause fairly clearly justified the first, for it explicitly requires judges to treat the Constitution as superior to state constitutions and laws. The power is less apparent in regard to congressional acts, and the courts were reluctant to exercise it. In 1792 a circuit court did declare an act of Congress unconstitutional, but the circumstances were special. A law passed early in the year provided that the circuit court judges should act as commissioners to settle the pension claims of wounded war veterans, which was not a proper judicial function. The Circuit Court for New York held that the assignment was not constitutional, but the judges professed willingness to serve on a voluntary basis out of respect for Congress. The Circuit Court for Pennsylvania, flatly refusing to act as commissioners when an invalid named Hayburn showed up with a claim, wrote a letter of protest to the president. Washington forwarded the protest to Congress, along with two more that had come from other circuit courts. Meanwhile, Attorney General Randolph brought suit in the Supreme Court, requesting that it order the Circuit Court for Pennsylvania to comply with the law. The Supreme Court delayed giving a decision, and in a few months Congress repealed the statute. Thus a confrontation was avoided.

By the time that issue had been successfully dodged, the Supreme Court had handed down its first full-fledged decision in a case—and stirred up nationwide howls of opposition. The case was *Chisholm* v. *Georgia* (2 Dallas 419), decided on February 18,

1793. Two citizens of South Carolina, representing a British cred-itor of the state of Georgia, brought suit for recovery of the debt. They initiated the case directly in the Supreme Court, for the language of the Constitution was unmistakable: The Supreme Court had original jurisdiction in all cases in which a state was a party. Georgia, however, refused to be represented in court, and despite the clarity of the Constitution, the state had a strong ground for its stand. No less ardent a nationalist than Alexander Hamilton had declared, in *Federalist* Number 81, that "it is inherent in the nature of sovereignty" that a state could not be sued by an indi-vidual *without its consent*. But the Supreme Court held otherwise, ruling against Georgia. Waves of protest swept the country when the decision was announced, and not merely on the abstract grounds of states' rights: The states' wartime confiscations and cancellations of debts due British subjects, involving many millions of dollars, were at stake. Demands for a constitutional amendment were made immediately, and in less than a year Congress pro-posed one that deprived the federal courts of jurisdiction in any case brought against a state by foreigners or citizens of another state. It was ratified as the Eleventh Amendment in 1798.

That unnerving response to the Court's first decision was symptomatic of things to come: For a decade and more, the ju-diciary would be in danger of destruction by the fierce currents of partisan politics. Most federal cases continued for a time to be handled by the circuit courts, and though their rulings invariably went against positions espoused by Republicans, the Supreme Court itself was thereby spared much attack. Even it, however, was somewhat embroiled in politics. Jay resigned as chief justice in 1795, and Washington appointed John Rutledge of South Car-olina to replace him; Rutledge accepted the appointment and heard two cases, but then it became known that he had delivered a speech denouncing Jay's Treaty, whereupon Federalists in the Senate blocked his confirmation. His replacement, Oliver Ell-sworth, had scarcely taken his seat when the Supreme Court handed down its decision in two hotly controverted cases, both involving Virginia and dealing with matters of intense concern to its citizens.

Ware v. *Hylton* (3 Dallas 199, decided March 7, 1796) was much like the Chisholm case except this time the debtor being sued was an individual. A Virginia law of 1777 had allowed citizens of the state to discharge their debts to British creditors by paying depreciated paper currency to the state. The peace treaty of 1783 provided that there be "no lawful impediment to the recovery of the full value" of all *bona fide* debts, but before 1789 British creditors had no place in which to sue. The Constitution made treaties part of the supreme law of the land, and that opened the new federal courts to the creditors. In *Ware* v. *Hylton* the Supreme Court ruled against the debtor on the ground that the Virginia act was contrary to the peace treaty and therefore unconstitutional. Significantly, however, though Virginians were extremely dissatisfied with the decision (and ultimately avoided its consequences by persuading Congress, after the Jeffersonian Republicans came to power, to pay their debts for them), they did not challenge the authority of the Court to declare the law unconstitutional.

Indeed, in the other case, which was decided the day after the Ware case, Virginians argued for the necessity of judicial review. In *Hylton* v. *United States* (3 Dallas 171) the Supreme Court was called upon for the first time to rule on the constitutionality of an act of Congress. A law passed in 1794 had imposed a tax of $16 on carriages; because Virginia planters owned many more carriages than did most northerners, they thought the tax discriminatory, and a group of them agreed to contest it on constitutional grounds. Their argument was as follows: The Constitution specifies that direct taxes must be apportioned among the states on the basis of population, the carriage tax was a direct tax and was not so apportioned, and therefore the act was unconstitutional. The Court ruled otherwise. Only taxes on land or taxes levied equally on persons, it held, were to be regarded as direct. The carriage tax was an "excise," a tax on commodities, and was thus indirect.

Unwelcome as these decisions were to Republicans, they provoked only a moderate amount of grumbling. Decisions rendered during the next three years, however, transformed the grumbling into an all-out attack. The occasion was provided by the outbreak of an undeclared naval war with France in 1798. Two separate but related kinds of court decisions at that time especially angered the Republicans. One decision was concerned with whether English common law was part of the national law in the United States. Obviously it was part of the law of the states in various and diverse ways, and no one contested that. Moreover, the procedural rights guaranteed by the Bill of Rights were essentially common law, and the Seventh Amendment explicitly and the Ninth Amendment implicitly recognized the common law. But these procedures protected defendants against actions by government; the question got sticky when government employed the common law as a basis of charges. Under the common law, certain deeds were crimes even if there was no statute saying so, and, in the absence of a national criminal code, federal officials had no way of stopping various undesirable activities except through common-law charges.

During the five years after 1793, when President Washington issued a neutrality proclamation to avoid involvement in the French revolutionary wars, the question took on a highly practical significance. The attorney general and several federal district attorneys brought common-law indictments against a number of people (invariably Republicans) for pro-French activities, and most of the Supreme Court justices, sitting in circuit courts, upheld the actions. Then, in 1798, Justice Samuel Chase—an intemperate and fiercely partisan Federalist but a first-rate constitutional lawyer— handed down a powerful and carefully reasoned decision to the contrary. A man named Worrall had been indicted and, upon jury trial, found guilty of attempting to bribe a Treasury Department official. The action was brought under the common law, for Congress had not yet made bribery a statutory offense. Justice Chase, pointing out that the common law had been adopted by the states piecemeal and in diverse ways, took the position that attempting to incorporate it as a whole into United States law would lead to infinite confusion and injustice, and he ordered the defendant released. Republicans cheered, but the cheering stopped abruptly when Chief Justice Ellsworth took precisely the opposite position in another circuit-court ruling. Republicans were enraged, for they were convinced, with some reason, that Federalist judges were using the common law to suit their political prejudices rather than the ends of justice. The question was indeed muddled, and both Federalists and Republicans took inconsistent positions on it. After the Republicans assumed control of the national government in 1801, they sometimes found it necessary to bring common-law indictments, and the practice lingered for another decade or so.*

Meanwhile, decisions in a related area were meeting reactions of almost hysterical proportions. At the height of the "anti-French phrenzy" in 1798 Congress passed, as part of a series of measures designed to prepare the country for the expected war with France, the so-called Sedition Act. That act prohibited conspiracy to obstruct the operation of the laws of the United States and made it illegal to "write, print, utter, or publish" anything intended to defame the government, Congress, or the president. Republicans denounced the act and contested it in both Congress and the courts on the ground that it violated the First Amendment's protection of freedom of speech and of the press. On the face of it, their argument would appear to be sound, but the matter was not so simple. The First Amendment forbids Congress to make any law "abridging" freedom of speech and press. To abridge means to shorten, to reduce. As a constitutional matter, the relevant ques-

---

*In 1813 the Supreme Court ruled definitively that there was no federal common law; *U.S.* v. *Hudson and Goodwin* (7 Cranch 32). In 1842, however, in *Swift* v. *Tyson* (16 Peters 1) it reopened the door for the development of federal common law, of a sort, in regard to interstate commerce. The Court handed down many interstate commercial decisions under that doctrine until it was overturned in 1938 by *Erie* v. *Tompkins* (304 U.S. 64).

tions were, how much freedom of speech and press legally existed before the passage of the Sedition Act, and in what ways, if any, did the act reduce that freedom? If common law applied, seditious libel was already a crime, and all the act did was prescribe the punishment, so there was no abridgment of rights involved. But the act went further. Under common law, the accused could not plead, in defense of himself, that what he had said or written was true; the Sedition Act expressly made truth a defense. It therefore had the legal effect of enlarging, rather than abridging, freedom of speech and the press—if, that is, there was such a thing as common-law crime under the Constitution.

The Republicans who opposed the passage of the Sedition Act—and of the Alien Acts, passed at the same time—made it clear that their objections arose not from concern for freedom of speech and press but from their view of the nature of the constitutional union.* They argued that the states could, should, and did suppress seditious libel (despite state bills of rights); the states did so, in fact, more ruthlessly than was provided for under the Sedition Act. What Republicans objected to, and regarded as unconstitutional, was such suppression (even though more moderate) by the national government rather than by the state governments. Their motivation was political as well as ideological: Federalists controlled the national government and could be expected to bring indictments under the Sedition Act in any state, whereas Republicans controlled several states and in them could indict Federalist critics and prevent indictments of Republicans.

Twenty-five persons were indicted under the Sedition Act and ten (all of whom were Republican newspaper printers) were convicted. In their defenses, the Republicans tried a novel tactic: They argued that juries, not judges, had the right to decide whether the

---

*The Republicans' position on the nature of the constitutional union, as expressed in the Virginia and Kentucky resolutions, is discussed in Chapter 4.

act was constitutional. The courts uniformly rejected the argument and upheld the constitutionality of the act.

Having lost in courts of law, Republicans had no recourse except to politics. They had long since taken that route; now they redoubled their efforts, and in the elections of 1800–01 they won control of the presidency and both houses of Congress. Clearly, the independence of the federal judiciary was in peril.

THE MARBURY CASE AND THE ATTACK ON THE COURTS

Upon assuming office, the Jeffersonian Republicans promptly came to realize that it was necessary to interpret the Constitution more loosely than they had previously been willing to admit. To be sure, they undid some of what they regarded as Federalist wrongs. They repealed the Sedition Act, President Jefferson pardoned all who had been convicted under it, and Congress restored all fines with interest. Moreover, the administration began dismantling the Hamiltonian financial system. But, as indicated, the Jeffersonians did resort to common-law prosecutions; they also negotiated the Louisiana Purchase, thus stretching the Constitution as far as Federalists ever had; and, in time, they even rebuilt the Hamiltonian system.

But any inclination Republicans might have had to go easy on the judiciary was ended by actions Federalists took at the very end of their tenure. On February 27, 1801, five days before John Adams' term as president ended, the outgoing Federalist-dominated Sixth Congress passed a new Judiciary Act, reducing the number of Supreme Court justices from six to five (to prevent Jefferson from replacing one who was about to retire), creating sixteen circuit courts and establishing separate judgeships for each, and adding a large number of federal attorneys, marshals, and clerks. In most respects the act was a long-needed reform, which Supreme Court justices had been requesting for a decade, for the requirement that they ride circuit was extremely hard on their health. Too, some of the jurisdictional changes made by the act, especially in regard to disputed land titles, were necessary to unsnarl a great tangle of cases that had developed in state courts. Nonetheless, the statute was also a blatant partisan measure, designed to continue Federalist domination of the courts after the Republicans had won control of the elective branches of government. President Adams underscored the political quality of the law by filling the new posts as fast as he could and by signing commissions until three hours before the expiration of his term.

The Republicans were appropriately outraged, no less so because Republicans in Virginia and Kentucky stood to lose claims to millions of acres of land by the removal of jurisdiction from state to federal courts. They retaliated soon after the Seventh Congress convened for its first session in December 1801. First they repealed the Judiciary Act of 1801, thereby abolishing all the positions created under it. Then they passed the Judiciary Act of 1802, which established six circuit courts and assigned one Supreme Court justice and one district judge to each. Finally, to deter challenges to these actions on constitutional grounds, they provided by law for the postponement of the term of the Supreme Court for one year.

These doings gave rise to two important Supreme Court cases. The Constitution states that judges, "both of the supreme and inferior Courts, shall hold their Offices during good Behaviour," and its prescribed method for ascertaining good behavior is the impeachment process. By repealing the 1801 act and replacing it with the one of 1802, Congress had, in effect, fired sixteen circuit-court justices. The repeal act and the Judiciary Act of 1802 were challenged on that ground in 1803 in the case of *Stuart* v. *Laird* (1 Cranch 309), brought in the Circuit Court in Richmond. The mere bringing of the case created a dilemma. Under the terms of the 1802 act, Chief Justice John Marshall (appointed by Adams in January 1801 to replace the retired Ellsworth) was required to preside over the Richmond circuit court. If he refused to do so until the Supreme Court next legally met, and if the Supreme Court upheld the constitutionality of the act, he would have been guilty of not obeying the law and would therefore be impeachable. If, on the other hand, he agreed to hear the case in the circuit court, he would be upholding both the repeal act and the 1802 Judiciary Act. The delay of the sitting of the Supreme Court had been cleverly designed to create just that problem. Marshall partially dodged the issue by holding that the plea raising the constitutional question was insufficient, and it was thus appealed to the Supreme Court. Meanwhile, all the other justices had complied with the 1802 act by sitting on circuit, and thus they had little option when *Stuart* v. *Laird* came before them. They ruled in March 1803 that the law requiring them to serve as circuit judges was constitutional as they had set a precedent by doing so since 1789. Though it avoided the question of the constitutionality of the repeal act, the Court indirectly confirmed its validity.

The other case, *Marbury* v. *Madison* (1 Cranch 137), resulted in Marshall's most famous decision, for in it the Supreme Court first declared an act of Congress unconstitutional. Immediately upon taking office, President Jefferson and Secretary of State Madison found that not all of the commissions for Adams' "midnight appointments" had been delivered. Hoping to block the appointments, Madison withheld some of the commissions, including one authorizing William Marbury to serve as a justice of the peace in the District of Columbia. Marbury brought suit under Article 13 of the Judiciary Act of 1789, which had not been altered by the recent changes. The article empowered the Supreme Court to issue writs of mandamus (orders requiring government officials to do their legal duty), and Marbury brought his action there. Trivial as the matter was, it attracted some attention because it seemed to be another trap: The Jeffersonians expected the Court to issue the mandamus, whereupon Madison would ignore it and the Court would become a laughingstock.

But Marshall, who wrote the decision, outflanked the Republicans. He declared that Marbury had a right to the commission and that a mandamus was the proper remedy; but then he ruled that the Supreme Court could not issue it, on the ground that Article 13 was unconstitutional because it gave the Court original jurisdiction, whereas the Constitution directed that its jurisdiction be original only in certain specified kinds of cases and appellate in all others. (Deliberately or not, Marshall misread Article 13; it did not in fact give the Court original jurisdiction in such cases.) By that means Marshall was able to assert judicial authority by striking down part of a congressional act, and yet, at the same time, to avoid a confrontation with the executive branch by allowing Jefferson and Madison to do what they pleased. Into the bargain, he included in his decision a lecture to the president and the secretary of state on what was proper behavior.

The maneuver was, however, more clever than prudent. For one thing, Marshall failed to consider the long-range constitutional implications of his decision, for it actually placed the Supreme Court on a shaky footing. By ruling that Congress could not change the Court's appellate jurisdiction into original jurisdiction, he had interpreted Article III, Section 2 of the Constitution to mean that the congressional power to make "exceptions" to the Court's appellate jurisdiction was the power to deprive the Court of jurisdiction entirely. Years later that decision would come back to haunt the Court.

The short-range effect of the decision was to antagonize the administration into seeking the virtual destruction of the Court. Marshall's calculated arrogance in sermonizing about Marbury's rights and the administration's duties was going too far—and besides, as he ruled that the Court had no jurisdiction in the case, it was *obiter dicta*, or irrelevant to the decision and thus improper. For some time, the less restrained Republicans had been insisting on sweeping the courts clean of Federalists; James Monroe, for example, had suggested that the Judiciary Act of 1789 should have been repealed along with that of 1801, so that the entire bench except for the chief justiceship (which is established by the Constitution, not by law) would have been vacated. After *Marbury v. Madison*, voices calling for a purge of the Court became a majority among Republicans.

Means to that end had already suggested themselves. Republicans in Pennsylvania, controlling the state legislature, had impeached the Federalist state judge William Addison, not for violations of the law but for partisanship, indiscretions, and explosions of temper. Many federal judges had behaved as high-handedly as Addison had, and when the state senate convicted Addison and removed him from office, just as the Marbury case was being decided, Republicans in Washington determined to follow Pennsylvania's example. On March 3, 1803, one week after Marshall announced his decision, the House took the first step in a trial run: It voted to impeach John Pickering of New Hampshire, a federal district judge whose failings were not high crimes and misdemeanors but drunkenness and insanity.

Pickering's impeachment came up for trial in the Senate a year later. Being totally insane, he could not appear in his own defense, and his son requested that he simply be removed from office and spared the disgrace of impeachment. But there is no way to get rid of a federal judge for incompetence; the Constitution's only remedy is impeachment. Moreover, because the purpose of impeaching Pickering was to test the procedure as a means of "purifying" the Supreme Court, the Senate proceeded with the trial. On March 12, 1804, Pickering was found guilty and ordered removed.

On the same day, at the urging of President Jefferson, the House voted to bring impeachment proceedings against Justice Samuel Chase—who, despite his great gifts, was politically the most vulnerable justice on the Supreme Court. Like Addison and Pickering, he was accused of no crimes, but he had aroused Republican hatred by his insulting treatment of Republican lawyers, by his impropriety in campaigning for Adams in 1800, and by his harangues to grand juries in which he predicted that Republican doctrines would lead to national ruin. Chase's impeachment came up for trial in the Senate on February 4, 1805, with the Virginian John Randolph of Roanoke managing the prosecution for the House. At stake, from the Federalist point of view, was whether there would be an independent federal judiciary, as the Constitution contemplated, and therefore a government of laws. At stake from the Republican point of view was whether the will of the people, as expressed at the polls in the elections of the other branches and at other levels, should determine what government would do.

Neither was the pivot on which the Senate's decision would turn. The real question was whether justices could be removed for political reasons or whether the Constitution was to be followed literally when it specified the grounds for removal. On March 1 the Senate voted on the charges and found Chase not guilty. That ended the Jeffersonians' direct attack on the Court and ensured the Court's continued existence as an independent branch of government.

WHO DETERMINES CONSTITUTIONALITY?

The survival of the Court after striking down an act of Congress did not usher in an era of judicial supremacy. The Jeffersonians did not object to judicial review as such; they merely insisted that each branch of the federal government—and, as we shall see in Chapter 4, each of the state governments as well—had an equal right and duty to determine constitutionality for itself. Nor did Marshall claim, in the Marbury case or at any other time, that the Court's opinion on constitutional matters was superior to that of the other two branches or binding in all cases upon them. Marshall's acceptance of the co-equal principle was illustrated during the trial of Aaron Burr for treason in 1807. Marshall issued a subpoena ordering President Jefferson to produce certain documents; Jefferson refused to comply, beyond submitting some of the documents to the district attorney, not the court, with instructions to withhold any he regarded as immaterial. Marshall had no alternative but to accept Jefferson's position.

Not until late in the nineteenth century did the Court begin to exert a claim to be the exclusive arbiter of constitutionality, and then only tentatively. In the meantime, presidents continued to be the principal guardians of the Constitution. The Supreme Court struck down only one more act of Congress before the Civil War, whereas during the same period presidents vetoed scores of congressional acts on grounds of unconstitutionality.

QUESTIONS FOR DISCUSSION

1. Who determines the jurisdiction of the Supreme Court? Can jurisdiction in specific areas be withdrawn from the Court? Could the Court or any part of it be abolished?

2. What office is charged by the Constitution to "preserve, protect and defend" it? Why was this made a specific part of the document? What powers go with this obligation?

3. What proposals were incorporated in the Bill of Rights? Which were rejected? If you were writing a Bill of Rights, what would you include?

4. How does a prime-ministerial system differ from ours? Would such a system be compatible with the Constitution?

5. During the controversy over Jay's Treaty, President Washington took a position that has come to be called the principle of confidentiality. What were his constitutional grounds? Did this precedent apply to President Nixon during the Watergate investigation?

6. What is judicial review? Does the Constitution mandate judicial review? Can you also argue against the principle of judicial review?

RECOMMENDED READINGS

WALTER BERNS, *The First Amendment and the Future of American Democracy* (New York: Basic Books, 1976).

ROBERT K. FAULKNER, *The Jurisprudence of John Marshall* (Princeton: Princeton University Press, 1968).

The Federalist (New York: Random House, Modern Library, 1937).

LEONARD W. LEVY, *Jefferson and Civil Liberties: The Darker Side* (Cambridge: Harvard University Press, 1963).

FORREST MCDONALD, *Alexander Hamilton: A Biography* (New York: Norton, 1979).

ROBERT RUTLAND, *The Birth of the Bill of Rights* (Chapel Hill: University of North Carolina Press, 1955).

3
THE CONSTITUTION AND THE NEW ECONOMIC ORDER

What may be called the Jeffersonian constitutional settlement—the understanding that each branch and level of government, and not just the federal courts, shared the right and duty to determine what was constitutional—would prevail until after the Civil War. As a consequence, the Constitution evolved along various and diverse paths. To be sure, there were overall trends that were generally evident throughout the country, notably trends toward the emergence of capitalism, democracy, and nationalism. Otherwise, however, there was a single "supreme law of the land" only to the limited extent that the Supreme Court could impose one. In the circumstances, it was no small achievement for the Court just to survive as a viable, independent institution; and it was a major achievement that it was able to provide some measure of consistency, order, and uniformity in the nation's laws.

For six decades following the Chase impeachment trial, the most important constitutional questions turned upon one or another of three related pivots: economic development, federal-state relations, and slavery. The economic growth of the United States during this period was phenomenal: In part, the growth reflected territorial expansion (the land area of the country trebled) and population increase (the number of people grew sixfold), but there were other reasons as well. One was financial: During the French revolutionary and Napoleonic wars, American merchants reaped enormous profits from the erratic and dangerous business of carrying the goods of the powers at war. Another was the rise of manufacturing, stimulated by periodic stoppages of international trade. Still another was technological innovation: The invention of the cotton gin, the steamboat, and later the railroad made possible an expansion of both agricultural and industrial production.

Underlying the growth and making it possible, however, was a profound transformation of American attitudes and institutions, a transformation that rapidly became embodied in the nation's constitutional and legal system. These changes are the subject of the present chapter; the constitutional questions arising from federal-state relations and slavery, though intertwined with those arising from economic development, will be considered separately in Chapter 4.

THE ECONOMIC
TRANSFORMATION

The most important change had to do with the nature of property rights. It will be recalled that property, in natural-rights theory, was one of the three basic human rights, along with life and liberty; and that concept was enshrined in the Constitution by the contract clause, the Fifth Amendment, and the very structure of the government. But there were two things about property rights, as protected in American constitutions and laws, that discouraged economic development and the emergence of capitalism.

The first deterrent was that only land was regarded as "real" property, all other kinds being "merely" personal. Personal property—whether in tangible forms such as goods, money, and ships or in intangible forms such as bonds, notes, and bank accounts— rested on shaky legal footing, when it was recognized at all. This is best understood through an example. Suppose a merchant named Smith sold a farmer named Brown a hundred dollars' worth of merchandise on credit and received in return a note from Brown promising to repay the sum in six months. Smith's property in the form of Brown's note had a standing in the law and could be collected by court action if necessary; but as the law then existed, if Brown claimed that the merchandise had been defective or overpriced or that he had been misled when he made the purchase, the jury in the case could cancel the obligation and was likely to do so. Moreover, the note was not always fully transferable. If Smith became pressed for cash and sold Brown's note to a third party, Jones, Jones might or might not (depending on the jurisdiction and the kind of note it was) be able to force Brown to pay. All such barriers to the free exchange of personal property stood in the way of the development of a modern, dynamic economy.

Second, even in regard to land the prevailing idea was that the holding of property was for personal enjoyment rather than to use or develop it as a productive asset. The law reflected and reinforced this attitude in hundreds of ways. For instance, there was the law governing improvements when title to land proved defective. If a farmer bought a hundred-acre tract and worked hard to clear it and make it productive, and then someone came along with proof that the land belonged to him—a frequent occurrence in early America when land titles were tangled in conflicting grants—the farmer was entitled to no compensation for the improvements he had made. Indeed, sometimes he was required to pay damages for the changes he had brought about. Or, there was the law of riparian (water-use) rights. A landowner could do anything he wanted to do with a stream flowing across his property, but only so long as it did not interfere with the rights of others, downstream. If he wanted to improve his crops by diverting some of the water for irrigation purposes, he could be blocked by the other property owners; if he wanted to erect a dam and build a mill, he could do so only if the state legislature granted him specific authorization. As long as the law continued to put the right of enjoyment ahead of productive use, America's economic growth would be stunted.

From the 1790s onward, Americans in increasing numbers became caught up in a spirit of development, and the law was changed to make development possible. In part, this was the work of legislatures, but in the main it was something the courts took upon themselves by reinterpreting existing law. Mainly, too, it was done by state courts on a case by case basis—the law of negotiable instruments being changed slightly here, that of nuisance there, that of insurance liability and waste elsewhere—without becoming involved in issues arising from the Constitution. In a few crucial areas, however, constitutional issues were of central importance.

One constitutional question was resolved fairly easily. The Fifth Amendment states that private property shall not be taken for public use except by "due process of law" and that if it is taken, government must pay the owner a "just compensation." In practice, state and local governments disregarded these restrictions from the outset. When they wanted land on which to build a road or a pier or a public building, they simply took it, rarely allowing the owner any means of contesting the action and even more rarely compensating him. Finally, in the 1830s, the owner of a wharf in Baltimore challenged, on Fifth Amendment grounds, damages done to his property by actions of the city. The Supreme Court (in *Barron* v. *Baltimore*, 7 Peters 243) ruled that the Fifth Amendment—and by implication the rest of the Bill of Rights—restricted only the national government, not the state and local governments. That gave the states a free hand in promoting economic development through the power of eminent domain (the condemning of private property for public use), and states were soon going so far as to convey the power to private individuals and groups. That is to say, the states granted private developers the right to take property from other citizens in order to put that property to productive use.

Such methods were not to be the norm. In other areas in which economic activity became entangled in constitutional questions, the process of determining the "supreme law" was far more involved.

THE NATIONAL GOVERNMENT AS PROMOTER OF ECONOMIC DEVELOPMENT

Once the American people—or a significant number of them—became infected with enthusiasm for promoting economic growth, it was understandable that they should try to enlist the help of government. As promotion-minded men saw things, economic development would benefit everyone, government in a republic was designed for the good of all, and therefore government should lend its support. Those people who objected in principle to government interference or sought to protect their vested interests used constitutional arguments to prevent governmental economic activity. Because economic enterprise was mainly local, it was within the states that the rivalry began. However, the Supreme Court's power to review state activity would bring it into the picture. In the meantime, the national government was called upon directly to promote economic growth in a variety of ways, most notably through protective tariffs, subsidization of "internal improvements" such as roads and canals, and fiscal policy. Each of these involved fundamental questions about the meaning of the Constitution.

That the Constitution gave Congress power to levy protective tariffs was generally agreed, though the initial reaction to that feature of the document had been mixed. Craftsmen in the cities— the "manufacturers" of the day—had petitioned the Confederation Congress and their state legislatures for protection against foreign competition through high taxes on selected imports, and they enthusiastically supported the Constitution because it made those taxes possible on a national basis. Many southern planters and importing merchants, on the other hand, fearing that protective legislation would be passed for the benefit of northerners at southern expense, sought an amendment requiring a two-thirds majority of both houses of Congress for the passage of such laws. At first, their fears proved to be groundless, for supporters of protection were few. Hamilton proposed, in his celebrated Report on Manufactures, that Congress enact a comprehensive program of protective duties, but the proposal was ignored.

It was not until the tariff of 1816 that Congress began to adopt the protective principle. Southerners did not object at that time, partly because the import duties were moderate, partly because they believed manufacturing with the use of slave labor might be profitable. Within little more than a decade, however, tariffs were increased sharply and the emergence of the factory system made free labor cheaper than slave labor in manufacturing, and southern fears were kindled anew. Having no way of halting the trend under generally accepted rules of constitutional interpretation, southern extremists came up with a radical constitutional doctrine: the assertion that state legislatures could declare acts of Congress null and void and prevent their enforcement within the state. That interesting doctrine and its implications will be considered in the following chapter.

The question of the constitutionality of internal improvements at federal expense was quite a different matter. It was almost universally assumed, at first, that Congress had no power to appropriate money for the building of roads and canals or for dredging rivers to make them navigable. Any such expenditure would necessarily be local, and the congressional power to tax was restricted to purposes of the common defense and the *general* welfare. Hamilton proposed a system of internal improvements in 1799 but thought that a constitutional amendment would be necessary to authorize the legislation. His Republican counterpart, Secretary of the Treasury Albert Gallatin, proposed in 1802 that receipts from the sale of public lands be used to build roads from the seaboard to the interior, but a majority in Congress thought even that would be unconstitutional and declined to act. In 1808, having a considerable surplus in the treasury, Gallatin went much further, proposing the building of a comprehensive transportation system for the entire country. That would qualify as spending for the general welfare, and Congress did vote funds for building the first section of a "national road" from Cumberland, Maryland, to Wheeling, (West) Virginia. Plans for extending the road were interrupted by the War of 1812. In 1816 President Madison recommended its completion; but when Congress passed instead a general internal-improvements bill, justifying its action on the ground that improved transportation was necessary for national defense, Madison vetoed the measure as unconstitutional. In 1822 Congress passed a more limited bill, to complete the national road, but President Monroe vetoed that.

Under the next two presidents, policy was reversed twice. John Quincy Adams approved legislation to extend the national road and to finance several other internal-improvement projects, and Congress overcame most of its constitutional scruples about such appropriations. Then Andrew Jackson reverted to a slightly loosened version of the earlier position. He approved the completion of the last section of the national road and also approved bills to improve rivers and harbors (on the ground that they fell within the congressional power to regulate commerce); but he vetoed bills for the construction of roads and canals within a single state. Jackson had an alternate approach to the financing of transportation facilities. The national debt was about to be retired, and the federal government would then have surplus revenues; Jackson proposed that the treasury surplus be returned to the states to pay for their own internal improvements. That was actually done for a brief period, but the surplus soon disappeared.

When Congress finally did begin to finance transportation development on a large scale—with railroads in the 1850s—it avoided the constitutional barrier by combining Jackson's approach with Gallatin's original proposal. It granted public lands to states, which, in turn, granted them to railroad corporations. Subsequently, Congress granted lands directly to the railroad companies.

Meanwhile, national fiscal policy as an instrument of economic development was undergoing a stormy constitutional history. Hamilton's measure for funding the public debts on a semipermanent basis had, by creating an enormous amount of liquid capital, been largely responsible for bringing about the developmental mentality. Much as Republicans opposed the Hamiltonian system, they did not seriously challenge that part of it on constitutional grounds. As we have seen, they did challenge the act establishing the Bank of the United States. When they gained control of the national government they were determined to dismantle the whole fiscal machinery, but that was not a simple undertaking. By the terms of the original funding act of 1790, only a small portion of the public debt could be retired each year; the Jeffersonians set about paying it off as fast as the law allowed, but their plans were frustrated by the expenses of the Louisiana Purchase and the War of 1812.

Destroying the national bank also turned out to be more difficult than anticipated. Because it had been chartered for twenty years it seemed necessary only to wait until the charter expired in 1811 and not renew it. But Gallatin and Madison, during their service as secretaries of the treasury and state departments under Jefferson, came to realize that the bank was of immense value to the nation, and when Madison became president in 1809 he let it be known that he would approve a recharter bill. The recharter bill, however, met the strange fate of being vetoed, in effect, by the vice president: The vote in the Senate was a tie and Vice President George Clinton, an old anti-Federalist who still believed the bank unconstitutional, cast the deciding vote against recharter. The calamitous disruption of public finance during the War of 1812, however, convinced most Republicans that a national bank was necessary, and in 1816 a Second Bank of the United States was created by act of Congress. It, too, was granted a renewable twenty-year charter.

The constitutionality of the second bank was soon confirmed

by the Supreme Court. The Maryland legislature passed an act requiring all banks not created by state authority to restrict their note issues or in lieu of that to pay an annual tax of $15,000. James M'Culloch, cashier of the Baltimore branch of the Bank of the United States, refused to comply on the ground that the state act was unconstitutional. The state sued, and the case was decided in 1819 as *M'Culloch* v. *Maryland* (4 Wheaton 316). In his decision, Chief Justice Marshall ruled on two constitutional questions: (1) whether the act creating the national bank was constitutional, and if so, (2) whether the state act taxing the bank was constitutional. To the first, his answer was yes; his reasoning and even his language closely followed that in the opinion Hamilton had written for Washington in 1791. To the second, his answer was no; because "the power to tax involves the power to destroy," states could undermine the national government, and thereby the Constitution itself, if they were allowed to levy such taxes. (Marshall said that the national government could, however, tax state-chartered banks; but in time the doctrine of reciprocal immunity developed, whereby neither federal nor state governments could tax the instrumentalities of the other.)

The Court had ruled that the bank was constitutional, but the matter did not end there. When Andrew Jackson became president in 1829, he raised the question anew. Jackson had some strange notions concerning the Constitution; for example, in his first annual message to Congress he proposed a constitutional amendment establishing two supreme courts, one for the area east of the Appalachians and another for the West. But he was within the traditions of Washington and Jefferson in regarding himself as a guardian of the Constitution, irrespective of what the Court had ruled; and in the same message he asserted that the constitutionality of the bank was "well questioned by a large portion of our fellow-citizens." In 1832, however, his secretary of the treasury, Louis McLane, praised the bank and recommended its recharter. When Jackson made no comment other than to say he would leave the question "to the investigation of an enlightened people and their representatives," friends of the bank took that to mean he would not oppose a recharter. They urged congressmen to pass a recharter act in 1832 rather than wait until the old charter expired four years later. Congress did so, but Jackson vetoed the bill. After the charter expired in 1836, the bank continued for a time to operate under a charter granted by the state of Pennsylvania, but it collapsed in the wake of the financial panic of 1837. It was never revived.

The overall result of the anti-nationalist and generally anti-developmental policies of the Jeffersonians and Jacksonians was to establish what amounted to local option in regard to economic policy. Each state could adopt such developmental programs as it chose. Ironically, in light of the Jeffersonians' and Jacksonians' antipathy to judicial authority, that result increased the strength of the federal judiciary, for the only restraint upon state action was the Constitution *as interpreted by the Supreme Court*.

THE COMMERCE AND CONTRACT CLAUSES UNDER THE MARSHALL COURT

For thirty-four years, the dominant influence in exerting that restraint was Chief Justice John Marshall. When Marshall was appointed to the bench in 1801 all his fellow justices were Federalists; when he died in 1835 all were either Jeffersonian Republicans or Jacksonian Democrats. Such was the force of his personality and power of legal reasoning, however, that the appointees of his political enemies came to share his ardent nationalism and most of his constitutional views. One of them, Madison's appointee Joseph Story, was more learned and probably had a better mind than Marshall; but that merely reinforced Marshall's influence, for Story's views, as they developed, were even more strongly Federalist than those of the chief justice.

The major decisions of the Marshall Court that concern us at present arose from the contract clause and the commerce clause. The contract clause of Article I, Section 10 forbids states to pass any law "impairing the obligation of contracts." The language seems plain enough, but as is often true of the language of constitutions and laws, its full meaning is complex. The idea of the sanctity of contracts was an ancient one, but in English and American law the obligations of contracts were limited by the concepts of just price and fair value. Everything was assumed to have an intrinsic worth, and if it could be shown that the "consideration" given by either party to a contractual agreement did not reflect that worth—if, for instance, one party had charged exorbitant prices or had taken advantage of the hardships of the other—that amounted to the use of force or fraud and the contract would be nullified by the courts. The courts of England had, during the two decades before the American Revolution, radically altered the law of contracts to bring it into accord with the idea of a free market. The new "will" theory of contracts, replacing the traditional "equity" theory, held that "it is the consent of the parties alone, that fixes the just price of any thing, without reference to the nature of things themselves, or to their intrinsic value." But that doctrine had, at the time of the writing of the Constitution, nowhere been established in America. Patrick Henry expressed the prevailing American view when he said that "there are thousands and thousands of contracts, whereof equity forbids an exact literal performance." In other words, few Americans, upon reading the Constitution in 1787, would have supposed that the contract clause prevented interference with contractual obligations through the equity principle.

The Marshall Court not only followed the will theory, at least in spirit, it also expanded the meaning of contracts. Its first major contract decision, in *Fletcher* v. *Peck* (6 Cranch 87), was a long time in developing. In the early 1790s the state of Georgia, though inhabited only on its seacoast and along the Savannah River, had extended from the Atlantic to the Mississippi, and thus its public domain included more than eighty million acres of unsettled land. The land was an irresistible source of fraudulent profits for the state's politicians. One governor signed away one and a half million acres to a single individual, and the legislature granted and regranted lands so extravagantly that individuals held titles to three times as much land as there was in a twenty-four county area. The most notorious sale was to four Yazoo Land Companies (named for the river that flows through what became Mississippi), whose directors paid handsome bribes to the legislature and a nominal sum to the state for title to thirty-five million acres. In 1796 a group of reformers gained control of the state government and passed a law rescinding the Yazoo sales, but in the meantime one of the companies had sold its claims to a group of presumably innocent investors in New England. The question of the legitimacy of the claims of the New Englanders was argued in the courts and in Congress for a number of years, until it was finally decided by the Supreme Court in 1810.

In the *Fletcher* case, as in the *M'Culloch* case, Marshall followed a line of reasoning earlier advanced by Hamilton. In a legal opinion written for the investors, Hamilton had argued that the contract clause did not apply only to private contracts, as most people assumed, but also to public contracts—those between individuals and government. Marshall so ruled, holding that the sale of the land by the state to the Yazoo company was a contract under the meaning of Article I, Section 10. The 1796 act repealing the sale impaired the obligations of that contract and was therefore unconstitutional. But the case also involved questions arising from the fraudulent circumstances of the original transaction. On this subject Marshall made two important pronouncements. The first concerned the rights of purchasers. If party *A* sells an item to party *B*, Marshall held, proof of fraud in the transaction would warrant setting aside the sale, but if party *B* had, before the fraud came to light, sold the item to party *C*, the rights of the latter "cannot be disregarded." If title to the item were valid, *C*'s claim to it would be upheld irrespective of fraud in the first instance. The second ruling had to do with the public nature of the fraud. It was not within the capacity of the Court, Marshall held, to inquire into the motives of a legislative body: That was a political question, and political questions could be resolved only by the people in the political arena. (The Court's self-imposed restraint in political matters was crucial to the preservation of a government of laws. Though its decisions often had political repercussions, the Court generally avoided interference in political questions for the next hundred and fifty years.)

The implications of the decision in *Fletcher* v. *Peck* were far-reaching, and in several other key cases the Marshall Court pursued some—but not all—of those implications. One clear implication was that if the contract clause applied to agreements between a state and an individual, it must apply also to agreements between states, and in the warmly disputed 1823 case of *Green* v. *Biddle* (8 Wheaton 1), the Court so ruled. When Kentucky became a state, after having been part of Virginia, it agreed that grants of Kentucky lands made earlier by the Virginia legislature would continue to be valid. But because the Virginia grants had been made when Kentucky was a wilderness and their exact locations were often unknown, a large number of conflicting claims arose. To remedy the confusion and also to benefit its own citizens, the Kentucky legislature passed a series of laws requiring claimants, upon proving title to land occupied by someone else, to compensate the occupant for his improvements. Although those laws were in keeping with the developmental spirit, they impaired the "contract" between Virginia and Kentucky and were therefore declared unconstitutional by the Court. (Decisions of this nature were, in fact, beyond the capacity of the Court to enforce, and as state courts were apt to do, the Kentucky courts generally ignored the ruling.)

More far-reaching, though less controversial at the time, was the Court's 1819 ruling in *Dartmouth College* v. *Woodward* (4 Wheaton 518) that a corporate charter was a contract. The college existed by virtue of a charter granted by George III during the colonial period; the charter entitled the trustees to fill vacancies in their own ranks and to govern the institution forever. In 1816 the state legislature, attempting to bring the college under public control, enacted legislation placing it under a board of overseers appointed by the governor. The New Hampshire Superior Court upheld the statute, ruling that the college was essentially a public corporation operating for a public purpose and thus subject to public control. On appeal, the Supreme Court overturned the state-court decision. Marshall, in giving the Court's opinion, conceded that the states reserved their powers to regulate their own civil institutions but went to considerable lengths to show that Dartmouth College was a private charitable institution rather than a public institution. The point on which the case turned, however, was that a corporate charter was a contract and therefore not subject to impairment by the state.

The implications of that decision were of enormous potential consequence. Corporations had long been used for carrying out public and charitable functions, but they had also been used for business purposes, and it was as agencies for private economic activity that they would be most used in America. The advantages of the corporate form of business organization over individual firms and partnerships were that corporations could, by attracting many investors, raise capital on a greatly expanded scale and that they existed, in the eyes of the law, as single entities independently of the persons who owned them. Several hundred corporations operating in the insurance, banking, transportation, and manufacturing industries had been chartered since 1790. In common practice, corporate charters were granted to individuals only by special acts of the state legislatures; in 1811, however, New York had passed a general incorporation law that allowed people to form corporations simply by complying with certain procedures and paying certain fees. During the next two decades most of the other states enacted similar legislation.

But the doctrine of the *Dartmouth College* case, if followed literally in all instances, would have meant that corporations once established were outside the authority of the states that created them: The terms of their charters could never be amended or annulled. The Court doubtless did not intend to go that far. Justice Story, in a concurring opinion, informed the states as to how they could avoid the trap, which was to include, in their acts of incorporation, a clause specifically reserving the right to repeal or modify the charter. The Court did not, during Marshall's lifetime, rule upon another possible implication of the *Dartmouth* decision—that corporations in certain fields, notably transportation, could claim that their charters gave them vested rights that could not be impaired by grants to new corporations, thus implying the creation of perpetual monopolies. In 1830 the Marshall Court did render a decision designed to prevent corporations from unduly stretching their privileges. In *Providence Bank* v. *Billings* (4 Peters 516), a bank contended that because it had not been subject to taxes under state law when it was chartered in 1791, it could not be taxed by a change in the law; the Court ruled that it was not exempt from taxation unless exemption were expressly granted in the act of incorporation. Despite such reservations, however, the corporation was the way of the future for large-scale business enterprise in America, and the *Dartmouth College* decision helped pave the way.

Two additional contract decisions, both involving bankruptcy acts, found the Marshall Court divided against itself. The Constitution had empowered Congress to establish a uniform system of bankruptcy laws, but Congress had declined to do so. As long as business relations remained essentially personal, most reputable people thought of bankruptcy as a refuge for scoundrels; but as economic activity became increasingly depersonalized, businessmen came to regard it as a convenient way of regularizing creditors' rights in the event of failure. Going with the new trend, New York enacted a general bankruptcy law when it passed its general incorporation act in 1811. The law was challenged and taken to the Supreme Court in 1819, in the case of *Sturges* v. *Crowninshield* (4 Wheaton 122). Two issues were involved. The first was whether a state, in the absence of congressional legislation, could pass a bankruptcy act; Marshall held that it could if it did not violate the contract clause. The second and decisive question was whether the specific act was constitutional; Marshall ruled that, because it relieved insolvent debtors of the obligation to pay debts contracted before the law was passed, it was unconstitutional.

Subsequently, New York and various other states passed new bankruptcy laws that covered all debts contracted thereafter but not those contracted before. In 1827 New York's revised law was reviewed by the Court in *Ogden* v. *Saunders* (12 Wheaton 213), and Marshall, for the only time in his career as chief justice, found himself dissenting from the majority. Justice Bushrod Washington, writing the majority opinion, declared that a bankruptcy law in force at the time a contract was made formed a part of the contract and was understood by the contracting parties to be included in their agreement. Marshall and Story, in dissent, insisted that states could not impair even future contracts. A side issue, on which the majority and minority agreed, was whether a state bankruptcy law could discharge a debt owed to a citizen of another state; unanimously, the justices held that it could not, because that would involve conflicts of sovereign powers and collide with the judicial power of the United States.

The Marshall Court's other major economic decisions arose under the commerce clause. The most significant of these cases was *Gibbons* v. *Ogden* (9 Wheaton 1), which concerned the newly developed steamboat. In 1807 the inventor Robert Fulton and his financial backer, Robert Livingston, procured from a skeptical New York legislature exclusive rights, for a period of years, to use a steamboat in the state's waters; provided they could produce such a craft. They succeeded, and in 1808 the legislature granted them a perpetual monopoly of steam navigation on New York waterways. Soon they had a number of steamboats in operation; but finding that their shortage of capital was hampering expansion, they began to lease rights to others. One such lease was to Aaron Ogden, giving him exclusive rights to steamboat traffic between New York and New Jersey. Then Thomas Gibbons, a Georgian who had once been a business partner of Ogden's, obtained a license from the federal government under the terms of a 1793 act regulating coastal trade and began a steamboat service in competition with Ogden. Ogden sued in the New York state courts and Chancellor James Kent, one of the most learned jurists in America, upheld the monopoly. Gibbons appealed to the Supreme Court.

The decision of the Court, given in an opinion written by Marshall, was delivered in 1824. Several issues were involved, and Marshall took them up one by one. The Constitution empowers Congress "to regulate Commerce with foreign Nations, and among the several States." Counsel for the monopoly argued that commerce meant "buying and selling, or the interchange of commodities," and did not comprehend transportation or navigation. Marshall disagreed: Because the power to regulate shipping was universally recognized as part of the power to regulate foreign commerce, he declared, navigation fell within the constitutional meaning of commerce. That in itself was a monumental ruling, for it would, within a few years, apply to another technological innovation, the railroad. The next question turned upon the meaning of the phrase "among the several states." The term "among," said Marshall, meant "intermingled with." Congress did not have power to regulate trade carried on wholly within a single state and not affecting that of other states, but its authority did extend to trade from one state to another and to the navigable rivers on which interstate or foreign commerce could be carried.

The third question was a sticky one. The power to regulate, the chief justice said, meant "to prescribe the rule by which commerce is to be governed." But Congress had not exercised the power; and in the absence of congressional action, it could be assumed that the states had a concurrent power to regulate, as they were not denied that power by the Constitution. Counsel for Ogden so argued; and Marshall himself had ruled in *Sturges* v. *Crowninshield* that states could enact bankruptcy acts in the absence of a congressional act. Counsel for Gibbons, Daniel Webster, argued on the contrary that the power of Congress was exclusive and that the absence of legislation meant that Congress intended for interstate commerce to be free: "All useful regulation does not consist in restraint; and that which Congress sees fit to leave free, is a part of its regulation, as much as the rest." Marshall dodged the issue. There was "great force" in Webster's argument, he said, but the Court was not certain. Instead, Marshall placed the burden of the decision on the 1793 licensing act. That law, under which Gibbons claimed the right to operate, was an act "in pursuance" of the Constitution and therefore took precedence over the state act of 1808 under which the monopoly operated. The monopoly was broken.

But, as happened in several other cases, Marshall had made some sweeping pronouncements from which he subsequently found it necessary to retreat. In *Brown* v. *Maryland* (12 Wheaton 419), he faced up to the question, at what point in the course of trade does the jurisdiction of the state begin? Maryland had passed an act requiring wholesale dealers in imported goods to pay a license fee. A dealer refused to pay the fee, contending that it was a tax on foreign commerce and thus unconstitutional. The state, whose case was argued by Roger Brooke Taney, regarded that claim as nonsense; the fee applied to wholesalers of a wide variety of goods, including some that incidentally had been shipped in interstate or foreign commerce. In his decision, rendered in 1827, Marshall coined the "original package" doctrine: After imported goods have been "mixed up with the mass of property in the country" they were subject to state taxation, but as long as they remained in the importer's warehouse in their original form or package, state taxes on them were unconstitutional duties on imports. States could control imports, Marshall conceded, as part of the "police power" to protect the health, safety, or well-being of their inhabitants, but that was not at issue in the present case.

The Court, however, was badly divided on the whole subject. Two years later, in *Wilson* v. *Black Bird Creek Marsh Company* (2 Peters 245), Marshall handed down a decision that was at least partially at variance with the opinion in the *Gibbons* case: A steamboat operator licensed under the same act as Gibbons had challenged a Delaware statute authorizing the building of a dam that closed off navigable waterways, and Marshall ruled in favor of the state. Then, in 1834, the Court was confronted with an extremely knotty problem. New York, overrun with penniless immigrants and faced with the prospect of feeding them or watching them starve, passed a law requiring ship masters to post bond that immigrants would not become public charges, else they could not be landed. The act was clearly a legitimate exercise of the police power and, equally clearly, it was a direct restriction on foreign commerce as Marshall had defined the term. The statute was challenged in *New York* v. *Miln* (8 Peters 120). Marshall and three associate justices thought the law was unconstitutional, but two of the latter were not present at the arguments and thus could not participate in the decision. The other three justices thought the law constitutional. But Marshall, outvoted three to two, postponed the decision by ruling that judgments in constitutional cases were not to be given unless four justices, a majority of the whole court, concurred in the decision. When the case was finally settled in 1837, Marshall was dead and the entire complexion of the Court had changed.

ECONOMIC ISSUES AND
THE TANEY COURT

The turnover in the personnel of the Court was almost total. Five justices died or retired during Jackson's presidency, leaving only Story and Smith Thompson of New York from the old Marshall Court. Moreover, in 1837 Congress increased the number of justices to nine, so that Jackson's appointees suddenly constituted a seven-to-two majority. They were all advocates of states' rights, and Roger Brooke Taney, Marshall's replacement as chief justice, had repeatedly criticized the nationalistic tenor of Marshall's decisions. He would remain on the bench until 1864, a tenure as chief justice second in length only to that of Marshall himself.

Taney took his seat in the 1837 term of the Court, just in time to participate in three long-pending decisions that altered the direction in which constitutional law had been moving. The simplest of these was the *New York* v. *Miln* case, which the Marshall Court had postponed: By a seven-to-one majority (Story alone dissenting), the Taney Court upheld the validity of the New York immigration law, which a majority of the justices on the Marshall Court had regarded as unconstitutional.

More subtle were the departures in a second case, *Briscoe* v. *Bank of Kentucky* (11 Peters 257), which turned on the constitutional provision forbidding the states to issue "bills of credit," or paper money. Seven years earlier, in the case of *Craig* v. *Missouri* (4 Peters 410), Marshall had construed the prohibition strictly and declared unconstitutional a state law issuing loan certificates receivable for taxes but not legal tender for private debts. In the Kentucky case it was not the state that issued paper money but a public banking corporation wholly owned by the state. With Story again dissenting, the Court held the Kentucky act to be constitutional. The significance of the ruling in respect to economic development was that—given the demise of the Second Bank of the United States—separate state systems of banking and currency would now replace the nationally monitored system. As a result, the nation's money supply would be unstable for a whole generation, until Congress restored some measure of order by passing a national banking act.

In the third important decision of the 1837 term, *Charles River Bridge* v. *Warren Bridge* (11 Peters 420), Taney rendered an opinion regarding corporate charters that was in spirit a radical departure from the *Dartmouth College* decision. In 1785 the legislature of Massachusetts had granted a forty-year charter authorizing the Charles River Bridge Company to build and operate a toll bridge from Boston to Charlestown, and in 1792 it extended the charter to seventy years. As the cities grew in population the venture became extremely profitable to the investors. Then in 1828 the legislature chartered a new corporation, the Warren Bridge Company, and authorized it to build a competing bridge a short distance from the original one. Tolls would be collected on the new bridge for six years, after which time it would be free. There was nothing in the charter of the first company stating it would be a monopoly, so the proprietors could not challenge a competitor on that ground. The terms of the Warren company's charter, however, were such as to drive the Charles River company out of business, thereby depriving its proprietors of legally and contractually vested property rights. The Charles River company brought suit for an injunction on the ground that the 1828 act was an impairment of the obligation of contracts.

The case was complicated by two questions, one constitutional and the other practical. The constitutional issue was the extent to which a corporate charter implicitly conveyed rights and privileges. Marshall had placed limits on the theory of implied rights when he ruled, in the *Providence Bank* case, that a corporation did not acquire immunity from future taxation simply because the law at the time of the grant did not provide for taxing it, but the circumstances in the *Charles River Bridge* case were quite different. Had the Rhode Island investors known they might someday be taxed, they would still have formed their bank. Had the Massachusetts investors thought the legislature would establish a toll-free competitor, they doubtless would never have undertaken the project; and it was agreed by all that the bridge provided a valuable public service. Underlying the problem was a deep-seated difference of opinion as to the best means of promoting economic development. An older school held that "certainty of expectations and predictability of legal consequences," together with the granting of special privileges to encourage developers, were the essential conditions of economic progress. An emerging school held that competition was a far more effective stimulus.

The practical question was one of changing technology. After centuries in which technological innovation was of trivial dimensions, a sudden burst of inventive activity had begun to bring profound changes in the way people worked, moved about, and lived. In Taney's own lifetime, primitive trails had been succeeded by turnpike roads, canals, and the steamboat, and the age of the railroad had begun. At any stage of this process a state, believing the improvement of transportation facilities to be in the public interest, might encourage investors to take the necessary financial risks by granting them exclusive franchises. But what was it to do when a better technology came along? The older school would have held that a monopoly grant to a turnpike company, say, precluded a subsequent grant to a railroad company, on the ground that the vested rights arising from a contract are inviolable. On the other hand, Taney, in a legal opinion given at the request of a turnpike company before he became chief justice, advanced the radical idea that a legislature had no power to grant monopoly privileges at all.

He did not go that far in his *Charles River Bridge* decision, for his associates did not agree with his extreme position; but he did, in ruling for the state and against the Charles River company, dismiss entirely the idea that there could ever be an implied monopoly. "In grants by the public," he declared, "nothing passes by implication." What the company was really claiming, Taney added, was that its charter was a contract conferring property rights in the form of a monopoly over "a line of travelling"; if that claim were admitted, it would be the end of the technological improvements "which are now adding to the wealth and prosperity, and the convenience and comfort of every other part of the civilized world." Chancellor Kent, writing to Story about the decision (Story had again been alone in dissent), said that "it abandons, or overthrows, a great principle of constitutional morality...injures the moral sense of the community, and destroys the sanctity of contracts." But Kent's and Story's were voices from the past.

During the next decade and a half the Taney Court handed down a number of additional decisions concerning corporations, all of the same general tenor—though often confusing. The most important was in an 1839 case, *Bank of Augusta* v. *Earle* (13 Peters 519). A Georgia bank had acquired some bills of exchange (checks drawn by merchants on accounts with other merchants) issued by citizens of Alabama, and in the post-1837 depression the debtors had refused to pay on the ground that an out-of-state corporation had no legal authority to do business in Alabama. To the shock of businessmen and lawyers throughout the country, Supreme Court Justice John McKinley, sitting on the Circuit Court for Alabama, upheld the debtors. When the case was appealed to the Supreme Court, Daniel Webster, as counsel for the bank, argued that a corporation was a person in the eyes of the law and as a "citizen" of one state was entitled by Article IV, Section 2 of the Constitution to "all Privileges and Immunities of Citizens in the several States." Taney, in his decision, rejected that argument and declared that a state had full power to prevent outside corporations from doing business within its borders. But it was common practice to allow them to do so, he went on, and in the absence of legislation specifically excluding them, the presumption must be that the state approves. On that narrow ground, Taney ruled in favor of the bank. Because of the outcome of the case, many people mistakenly assumed that the Court had ruled that a state could not exclude outside corporations; but the principle of exclusion stood, and many states soon began to act upon it.

In its other contract and corporation cases the Taney Court tended to be inconsistent, in no small measure because the chief justice lacked his predecessor's powers of persuasion and could not bring the associate justices into agreement with any regularity. Taney often found himself in the minority, cases were frequently settled by a five-to-four vote with alignments shifting, and, significantly, the justices commonly wrote separate opinions even when they agreed with one another. The result was a considerable amount of confusion.

Possibly the greatest confusion arose from the Court's decision in *Swift* v. *Tyson* (16 Peters 1), decided in 1842. Article 34 of the original Judiciary Act had provided that state laws would control trials at common law. In previous decisions of the Supreme Court it had been generally assumed that "state laws" included decisions of state courts as well as statutes. But now the Court ruled—in a case involving the law of negotiable instruments in New York—that decisions of state courts were not necessarily binding and that there existed a general commercial law of the United States that overrode state-court rulings, even in the absence of constitutional provisions or acts of Congress. Gradually, under this doctrine, the Supreme Court attempted to work out a uniform national commercial law; but in the meantime, businessmen and their lawyers could never be entirely certain as to what the Court would declare the law to be.

In one economic area, however—cases involving the commerce clause—the Taney Court managed to be more consistent and clear than the Marshall Court had been, even though it continued to be internally divided. In general terms, the tendency of its decisions was to expand national authority in regard to foreign commerce and to expand state power in regard to interstate commerce. The Constitution gave the federal courts jurisdiction over maritime and admiralty cases. In English law, and in American law when Marshall was on the Court, admiralty jurisdiction extended only to tidewater—that is, to the seas and coastal rivers. With the coming of the steamboat, a large volume of traffic began on the Great Lakes, and in 1845 Congress passed a law extending federal admiralty jurisdiction to cover cases involving the inland lakes. The constitutionality of the act was strongly challenged, but in *Propeller Genessee Chief* v. *Fitzhugh* (12 Howard 443), Taney upheld the extension, thus reconciling (as he had in the *Charles River Bridge* case) constitutional doctrine with changing technology.

In the *Passenger* cases (7 Howard 283), decided in 1849, the Taney Court ruled that congressional power over foreign commerce was exclusive and that states could not act upon it even in the absence of congressional legislation. The states of Massachusetts and New York had passed laws imposing a head tax on all immigrants landed in their jurisdictions. The Supreme Court held that the tax was, in effect, a duty on imports and thus prohibited by Article I, Section 10. Taney himself dissented, contending that in the absence of congressional regulation the states had concurrent power to regulate foreign commerce.

In regard to interstate commerce, the justices were likewise divided and likewise, on the whole, consistent. The *License* cases (5 Howard 504), settled in 1847, involved the constitutionality of laws enacted by Rhode Island, Massachusetts, and New Hampshire to restrict and tax the sale of alcoholic beverages. The Court upheld all three laws, though six different judges wrote nine different opinions in the three cases, not one of which was supported by a majority of the Court. The statutes of Rhode Island and Massachusetts were reasonably simple; because they taxed imported liquor only after it was broken into small quantities for retail sale, they were not contrary to the original-package doctrine. The New Hampshire law, however, taxed imported liquor in its original and unbroken package. Taney and three other justices declared in their opinion that state power over interstate commerce was concurrent with federal power and could be exercised whenever Congress failed to act. Justice John McLean disagreed, holding that congressional power was exclusive, but he voted to uphold the New Hampshire law anyway, on the ground that it was not a regulation of commerce but a valid exercise of the state's police power.

If the *License* cases puzzled lawyers as to whether the states did or did not have concurrent power over interstate commerce, their confusion was removed four years later. In *Cooley* v. *Board of Wardens of the Port of Philadelphia* (12 Howard 299), the Court ruled in favor of concurrent jurisdiction, having come to realize that Congress itself had long since acted on the question. The First Congress, in 1789, had directed harbor pilots to "continue to be regulated in conformity" with existing or future state laws "until further legislative provision shall be made by Congress." Pennsylvania's pilot act of 1803, under which the *Cooley* case was brought, was thus authorized by act of Congress. Obviously, then, the members of the First Congress had regarded the power to regulate interstate commerce as concurrent. The Court agreed with that determination and upheld the Pennsylvania act.

THE DIRECTION OF CONSTITUTIONAL LAW CONCERNING THE ECONOMY

The overall drift of constitutional and legal decisions in regard to economic activity during the first half of the nineteenth century was in a single general direction, but the movement was erratic. Development replaced enjoyment as the central concern of the law of property rights, a variety of new forms of property rights came to be recognized and protected under the law, and a free-market theory of contracts was substituted for the equity theory. Yet the breakthrough was far from complete. The proper role of government in economic life remained subject to serious debate. Different sections, interest groups, and states took different positions. With the general decline of the authority of the central government, the Founding Fathers' ideal of a common national market having a uniform currency and uniform commercial regulations gave way to a multiplicity of bodies of economic law. Whether a national system or state systems would prevail remained an open question.

QUESTIONS
FOR DISCUSSION

1. Were John Marshall's decisions consistent? Did they flow in a single overall direction? Do you expect justices and especially the chief justice to be always consistent? Do you want them to be?

2. Can one refer to the "Taney Court" in the same way one refers to the "Marshall Court"? How did the Taney Court differ from the Marshall Court?

3. How did the developments in business and technology affect the interpretation of the Constitution? Do you think the Constitution can encompass future technological changes such as interplanetary navigation, subaqueous farming and mining, computerized health care?

4. What is a contract? What kind of protection does the "contract clause" provide?

5. Is a corporation a "person" in the eyes of the law today? What legal rights does a corporation have? What legal remedies exist if a corporation violates the law? How could the Ford Motor Company be tried for murder?

RECOMMENDED
READINGS

MORTON HORWITZ, *The Transformation of American Law, 1780–1860* (Cambridge: Harvard University Press, 1977).

STANLEY I. KUTLER, *Privilege and Creative Destruction: The Charles River Bridge Case* (Philadelphia: Lippincott, 1971).

PETER MAGRATH, *Yazoo* (Providence, R.I.: Brown University Press, 1966).

R. KENT NEWMYER, *The Supreme Court under Marshall and Taney* (New York: Crowell, 1968).

HARRY N. SCHEIBER, "Property Law, Expropriation, and Resource Allocation by Government, 1789–1910," *Journal of Economic History* 33 (1973).

4
FEDERAL-STATE RELATIONS

*I*n creating a federal system of government, the framers of the Constitution devised what James Wilson accurately described as a "system hitherto unknown." Doing that was hardly a vision and even less of a decision; it was a compromise. Several of the delegates would have been willing to abolish the state governments entirely, had they been able to get the voters to approve; a few of the delegates, most politicians, and a sizable majority of the electorate would have been content to give the Confederation Congress a few additional powers and otherwise leave the states in full control. What was worked out instead was something that jurists and legal theorists had long regarded as impossible, namely, a division of sovereignty. The national government (or, as we have come to call it, the federal government) had, in the words of Gouverneur Morris, "compleat and compulsive power" over individuals in its designated sphere of authority. The states had such power in the sphere of authority reserved for them. In a few areas—very few—both levels of government were forbidden to act; in a somewhat larger area, both were free to act, but in the event of conflict, federal law took precedence over state law.

The two principal authors of *The Federalist*, Madison and Hamilton, had different opinions as to how effective the federal system would be in practice. Madison, who was fond of complex theoretical schemes, was inclined to believe the system would work without much friction or at least without destructive friction. Hamilton, a practical man, feared that either the states would swallow the national government or the national government would swallow the states, and thought the states more likely to win. Neither prediction turned out to be entirely accurate. Resistance to federal authority, sometimes by individuals though more effectively by state governments, proved to be as frequent and almost as strong as Hamilton had feared, yet the system somehow survived challenge after challenge, decade after decade. But no one could be sure, even after sixty years, how much longer the Union would endure.

DEFIANCE OF FEDERAL AUTHORITY TO 1816

The first serious defiance of the federal government arose in response to one of Hamilton's measures, an excise tax on liquor levied in 1791. In the backcountry of Pennsylvania and North Carolina, where frontiersmen distilled and drank great quantities of whiskey, had never paid taxes on it, and resented every intrusion of government, the excise was resisted from the outset. In 1792 gangs of armed men terrorized a number of tax collectors, and it appeared for a time that the army or the militia might have to be employed to enforce the law. To facilitate that, should it become necessary, Congress passed the Militia Act of 1792, authorizing the president to call out state militias whenever a federal judge certified that the laws of the United States were being opposed "by combinations too powerful to be suppressed by the ordinary course of judicial proceedings." Things quieted down, however, and for a year or two most of the backcountry men paid their taxes without much protest.

In the meantime, the Washington administration was learning that the law-enforcement machinery provided by the Constitution was inadequate. To be sure, federal marshals, as officers of the court, could handle infractions after a district attorney obtained the appropriate court order, and the Coast Guard, as a branch of the Treasury Department, could police smuggling. But between these regular means and the extreme measure of employing armed force lay a large twilight zone in which there was no federal machinery, and it was politically impracticable, if not constitutionally impossible, to create any. The solution adopted was to use state officials to enforce federal laws. In the Fugitive Slave Act of 1793 Congress did so, and in the same year President Washington requested the state governors to enforce a neutrality proclamation. For the most part, state officials complied, and the practice became an established norm.

The weakness in that approach was that it made federal authority dependent to a considerable extent on the voluntary cooperation of state officials, and cooperation could not be counted upon when state and federal interests clashed. A showdown came as early as 1794. To facilitate the enforcement of the excise law, Congress removed jurisdiction over collection disputes from the federal district courts, which were sometimes hundreds of miles away from the backcountry distilleries, and placed it in state courts, which existed in every county. For that and other reasons, western Pennsylvania erupted in the so-called Whiskey Rebellion. The mails were robbed; several hundred men laid siege to the home of the excise inspector, defended by seventeen soldiers of the regular army; several thousand armed men paraded in Pittsburgh, and talk of murdering federal officials caught in the area became common. President Washington and several of his advisors conferred with Pennsylvania Governor Thomas Mifflin, but Mifflin was reluctant to do anything, partly from fear that, if called, the Pennsylvania militia would refuse to serve, partly from fear that his political future was in jeopardy. Finally, Washington invoked the Militia Act of 1792, mobilized 12,950 militiamen from four states, and personally marched at the head of the troops into the interior of Pennsylvania. In the face of that massive display of federal power, the "rebellion" vanished. Scarcely a shot was fired, two thousand troublemakers fled to Kentucky, and resistance to federal law in the region disappeared.

Five years later a much more dangerous situation arose. In response to the Alien and Sedition acts of 1798, the Republican-controlled legislatures of Virginia and Kentucky defied the federal government and prepared to back their defiance by force. Both states adopted resolutions endorsing the doctrine that the Constitution was a compact between states, and both declared the Alien and Sedition acts unconstitutional. The Virginia resolutions, which were written by Madison, advanced the doctrine of interposition: that when Congress exceeds what the states regard as the limits of its constitutional authority, the states have the right and duty "to interpose for arresting the progress of the evil." The Kentucky resolutions, drafted by Jefferson, went further, saying in one set of resolves that each state has "an equal right to judge for itself" whether an act is unconstitutional and, if it so decides, to resist in whatever way it sees fit. In a second series of resolutions Kentucky declared that "a nullification...of all unauthorized acts" was the proper remedy. In addition, the Virginia legislature bought five thousand muskets and levied taxes for further military measures, to enable the state "to resist by force the encroachments of the...administration upon her indisputable rights."

The doctrines of interposition and nullification were not put to the test of force. Hamilton wanted to handle the Virginia "rebellion" in the same way that the Whiskey Rebellion had been handled: He proposed to lead a new twelve-thousand-man federal army, of which he was major general, to the South and "put Virginia to the test of resistance." As it happened, the prospect of war with France—for which the army had been authorized—blew over and Hamilton was unable to recruit many men. Whether he actually would have invaded Virginia and whether Virginia actually would have met force with force are unanswerable questions. More important is another question that went unanswered, one that was implicit in the Virginia and Kentucky resolutions: If the Republicans had not gained control of the federal government and repealed the Alien and Sedition acts, and if Virginia and Kentucky had stuck by their positions, what constitutional remedy would the federal government have had?

The Republicans' accession to power by no means ended state challenges to federal authority. Rather, the center of resistance shifted from the South to New England. From 1803 until 1815 New England Federalists repeatedly hampered or blocked the enforcement of federal laws, and Yankees repeatedly flirted with an idea that went beyond the doctrine of nullification, namely, secession. Although resistance was stimulated by the whole tenor of the Republican administration, it grew most intense in response to three particular actions: the Louisiana Purchase, the Embargo Act, and the War of 1812.

Opposed to the Louisiana Purchase mainly for narrow economic and political reasons, New Englanders nevertheless justified their stand on constitutional grounds. As they were quick to point out—and as Jefferson admitted—the purchase ran directly counter to the doctrine of strict construction, for the authority to buy territory from foreign governments is nowhere to be found among the enumerated powers of Congress. More fundamentally, the purchase contradicted the compact theory, with which Jefferson had been identified and which underlay the doctrine of states' rights. If the national government could buy a tract of land so large as to be divided into more states than had been party to the original compact, then the state governments could no longer claim that the national government was their creature. When Louisiana was admitted to statehood a few years later, Massachusetts Congressman Josiah Quincy declared that the action made it the right of all states to secede.

Though the New England state governments took no official steps to block the purchase, a number of Federalist leaders, headed by former Secretary of State Timothy Pickering, attempted a more ominous undertaking. The details are shrouded in mystery, but Pickering apparently devised and gained some support for a scheme whereby the five New England states and New York would secede from the United States and form their own union. He considered New York essential to the plan, and he sought, and possibly received, a pledge of support from Vice President Aaron Burr, conditional upon Burr's winning the governorship of New York in the state elections of 1804. When Burr was defeated, the scheme temporarily collapsed.

There was little popular or political support for secession at the time, but that soon changed. In December 1807 Congress, in an effort to combat commercial restrictions imposed by warring France and Britain, passed the Embargo Act, which, when amended at President Jefferson's request, prohibited all shipping and exports. The means for enforcing the law, also enacted at Jefferson's request, were extreme; they included the use of federal troops and the seizing of cargoes without a warrant or the prospect of a trial on the mere suspicion that a merchant or shipper *contemplated* a violation of the embargo. Resistance was widespread, often violent, and ruthlessly suppressed. By midsummer 1808 much of upper New York and New England were under martial law. In Charleston, South Carolina, a ship was detained by the collector of customs on instructions from the president, then ordered released by Supreme Court Justice William Johnson, sitting on circuit, on the ground that the president had exceeded his statutory authority. Jefferson disregarded the order and his attorney general, Caesar Rodney, rebuked Johnson for attempting to interfere with the executive.

In that turbulent context and amidst severe economic dislocations, Timothy Pickering called upon the New England states to nullify the embargo and revived his secession plan. Town meeting after town meeting drew enormous crowds—four thousand adult males in Boston, out of a total population of less than thirty thousand—and adopted resolutions condemning the embargo and the administration and hinting at dismemberment of the Union. The legislatures of Massachusetts and Connecticut adopted interposition resolutions, pointedly using the language Virginia and Kentucky had previously employed. Jefferson responded with an increase of military force; but early in 1809 Congress terminated the crisis by voting to repeal the embargo as of March 4, Jefferson's last day in office.

The War of 1812 evoked the most direct challenges to federal authority by the New England states. The war was extremely unpopular with the people of the region, who considered it unnecessary, contrary to American interests, and waged for the gain of the South and West. A critical question arose almost as soon as war was declared: President Madison called out the state militias for national service, and the legislature of Massachusetts challenged the constitutionality of his action. The problem was turned over to the state supreme court, which issued a carefully worded opinion. The federal government had constitutional authorization to use the state militias for three specified purposes— executing national laws under certain conditions, suppressing insurrections, and repelling invasions—but, the judges added, no power was given to either the president or Congress to determine that the necessary "exigencies do in fact exist." As the power was not delegated to the federal government and not denied to the states, it was reserved to the states by the Tenth Amendment. That position was confirmed by the Massachusetts legislature and adopted by the legislatures of Rhode Island, Vermont, and Connecticut. Connecticut went even further than to deny the federal government the use of the state militia: In 1815 it passed an act directing state judges to release from the United States Army, by writ of habeas corpus, any minors who had enlisted without the written consent of their parents. Moreover, people throughout the region openly furnished supplies to the British army in Canada, and the state governments refused to enforce federal laws forbidding this practice.

The climax of resistance to the war came at the Hartford Convention in December 1814. The legislatures of three of New England's states officially sent delegates, as did local conventions in the other two states. Most people at the time thought the convention represented the culmination of a conspiracy to break up the Union, and historians long believed the same; but recent scholarship suggests that moderate Federalists really called the convention to head off a secession movement by proposing a series of constitutional amendments. In any event, after endorsing the doctrine of interposition, the convention actually did propose amendments. It also appointed a committee of three to negotiate with the national government, but before the committee could set to work, news arrived from Europe that a peace agreement had been reached. Thus once again a crisis passed.

STATE CHALLENGES TO THE MARSHALL COURT, 1816–1832

Meanwhile, state courts had begun to defy the Supreme Court. The strongest defiance set off a running battle between Chief Justice Marshall and Virginia Court of Appeals Judge Spencer Roane—the man Jefferson would have appointed chief justice if he had had the opportunity—though when the fracas started, Marshall was not an active participant. The first of the cases involved, *Fairfax's Devisee* v. *Hunter's Lessee* (7 Cranch 603), had been a long time in developing. During the Revolution, Virginia had confiscated the vast estate of Lord Fairfax. Ignoring the claims of Fairfax's heir, Denny Martin, that the confiscation was invalid, the state sold parts of the land to a number of buyers, including John Marshall and his brother James. Suits over the title dragged along in the courts for many years until 1810, when the Virginia Court of Appeals unreservedly annulled Martin's claim. Martin appealed to the Supreme Court under Article 25 of the Judiciary Act of 1789, which authorized appeals when a state-court decision was alleged to be unconstitutional. Marshall, as an interested party, did not participate, two other justices were absent, and one dissented; consequently, the case was settled by less than a majority of the full Court. Story, in the opinion, declared that the Fairfax estate had been protected by the terms of Jay's Treaty of 1794 and, as treaties take precedence over state laws, reversed the Virginia court's ruling. The Supreme Court directed the Virginia court to carry out the decision.

The matter by no means ended there. Roane and the other Virginia judges convened the state's leading lawyers to argue the question whether they should obey the Supreme Court's order; after six days of argument, the state court held that Article 25 of the Judiciary Act was unconstitutional and therefore that the Supreme Court had no jurisdiction in the case. That decision, in turn, was appealed to the Supreme Court as *Martin* v. *Hunter's Lessee* (1 Wheaton 304), settled in 1816. This time the issue was not title to the land but the constitutionality of Article 25 of the Judiciary Act. Story, as expected, ruled in favor of constitutionality, but he faced a serious problem: What could the Court do if the Virginia Court of Appeals again refused to abide by his decision? To stave off an immediate confrontation, he returned the case not to the court of appeals but to the lower state court in which it had originated.

What was needed, if the Court was to maintain its authority, was a case from which Marshall was not disqualified, so that he could match his wits and prestige against Roane's. A suitable case was arranged in 1819 and settled in 1821. Congress had passed an act authorizing a lottery in the District of Columbia. Lotteries were illegal in Virginia. A man named Cohens, licensed under the congressional act to sell lottery tickets in the District, sold some in Virginia, was arrested and convicted, and appealed to the Supreme Court. This time, in *Cohens* v. *Virginia* (6 Wheaton 264), Marshall wrote the decision, and it was masterful. He addressed himself to the compact doctrine and demolished it. He spelled out in careful detail the doctrine of divided sovereignty. He pointed to the supreme-law clause of the Constitution, which explicitly bound "the judges in every state" to place the Constitution above state constitutions and laws. Because the power to determine whether the state judiciaries were obeying that mandate had to rest somewhere, it was only reasonable that Congress should have vested the power in the supreme federal judiciary.

Having rebutted Roane's argument regarding jurisdiction, Marshall proceeded to rule in favor of Virginia. The case, he said, raised two substantive questions, whether the congressional act was intended to authorize the sale of the lottery tickets in states where such sale was prohibited by law, and if so, whether the act was constitutional. The answer to the first question being in the negative, the second did not arise.

Marshall followed the same tactic, with a more telling effect, a few years later. In *Green* v. *Biddle*, as we have seen, he ruled in favor of Virginia's claims to Kentucky lands. Because Virginians had a large financial stake in the question, they welcomed Marshall's decision; but they could benefit from it only if they recognized the Supreme Court's jurisdiction. They did so, whereupon the Kentucky courts substantially ignored the Supreme Court.

By that time a new challenge had arisen, this one from Ohio. In 1819 the state legislature passed a law imposing a $50,000 annual tax on the Ohio branch of the Bank of the United States. Though the Supreme Court ruled a few weeks later, in *M'Culloch* v. *Maryland*, that such taxes were unconstitutional, Ohio officials chose to ignore the decision. The bank obtained, from the federal circuit court, an injunction prohibiting the state auditor, Ralph Osborn, from collecting the tax. Osborn responded by sending his assistant to the branch bank to enter the vaults by force, if necessary, and remove all the assets he could find. More than $120,000 in gold and notes was removed. The bank sued Osborn for damages and the case began making its way to the Supreme Court, where it was decided in 1824.

Osborn v. *United States* (9 Wheaton 738) involved three major questions. Two of them, concerning the constitutionality of the bank and the power of a state to tax it, were the same as in *M'Culloch* v. *Maryland* and were answered in the same way, though Marshall did add one point to his earlier opinion. Directing his remarks to critics of judicial power, he asserted that judicial power as such "has no existence.... Courts are the mere instruments of the law, and can will nothing.... Judicial power is never exercised for the purpose of giving effect to the will of the judge; always for the purpose of giving effect to the will of the legislature; or, in other words, to the will of the law."

The third question resulted in a considerable extension of the power of the Supreme Court. Ohio contended that the suit against Osborn was in reality a suit against the state by a corporation that was not a "citizen" of Ohio, and thus that the Eleventh Amendment deprived the Supreme Court of jurisdiction. Marshall ruled to the contrary, on two grounds. The first was that in the present case the state was not officially a party of record. The other was that a state officer who had committed a trespass under authority of an unconstitutional act was to be held personally responsible. The first would be overturned by later Court decisions, but the second held and provided the Court with an invaluable weapon against defiant state officials.

It needed every weapon it could find, for challenges to national authority were soon to mount in intensity. Andrew Jackson, in his first message to Congress in December 1829, proposed, among other things, that all southern Indians be removed from their existing lands, even though those lands were guaranteed by treaties, and relocated across the Mississippi River in what was then thought of as the Great American Desert (present-day Oklahoma). The state of Georgia took Jackson's announced position as a blank check for any policy it wished to pursue with respect to the Indians within its borders. The lands of the Creek Indians in Georgia had been obtained through a treaty negotiated by the administration of John Quincy Adams, but the Cherokees continued to hold a large area in the northwestern part of the state. Georgians had long resented the presence of the Cherokee, and two recent developments had sharpened their enmity. One was that the Indians, under the guidance of missionaries (mainly from New England), had been attending schools supported by government funds and were making large strides toward becoming "civilized," white style. They developed a written language, adopted an Anglo-

American system of property rights, and, in 1827, established a constitution organizing tribal law and government along the lines of the United States Constitution. To Georgians, that implied permanency as a self-governing state within the state. The other recent development was the discovery of large deposits of gold in the heart of the Cherokee territory.

In these circumstances, Georgia responded quickly to what it regarded as Jackson's invitation to plunder. Eleven days after Jackson addressed Congress, the state passed a series of laws nullifying the treaties between the United States and the Cherokees and all Cherokee laws and constitutions adopted under the authority of those treaties. The state also prohibited further meetings of the Cherokee government, extended Georgia's jurisdiction over a large section of Cherokee territory, prohibited the Indians from digging for gold on their remaining lands, and extended the laws of Georgia to apply to all Cherokees. These enactments were to become operative as of June 1, 1830.

Two days before the acts went into force, Congress passed the Indian Removal Act that Jackson had requested. The president was thereby authorized to offer all the eastern tribes a nominal compensation for their lands if they would voluntarily move west of the Mississippi. Most Indian tribes were too weak to resist government pressure, but two tribes decided in vain to fight. The Cherokees were determined to protect their rights in the federal courts. For that purpose, they engaged two of the country's most distinguished lawyers, former Attorney General William Wirt and John Sergeant, chief counsel for the Bank of the United States. The attorneys promptly began readying themselves for a test case in which they would attempt to establish the tribe's territorial rights and secure its exemption from the authority of the state of Georgia.

Then a different case diverted the issue. An Indian named Corn Tassel had murdered another Indian, and though the crime took place on Indian territory, state officials arrested, tried, and sentenced Corn Tassel to be hanged. The case was quickly appealed on the ground that the state law under which Corn Tassel was tried violated the Cherokee Treaty of 1791 and thus that his conviction was unconstitutional. On December 22, 1830, the Supreme Court issued a stay of execution and ordered Georgia to appear before the Court the following month. The governor disregarded the writ and the legislature formally ordered all state officials to ignore orders from the Supreme Court. Two days later, Corn Tassel was hanged. Other states had talked of nullifying the authority of the national government; Georgia had acted—openly, contemptuously, and irrevocably.

The Jacksonians in Congress, instead of bringing pressure on Georgia, moved to crack down on the Court. The House Judiciary Committee drew up a bill to cancel the Supreme Court's authority to hear appeals from state trial courts. That would have deprived the national government of a means of requiring the states to abide by the Constitution and would have made it possible for state legislatures to nullify acts of Congress by making their enforcement a crime. After a month of heated debate, however, the bill was defeated.

Meanwhile, Wirt and Sergeant proceeded with their legal action in behalf of the Cherokee nation. They brought suit as an original case before the Supreme Court, on the ground that the Cherokee were an independent nation, and sought an injunction preventing Georgia from enforcing its laws regarding the Indians. The governor, echoing President Jackson's flat declaration that Georgia could do what it pleased with its Indians, refused to obey a subpoena to appear for his state; consequently, Georgia was unrepresented at the hearing. Marshall nevertheless heard the Indians' argument, only to rule, in *Cherokee Nation* v. *Georgia* (5 Peters 1), that the Supreme Court had no original jurisdiction in the case because the Cherokee tribe was not a nation under the meaning of the Constitution. He made it clear, however, that he would rule in favor of the Indians if a suit were properly brought.

The proper suit, *Worcester* v. *Georgia* (5 Peters 515), was brought the next year. One of Georgia's restrictive laws required all white persons living in Cherokee territory to take out licenses and swear an oath of allegiance to the state. Two New England missionaries, Samuel Worcester and Elizur Butler, refused to take out a license and refused to obey an order banishing them from the state. In July 1831 they were arrested. Subsequently, they were tried and sentenced to four years at hard labor. On appeal, the Supreme Court agreed to hear the case, and in October it ordered Georgia's governor and attorney general to appear in behalf of the state. The Court clearly had jurisdiction this time, but the Georgians again refused to appear. Argument for Worcester and Butler was heard in February 1832 without counterargument. In March Marshall announced his decision. He declared the Georgia statute unconstitutional on the ground that the federal government's jurisdiction over Indians was exclusive, no state having power to pass any laws affecting them or their territory. Worcester and Butler were to be released, but the order to carry out the decision was delayed, apparently in the hope that Georgia would voluntarily comply.

Instead, the governor and attorney general of Georgia denounced the decision and said that they were willing to resort to armed force to prevent its execution. President Jackson unreservedly supported them, though he apparently did not say, as he has been quoted as saying, that "Chief Justice Marshall has made his decision; now let him enforce it." Only after some time did Georgia agree to release the missionaries, and then only after they agreed to leave the state—which is what the state had ordered in the first place. Clearly, state resistance to the Supreme Court was out of control.

THE NULLIFICATION CONTROVERSY

Soon it was Jackson's turn to be challenged. In 1828 Congress had passed the so-called Tariff of Abominations, imposing higher protective duties than ever before. Southerners were furious, and many people in South Carolina, goaded by a document secretly written by John C. Calhoun, began to talk of nullifying the law. Nullifiers were unable to gain control of the state for some time, partly because Calhoun, the state's most powerful politician, did not openly support them and partly because Jackson recommended a moderation of the tariff. But in 1831 Vice President Calhoun, having undergone a break with Jackson and having given up hope of becoming his successor, cast his political future with the South Carolina nullifiers. In his Fort Hill Address that summer he gave the doctrine of nullification its ablest philosophical justification. A year later Congress finally revised the tariff but reduced duties only slightly, and in October 1832 the nullificationists swept the South Carolina elections.

Immediately, Governor James Hamilton called the legislature into special session, and the legislature passed a law calling for a popularly elected state convention. That was a carefully chosen maneuver: As the Constititution had been ratified in South Carolina by a popularly elected convention, the state was now returning to such a convention as the ultimate source of sovereignty. The convention met and adopted ordinances declaring the tariff acts of 1828 and 1832 null and void, prohibiting the collection of the duties after February 1, 1833, forbidding appeal to the Supreme Court of cases arising under the ordinance, and declaring that South Carolina would have just cause for seceding from the Union if the federal government should attempt to use force to execute the tariff.

For Georgia to defy the Supreme Court was one thing; for South Carolina to defy an act passed by Congress and signed by Andrew Jackson was quite another. Jackson took the challenge personally, especially as South Carolina's cause was identified with his archenemy Calhoun, and prepared a show of force. He alerted the federal troops in Charleston harbor and ordered General Winfield Scott to take command of the army forces in South Carolina. The state legislature responded by enacting the nullifying convention's ordinances into law. The president again recommended a reduction of the tariff, but he also issued a proclamation to the people of South Carolina denouncing nullification as an "impractical absurdity," declaring that the laws of the land would be executed by force if necessary, and warning the Carolinians that any attempt to secede would be regarded as treason and be punished accordingly. The newly installed governor of that state, former Senator Robert Y. Hayne, issued a counterproclamation defying the president, and the legislature thumbed its nose at Jackson by electing Calhoun to the Senate in Hayne's place. Jackson countered by requesting Congress to pass a Force bill authorizing him to use the army to collect the national revenues. Governor Hayne advised the people of his state to arm themselves for resistance.

It was time for someone with a cool head to intervene, lest the president and the state of his birth blunder their way into a civil war. The man for the task was Senator Henry Clay of Kentucky, who saw, as no one else had seen, the elements of a successful compromise. Reluctantly, he supported the Force bill but coupled it with a compromise tariff that would reduce both nullification and the Force bill to academic questions. Clay's tariff bill would affect the duties only on goods being taxed at more than 20 percent: It would reduce them at two-year intervals until, in 1842, they were down to the 20 percent level. That would appease South Carolinians and other opponents of the tariff by phasing out the protective principle and would retain for manufacturers the benefit of at least some protection for nine years. Too, as Clay pointed out, if this system had flaws they could be remedied later, when tempers had cooled. Both measures were passed on March 1, 1833, and signed by the president the next day.

That broke the crisis, though the overcommitted actors in the drama still had to play out their parts. South Carolina had rescinded its nullification of the earlier tariff as soon as it learned of the introduction of Clay's compromise, and it accepted the new tariff with relief. But, consistent to the last, it formally nullified the Force bill. No showdown was necessary, and that was that.

Jackson, for his part, had occasion a few months later to show how much stomach he had left for a contest of force with a defiant state. In Alabama, most Indians had signed removal agreements under the act of 1830, but the Creeks ceded about three million acres and were guaranteed, by the treaty of cession, the remaining two million acres in their possession. Federal marshals and army troops were ordered to protect them in their reserved area, but speculators and settlers had already swarmed into it, and they defied the federal authorities and looted Indian property almost at will. Then in July 1833 soldiers killed a county commissioner who favored the settlers and was especially obnoxious to the Indians. Alabama whites started forming volunteer companies to expel the army. General Winfield Scott advised Jackson's secretary of war, Lewis Cass, that if he tried to use the army to enforce federal law in Alabama, then Georgia, Mississippi, Virginia, and both Carolinas would join Alabama in armed resistance. Cass conferred with Jackson, and it was decided that white men should not kill one another to protect mere Indians. So the Force bill was not invoked, and Jackson, too, was consistent to the last.

STATES' RIGHTS, SLAVERY, AND THE TANEY COURT

By the time of John Marshall's death it had begun to appear that Hamilton's prediction would be fulfilled, that the state governments, indeed, would swallow the national government. It is only a slight exaggeration to say that, for the most part, the Supreme Court under Roger B. Taney avoided the defiance of the states by letting them do what they wanted. The general trend of the economic decisions discussed in the preceding chapter was definitely in that direction.

In one important case, the Taney Court wisely refused to deal with a state's problems in any way. Most states had, since the beginning of the century, been steadily expanding the right to vote, in large measure by abolishing property qualifications for voting. Almost all states that had not already done so adopted new and more democratic constitutions after the panic of 1837. The state of Rhode Island stubbornly refused to go along with the movement, retaining as its constitution the royal charter of 1663, even though the charter limited voting to owners of several acres of land and most of the tiny state's inhabitants lived in urban areas. A group of Democrats, led by Thomas W. Dorr, demanded reform, and upon being turned down by the legislature, they called an extra-legal convention, which drafted a constitution and submitted it to the state's adult males for ratification. The document was ratified, elections were held under it, and Dorr was elected governor. The existing government proclaimed the new one illegal, and after some minor fighting it won control. Dorr and several of his followers were arrested, Dorr being imprisoned for treason. Though Dorr attempted to have his case reviewed by the Supreme Court, the issue was brought to the Court in a different manner.

The case was *Luther* v. *Borden* (7 Howard 1), decided in 1849. Borden, a militia officer in service of the old government, broke into the home of Luther, a Dorr supporter, to arrest him. Luther sued for trespass on the ground that Borden lacked authority because the Dorr government was the legal one. This argument was based upon a doctrine that was closely related to the argument for nullification: that the people of a state are sovereign and that they thus can form a new government whether their existing government consents or not. The case obviously involved a constitutional issue, for Article IV, Section 4 declares that "the United States shall guarantee to every State in this Union a Republican Form of Government." But Taney, in rendering the decision, said that the matter was not a proper one for the Court to determine. The question, which of the governments of Rhode Island was legitimate, was a question of political power, to be resolved by the political departments of government. By implication, it was up to the president and/or Congress to enforce Article IV, Section 4.

The most crucial constitutional issues arising after Taney became chief justice were those concerning slavery. The Constitution clearly recognized slavery, though it did not use the term. At the time the Constitution was adopted, however, slavery was thought to be a dying institution except in South Carolina and Georgia. It was being phased out by law in the North and was prohibited in the Northwest Territory by the Northwest Ordinance.

In the tobacco-growing regions of the upper South slavery was unprofitable, and there was considerable sentiment for some form of gradual emancipation. But the rapid expansion of cotton growing after the invention of the cotton gin revitalized slavery and ensured its continuation, at least in the lower South.

Prior to the 1830s, the issue had not often excited much controversy, and such dispute as there was turned not on moral considerations but on the question of political power. Few northerners had strong feelings about slavery, but they resented the disproportionate voice in national affairs that the South derived from the constitutional provision that counted slaves as three-fifths of a person for purposes of representation and direct taxation. Because direct taxes were rarely levied, the South had all the benefits of what had originally been a compromise. As a result, southern states were overrepresented. In 1820, for instance, South Carolina and New Hampshire each had about 245,000 free inhabitants, but the former had nine seats in the House of Representatives and the latter only six; Virginia and Georgia combined had something over 800,000 free inhabitants and thirty-three electoral votes, whereas Massachusetts, with roughly the same free population, had but twenty-two. The South's advantage was being overcome, however, because the North's population was increasing faster. Yet the South was expanding territorially, which gave it hope of creating enough new states to preserve at least an equal voice in the Senate.

It was those circumstances that underlay the Missouri Compromise of 1820. Maine was admitted as a free state, against the wishes of southerners, and Missouri was admitted as a slave state, contrary to northern wishes, and slavery was excluded in the remainder of the Louisiana Purchase area north of Arkansas. Subsequently, admissions of new states were paired, one slave and one non-slave.

The issue took on new and more dangerous proportions in the 1830s. On the one side, southerners feared that the North's rapid growth would bring total northern control of the federal government and, with it, protective tariffs and a host of other policies designed to promote northern economic growth at the South's expense. On the other side, antislavery sentiment began to spread in the North, and by the end of the decade a full-blown, fiercely uncompromising abolitionist movement had come into being. Slavery could not, of course, be abolished except by a constitutional amendment, but the activities of the abolitionists could and did raise a number of constitutional issues.

Two of these came up during Jackson's presidency and were temporarily resolved outside the court. Abolitionists began deluging Congress with petitions, and John Quincy Adams (who was returned to the House for nine terms after he left the presidency) insisted upon reading them on the floor. That seriously disrupted business, but the right to petition the government was explicitly guaranteed by the First Amendment. Finally, in 1836 the House adopted the so-called Gag Rule, whereby abolitionist petitions were received but automatically tabled without being discussed. The rule was renewed, with variations, for the next eight years. Meanwhile, abolitionists, after having been expelled from the South, were sending propaganda tracts into the region by the mails. In Charleston in the summer of 1835, the postmaster impounded a boatload of antislavery materials, and a mob seized and burned them. When the postmaster reported the incident to Postmaster General Amos Kendall, Kendall officially replied that he had no legal authority to bar the publications from the mails. Unofficially, despite the protection of a free press by the First Amendment, he advised southern postmasters to intercept all such material, for "we owe an obligation to the laws, but a higher one to the communities in which we live."

The first major case concerning slavery that reached the Supreme Court was decided in 1842. At issue were the Fugitive Slave Act of 1793 and the principle of using state officials to enforce federal laws. A number of northern legislatures, beginning with Indiana's in 1824, passed "personal liberty" laws refusing to cooperate. A Vermont law enacted in 1840 made it a criminal offense for any citizen to aid in the capture of a runaway slave. A case testing the personal-liberty laws was arranged between officials of Maryland and Pennsylvania: A man named Prigg carried a runaway slave woman and child from Pennsylvania back to Maryland, in violation of Pennsylvania's act of 1826 declaring the removal of an alleged fugitive, without a certificate from a state official, to be kidnapping. Prigg returned to Pennsylvania to be tried and convicted, then appealed to the Supreme Court. In *Prigg* v. *Pennsylvania* (16 Peters 539) Justice Story delivered the opinion that the Pennsylvania act was unconstitutional. The reasoning, however, drew some careful distinctions. Slaveowners had a constitutional right to have runaways returned, and no state could interfere in any way, for power to legislate on the subject was vested exclusively in Congress. When Congress delegated enforcement powers to state officials in the 1793 act, it had every right to do so; but because state officials were not federal officials, they could not be *required* to enforce the federal law if state law prohibited them from doing so. The doctrine of states' rights, obviously, could work either for or against slavery.

Four years after the Prigg decision, the Mexican War broke out, and with it came intensification of the sectional divisions. The war was extremely popular among southerners, for they saw in it the prospect of annexing a large area into which the slave plantation system might be expanded. It was unpopular in the Northeast, for the same reason. In Massachusetts, the state House of Representatives adopted a resolution declaring the war unconstitutional, and abolitionists sought from the state supreme court an order prohibiting the recruitment of soldiers in the state. Though that effort failed, the legislature did refuse to supply the volunteer companies that were recruited in Massachusetts. In Congress, John Quincy Adams sponsored a resolution stating that the war was unconstitutional—even though Congress itself had declared it—and the House passed the resolution in a purely sectional vote. Then Congressman David Wilmot of Pennsylvania made a proposal that would bitterly divide the nation for years. He offered, as a rider to an appropriation bill, a provision that slavery be forever prohibited in any territory acquired as a result of the war. The "Wilmot Proviso," though passed by the House, was rejected by the Senate; but the issue of slavery in the territories inflamed passions all over the country.

A grave crisis followed during the winter of 1849–50. Southerners threatened secession if the Wilmot Proviso were passed, and they were doubly alarmed by the prospect that California would be admitted to statehood, tipping the balance of power in the Senate, sixteen free states to fifteen slave states. Conflict was avoided, however, by the Compromise of 1850. California was admitted as a free state, but the rest of the newly acquired territory was organized with no prohibition against slavery. The slave trade in the District of Columbia, which had long outraged opponents of slavery, was abolished, but a new and tougher fugitive slave act was passed. The crisis was over for the time being.

The Supreme Court had occasion, a year later, to render its second major decision regarding slavery. A slaveowner in northern Kentucky had a black minstrel show, and several times he sent his blacks across the Ohio River to perform in Cincinnati. One day three of them crossed into Ohio and escaped to Canada. The slaveowner sued the ferryboat owner for helping in the escape; the ferryman argued that the runaways had become free by having previously been in Ohio, where slavery had been banned by the Northwest Ordinance. But the Court, in *Strader* v. *Graham* (10 Howard 82), decided to the contrary. It ruled that the ordinance ceased to have effect after the territory was carved into states. It also ruled that, whatever the status of the blacks when they were in Ohio, the Kentucky law applied upon their return to Kentucky and under that law they were slaves.

The issue flared up in Congress again in 1854 with the passage of the Kansas-Nebraska Act, which provided for the organization of the two territories on a "popular sovereignty" basis— that is, the settlers could decide for themselves whether they would have slavery. As both territories lay north of the Missouri Compromise line, the act repealed that compromise. Abolitionists were furious, protest demonstrations were held all over the North, and people from North and South alike sent settlers rushing to Kansas in an effort to capture the area for their sides. A considerable amount of violence ensued.

It was in that atmosphere that the Supreme Court handed down its decision in *Dred Scott* v. *Sandford* (19 Howard 393). Scott was a slave in Missouri. His owner, an army surgeon, took him to Illinois, part of the Northwest Territory, resided there for more than a year, and subsequently took him to what became the state of Minnesota. Thereafter, Scott returned with his owner to Missouri. After a change of ownership through inheritance, Scott brought suit in a local Missouri court, claiming that his periods of residence in free territory entitled him to his freedom. He won in the lower court but the state supreme court, following the precedent of *Strader* v. *Graham*, reversed the verdict. Persons helping Scott then sought a trial in the federal courts by arranging a fictitious sale of the slave to a New Yorker—which, because the case now involved residents of different states, was presumed to be a constitutional ground for the exercise of federal jurisdiction. The suit was tied up in technicalities for several years but finally reached the Supreme Court in 1856.

The matter could have been resolved simply, but the justices allowed personal attitudes and feelings to interfere with the Court's functioning as a "mere instrument of the law." The easy and proper course was to follow the ruling in *Strader* v. *Graham*. Most of the justices were, at first, agreed to do that, but apparently Justices John McLean of Ohio and Benjamin Curtis of Massachusetts, both ardent abolitionists, were determined to write dissenting opinions arguing that Congress had power over slavery in the territories. Moreover, the five southern justices on the Court actually welcomed the opportunity to rule to the contrary, and Taney—publicly the essence of judicial impartiality—was seething with sectional animosity. Accordingly, plans were changed and the chief justice took over the task of writing an opinion that would deal with all the controversial questions. It turned out that the other justices, though agreeing with his decision, disagreed with various parts of the reasoning by which he reached it. When the decision was rendered early in 1857, all nine justices presented separate opinions.

Taney began his opinion with a strange assertion: that Negro slaves and their descendants, even if born in freedom, were not and never could become citizens of the United States, though they might become citizens of a particular state. The inference to be drawn from that proposition was that Dred Scott was not a citizen and therefore had no right to sue in a federal court under the diversity of citizenship clause of the Constitution. That had been the ruling of the federal circuit court in Missouri, and the opinion could have ended there, had a majority of the Court agreed with Taney, because it meant that the Supreme Court had no jurisdiction in the case. But only three justices agreed, and two explicitly disagreed, so it was necessary for Taney to go on and establish another ground for Scott's inability to sue, namely, that he was a slave. Establishing that ground permitted Taney to deal with two substantive issues.

The first concerned whether Scott's residence in free territory liberated him. It did not, Taney said, because his status was determined by the laws of the state in which he resided when he commenced the suit, and the Missouri courts had ruled that under state law he was a slave. On this point the justices were agreed, six to three, for it was the same ruling as in the *Strader* case. Taney might have stopped there, but he went on to deal with a second substantive issue.

The second issue was a bombshell, the questions of the constitutionality of the Missouri Compromise and thus of congressional exclusion of slavery from any of the territories. The Constitution recognized slaves as property, Taney pointed out, and the Fifth Amendment prohibits the taking of property without due process of law. From this he concluded that "an act of Congress which deprives a citizen of the United States of his liberty or property, merely because he came himself or brought his property into a particular territory of the United States, and who had committed no offense against the laws, could hardly be dignified with the name of due process of law." The Missouri Compromise was thus unconstitutional. On this point the Court was agreed, six to three.

Apparently Taney hoped that the Court, by going beyond what was strictly necessary in clarifying its interpretation of the Constitution on the subject, could stop all the divisive political agitation over slavery in the territories. It had precisely the opposite effect. The dissenting opinions of McLean and Curtis, pointing out some of Taney's inconsistencies, were widely circulated; political collusion was charged; and the Court all but lost its credibility north of the Mason-Dixon line. The loss of credibility was more devastating than the immediate storm of protest over the decision itself, for the Court is constitutionally the most vulnerable of the three branches of the federal government. Within a year, abolitionists in Congress were talking of removing the Court's appellate jurisdiction in cases concerning slavery. The Court's only defense against such a move—then or ever—is general public confidence in its integrity.

THE BOOTH CASES

The *Booth* cases offer an interesting postscript to the *Dred Scott* decision. An abolitionist newspaper publisher in Wisconsin, Sherman M. Booth, was arrested for aiding the escape of a fugitive slave from a federal marshal. There being no federal jail in the area, Booth was put in a local jail. He sued to be released on a writ of habeas corpus and the state supreme court granted the writ, taking the position that the Fugitive Slave Act of 1850 was unconstitutional. The marshal appealed to the United States Supreme Court. While the appeal was pending, Booth was tried in the federal court in Milwaukee, convicted, and sentenced to fine and imprisonment. He appealed again to the state supreme court, which ordered his release on the same ground as before. The two cases were argued together as *Ableman* v. *Booth* (21 Howard 506).

For once, the Taney Court was unanimous, and Taney delivered a powerful opinion justifying the supremacy of the federal judiciary. This was the first time, Taney said, that the supremacy of state courts over federal courts had been asserted in a formal decision. That could not be allowed; had it been, the Union could not have lasted a year, "for offenses against its laws could not have been punished without the consent of the state in which the culprit was found." But nullificationist doctrines, now denounced by a strongly states' rights court, spread rapidly throughout the North, being justified by the language South Carolina had used in the 1830s.

Before the controversy could proceed very far, however, there was a change of jurisdiction: The question of the nature of the constitutional union was removed from the courts to be decided on the field of battle.

QUESTIONS
FOR DISCUSSION

1. What is the theory of divided sovereignty? How and why did it develop in America? Had such a political theory existed in the 1770s could America have remained a British colony?

2. What techniques did Marshall employ to protect the Court? How did he handle direct attacks by the states and the other branches of the federal government? Is the Court vulnerable today?

3. Was Taney right in declaring the Missouri Compromise unconstitutional in the *Dred Scott* case? If you were writing a strict-constructionist opinion, how would you decide the case? Do you think your opinion would be influenced by the part of the country in which you live?

4. Do the doctrines of interposition, nullification, or secession have validity today? What is the current balance of federal/ state relations? What remedies exist for a state that feels encroached upon by the federal government?

5. Did South Carolina have a reasonable ground for its stand in the nullification crisis? What would have happened if neither side had compromised?

RECOMMENDED
READINGS

EDWIN S. CORWIN, "National Power and State Interposition, 1787–1861," *Michigan Law Review* 10 (1912), 535–551.

MARTIN DIAMOND, *A Nation of States: Essays on the American Federal System* (Chicago: Rand McNally, 1964).

DON E. FEHRENBACHER, *The Dred Scott Case: Its Significance in American Law and Politics* (New York: Oxford University Press, 1978).

BERNARD SCHWARTZ, *From Confederation to Nation: The American Constitution, 1835–1877* (Baltimore: Johns Hopkins University Press, 1973).

DIANE TIPTON, *Nullification and Interposition in American Political Thought* (Albuquerque: University of New Mexico Press, 1969).

WILLIAM M. WIECEK, *The Sources of Antislavery Constitutionalism in America, 1760–1848* (Ithaca: Cornell University Press, 1977).

5
CIVIL WAR, RECONSTRUCTION, AND THE FREEDMAN

*T*he Civil War and the Reconstruction that followed were as grave a constitutional crisis as could have befallen the nation. And yet, though the existence of the constitutional union was at stake, the survival of the Constitution itself was not. Belief in the sacredness of the written Constitution had taken such deep roots in all parts of the country that each side made a point of insisting, from beginning to end, that its position was constitutionally the proper one. Indeed, the very intensity of that belief is what underlay the conflict. Whatever the economic, social, and political causes and consequences of the war may have been, the fact remains that Americans, in North and South alike, believed so devoutly in the Constitution—as they interpreted it—that they were willing to fight and die for it.

THE CONSTITUTIONAL
NATURE OF THE WAR

The abolition of slavery was not the issue. People on both sides were fully aware that slavery could have been abolished only by a constitutional amendment, which required the approval of three-fourths of the states; and as there were fifteen slave states, abolitionists would have had to wait until there were sixty states before they could hope to pass an abolition amendment. But northern willingness that slavery continue to exist went further than mere recognition of an insurmountable constitutional obstacle. In February 1861—after Lincoln and a Republican Congress had been elected and after seven states seceded and formed the Confederacy—Congress passed and sent to the states (including those that had seceded) for ratification an unrepealable amendment protecting slavery forever in those states where it already existed. Lincoln announced that he had no objection to the amendment, and three states, two of them northern, actually ratified before the war made the question irrelevant.

Nor was states' rights the issue. For more than a generation, as we have seen, a states' rights interpretation of the Constitution, sometimes including virtual nullification, had prevailed throughout the country. When the war began, northern states plunged into it as states: Wisconsin, New York, New Jersey, Indiana, Ohio, and Illinois recruited troops and supplied them at state expense. Indiana cared for its wounded through its state sanitary commission and objected when the United States Sanitary Commission tried to take over the function. Illinois, whose motto was State Sovereignty and National Union, followed the vigorous lead of Governor Richard Yates in its war efforts; but that same governor proclaimed that he "would be the first to resist" if the federal government tried to encroach upon the powers of the states. No southern governor was firmer or more clear on that point.

Rather, the issue was the proper interpretation of the Constitution, in regard to two questions above all others. The first was the long-agitated issue of slavery in the territories. The *Dred Scott* case had decided the matter, but there was no way of knowing whether that decision would be lasting. Opponents of slavery hoped and believed it could be overturned. They hoped so, fervently, because of the strategic limitations imposed upon their crusade by the Constitution: Being unable to abolish slavery, they were vitally concerned to stop its expansion, and many thought a policy of containment would ultimately destroy it. The prospects of a reversal were in fact promising. One of the six justices who had been in the majority in the case died in 1860, and Taney was eighty-three years old and in frail health; their replacements needed only to agree with the abolitionists' contention that the decision was contrary to Article IV, Section 2, which gives Congress power "to dispose of and make all needful Rules and Regulations respecting the Territory or other Property belonging to the United States." President-elect Lincoln flatly predicted that the necessary turnover would take place.

To southerners, Lincoln's election seemed to ensure that the Court would overturn the *Dred Scott* decision, and in their eyes such a reversal would make them second-class citizens. Northerners could take their property anywhere in the country, and local jurisdictions were obliged to recognize their rights in that property; if the territories were closed to slavery, slaveowners would be denied the equal right. And, though the prospect had been hinted at by only a few extreme abolitionists, a federal government firmly under antislavery control could, under the power to regulate interstate commerce, prohibit the movement of slaves from state to state within the South. Southerners were convinced that the Republican victory in 1860 meant that such an attack on their domestic institutions was coming. That, paired with the Republicans' clear commitment to high protective tariffs, internal improvements at federal expense, and other national economic promotional activities that had been substantially abandoned since Jackson's time, was more than southerners were willing to tolerate.

The southern response—secession—was the second irreconcilable constitutional issue. The eleven states that seceded (seven between Lincoln's election and his inauguration, the other four after Lincoln ordered the use of the army against the first seven) believed they had every constitutional right to secede, and they were careful to follow the constitutional procedures they thought were appropriate. South Carolina, the first to go out, set the pattern: The state had entered the Union by the action of a special convention of delegates elected by the people, and it left the Union by the same procedure. In its Declaration of Causes of Secession, the convention affirmed the compact theory of the Constitution, declared that the obligations of a compact are mutual, and charged that fourteen northern states had, by passing laws and otherwise obstructing the constitutionally mandated return of fugitive slaves, "deliberately refused for years past to fulfil their constitutional obligations." Northern states, in other words, not southern states, had broken the compact. And now a "sectional combination for the subversion of the Constitution"—the Republican party—had elected to the presidency a man who had declared that "government cannot endure permanently half slave, half free." When the new administration took office, "the guarantees of the Constitution will then no longer exist." Each of the other seceding states justified its action with similar constitutional arguments.

In drafting a constitution for the newly formed Confederate States of America, the seceding states adopted the United States Constitution almost word for word, the main exceptions being designed to make sure that the new constitution be interpreted as southerners had interpreted the old one. The preamble begins: "We, the people of the Confederate States, each State acting in its sovereign and independent character." Bounties, protective tariffs, and internal improvements at Confederate expense were prohibited. Property in slaves was explicitly recognized, along with full rights of owners to move them within the Confederacy; but, interestingly, African slave trade was prohibited. In sum, the constitution the southerners established was essentially the one they thought they had had.

Northern opinion about all this was by no means unanimous. Some believed the southern states had acted constitutionally, and others believed the southern position was justified even if not constitutional. Most disagreed entirely on both counts, but many thought that the seceding states should be allowed to leave the Union in peace. The mayor of New York embraced this position and recommended that the city also secede. Four slave states chose to remain in the Union, but large numbers of their citizens favored secession or favored letting the seceding states go peaceably.

The most important opinion, however, and possibly the one most widely shared in the North, was that of Abraham Lincoln. The Union, he insisted, was perpetual, because "perpetuity is implied, if not expressed, in the fundamental law of all national governments." Even if the compact theory were accepted, the assent of all parties to the compact would be required to dissolve it. It followed, Lincoln said, "that no State upon its own mere motion can lawfully get out of the Union," and that any forcible resistance to the authority of the United States was "insurrectionary or revolutionary, according to circumstances." When the president of the United States took that position, war was assured.

CONSTITUTIONAL ISSUES OF THE WAR

President Lincoln, faced with the secession crisis, was a good deal less fussy about legal and constitutional niceties than were the southerners. When South Carolina forces fired upon and seized the federal army installation at Fort Sumter on April 12, 1861, Lincoln declared that an insurrection existed and took measures to suppress it. He called into federal service seventy-five thousand militia troops, which he was authorized by law to do; and, as the law provided that no militiaman could be compelled to serve on active duty for more than three months, he summoned Congress into a special session to begin on July 4. But he also went beyond the law. He proclaimed a blockade of southern ports and ordered the navy to enforce it. That raised a knotty constitutional problem. Under international law, a country could establish a blockade to prevent the arrival of foreign ships in time of war, but war could be conducted only between sovereign nations. The blockade was either a tacit recognition of the constitutional legitimacy of secession or a violation of international law.

Lincoln acted illegally in two other respects as well. On May 3 he issued a proclamation calling for forty-two thousand volunteers to serve for three years in the army—an unconstitutional as well as an illegal action, for it involved the expenditure of public funds without congressional authorization. However, when Congress convened, the president asked for and received retroactive legal sanction for what he had done. The other main area in which he acted illegally proved to be more controversial. In the border states and the southern parts of Illinois, Indiana, and Ohio, Confederate sympathizers were numerous and active. To avert the danger they posed, Lincoln ordered military commanders to arrest them and hold them without trial. When innocent people are arrested and detained, their legal remedy is to obtain from a court a writ of habeas corpus ordering their release. The Constitution provides that "the privilege of the writ of habeas corpus shall not be suspended, unless when in cases of rebellion or invasion the public safety may require it." There are no guides as to who decides when the public safety requires it. Lincoln did not hesitate in instructing the army to suspend the writ, and a number of innocent persons, along with many more who were rebellious, were imprisoned without evidence, charges, or trial.

Properly, the question was one for the courts to decide, as was the question of the legality of the blockade; but in 1861 the Supreme Court was in disrepute. The justice who died in 1860 had been a Virginian, and Justice John A. Campbell of Alabama resigned when his home state seceded, but Taney lived on and the Court's integrity continued to be suspect. The Chief Justice scarcely increased its prestige in a decision he rendered during the first months of the war. An army officer in Maryland arrested a Baltimore secessionist, John Merryman, and imprisoned him without formal charges. Through his attorney, Merryman petitioned Taney, sitting as a circuit judge, for a writ of habeas corpus, and

Taney granted the writ. The military commander refused to release the prisoner, however, whereupon Taney cited him for contempt of court and issued an opinion holding that the power to suspend the writ was vested in Congress, not the president, and denouncing the suspension of constitutional rights by military order. Lincoln defied the decision, defended his policy in a message to Congress, and continued to order military commanders to suspend habeas corpus as they saw fit. Indeed, at one point Lincoln refused a request from the House to provide information about people who had been arbitrarily arrested. A large number of loyal citizens began to fear that the war to defend the Constitution would result in its destruction.

Then the awaited turnover in the personnel of the Court took place. Another justice died, and in 1862 Congress increased the number of justices to ten, with the result that there were suddenly four new members. Still another judge died in 1863, and Taney died at last in 1864. Lincoln appointed Salmon P. Chase of Ohio to his seat as chief justice. Thus from 1862 onward it was a new Court, and after 1864 it was a Lincoln Court.

This Court soon had occasion to pronounce upon the constitutional nature of the war. Congress never declared war, but in a series of acts it authorized everything necessary to carry it out, including the blockade that Lincoln had proclaimed. For two years, over the protests of several foreign governments, the United States Navy enforced the blockade, capturing and confiscating the ships of neutrals that tried to land in southern ports. Owners of several of the vessels appealed to the Supreme Court, which in the *Prize* cases (2 Black 635) of 1863 ruled that the seizures were legal. Justice Robert Grier, delivering the majority opinion, followed a careful line of reasoning that gave the government all the advantages of a belligerent power without sacrificing the principle that the southern states had no constitutional right to secede. "A civil war," Grier wrote, "always begins by insurrection against the lawful authority of the government." The president, as commander in chief, has the duty of suppressing insurrections, and it is solely up to him to determine what amount of force a crisis demands. At some point, the present conflict became a war in fact though not in name. "A civil war is never solemnly declared"; but it is not the less a war because one side refers to the other as rebels or traitors. As abolitionist Senator Charles Sumner put it in commenting on the decision, "you may call it a rebellion or war as you please, or you may call it both." The entire Court agreed with that interpretation, though four justices dissented on one point: They insisted that because Congress alone had the power to declare war, the blockade had not become legal until Congress confirmed the existence of a de facto war by enacting its war measures.

The Court was equally cooperative in regard to Lincoln's method of dealing with southern sympathizers. In 1863 Congress passed an act imposing restraints upon the use of military authority against civilians, but the president made no appreciable changes in his policy. A month after the act was passed, General Ambrose Burnside, commanding the military department that included Ohio, issued an order declaring that anyone committing acts favorable to the enemy would be executed. A southern sympathizer and ex-congressman named Clarence Vallandigham was arrested, under that order, for giving a pro-southern speech, and was tried and found guilty by a military commission. Vallandigham's attorney applied to the United States circuit court for a writ of habeas corpus, but the application was denied. The attorney then appealed to the Supreme Court for review. Early in 1864 the Court held, in *Ex parte Vallandigham* (1 Wallace 243), that it had no power to review the proceedings of a military tribunal, as its jurisdiction extended only to judicial courts and a military commission was not a court under the meaning of the Constitution. (Vallandigham was, however, ultimately released on a technicality.)

This is not to suggest that the justices, from lack of scruples or out of fear of the president and Congress, were abandoning their constitutional duties. Except in regard to the war, the Court carried on its business as usual, and in some respects it was bolder than ever before. The Chase Court, for example, declared ten acts of Congress unconstitutional, compared with only two such rulings in the entire period before the war, and it overturned forty-six state laws. But as long as the fighting continued, the Court would have jeopardized its very existence had it attempted to interfere with the way Congress and the president chose to conduct the war.

A goodly number of points of constitutional law were thus determined non-judicially. For instance, in March 1863 Congress passed the Conscription Act, requiring all males between the ages of twenty and forty-five to register for military draft. The draft was extremely unpopular, riots against it erupted in New York City, and many people thought it unconstitutional, but no case challenging the law reached the Supreme Court. Lincoln gave his own interpretation: "The Constitution provides that the Congress shall have power to raise and support armies; and by this act the Congress has exercised the power to raise and support armies. This is the whole of it."

It was as a by-product of the way Lincoln and Congress conducted the war that abolition of slavery came about. An element that could influence the outcome of the war was the position taken by European powers, especially Great Britain and France. Britain, needing the South's cotton for its textile mills and habitually sympathetic to the underdog, granted diplomatic recognition to the Confederacy and leaned toward intervening in its behalf. France, just then engaged in an attempted take-over of Mexico, believed southern independence would be to its advantage; and French mediation could succeed if the British cooperated. But the British were strongly opposed to slavery, and if emancipation were made a goal of the war they might change their position. These circumstances created considerable pressure for emancipation. Additional pressure came from radical abolitionists in Congress, who, though distinctly a minority, became more insistent in their demands as the war continued.

The movement toward emancipation took place in several steps. In August 1861 Congress passed the First Confiscation Act, declaring lawfully free any slaves whose masters required them to take up arms or work for the Confederate army or navy.

The following spring, Lincoln recommended and Congress enacted legislation offering financial compensation to the loyal slave states if they would provide for gradual emancipation. In July 1862 came the Second Confiscation Act, providing for the freeing of all rebel-owned slaves who were captured by the army or who voluntarily went beyond Union lines. Two months later Lincoln issued the Emancipation Proclamation, declaring that as of January 1, 1863, all persons held as slaves in rebellious states were to be freed. The proclamation was of questionable constitutional status, and as it applied only to states that had declared themselves independent, it actually freed no one. On the other hand, the proclamation and the congressional enactments taken together effectively authorized military commanders to free the slaves in any areas captured by the Union army, and many were liberated by that means as the army advanced.

Though some people thought that abolition could be accomplished by such means, most continued to recognize that it could be legitimately done only by constitutional amendment. In his second annual message to Congress, Lincoln recommended an amendment providing compensation to any state that would abolish slavery before the year 1900. Several different amendments were proposed in Congress in 1863, but none passed in either house. Then, in April 1864, the Senate adopted an abolition amendment by the requisite two-thirds majority, but the House failed to concur. It was argued in the House that an amendment abolishing slavery would require ratification not by three-fourths of the states but by all, because slavery as an institution lay within the dominion constitutionally reserved to each state for itself. Finally, however, in February 1865 the House concurred by the necessary majority, and an amendment abolishing slavery except as punishment for a crime was submitted to the states for ratification. Two months later, Confederate General Robert E. Lee surrendered to Union General Ulysses S. Grant, and the war was over. In December, Secretary of State William H. Seward announced that the Thirteenth Amendment had been ratified by twenty-seven of the thirty-six states, including eight from the former Confederacy, and was therefore part of the Constitution.

RECONSTRUCTION: POLITICAL

Reconstruction proved to be a turbulent affair. President Lincoln urged the nation to bind up its wounds, "with malice toward none, with charity for all," and his reconstruction plan was designed to readmit the southern states quickly and with little disruption. He held that the southern states had never legally seceded, that the war was a rebellion, and that it was up to the chief executive to decide when the rebellion was over and when legal government had been restored. He proposed to grant pardons to all southerners who would take an oath of loyalty to the Union, excepting only the highest ranking civil and military officers of the Confederacy, and to grant executive recognition to the governments of the states where 10 percent of the voters took the oath, formed a government, and accepted emancipation of the slaves. In 1864 he recognized governments on that basis in Arkansas, Tennessee, Virginia, and Louisiana.

But things did not work out that simply. Northerners, or at least many northern politicians, were determined that the South should be punished, and the more radical Republicans thought it irresponsible to leave the newly freed blacks to the government of their former masters. The Radicals' constitutional position was that the seceding states had committed suicide as states and that they were "conquered provinces." Congress refused to seat the representatives and senators elected by the states Lincoln had recognized, and in July 1864 it passed the Wade-Davis bill, imposing its own much harsher terms for readmission. A full majority of the voters would be required to take a loyalty oath and select a constitutional convention to form a new state government. No one who had served in the Confederate army or held a Confederate or state office could participate. The state constitution must prohibit slavery, exclude from voting or officeholding all former

Confederate officials, and repudiate Confederate and state war debts. Lincoln killed the bill by "pocket veto," holding it unsigned until Congress had adjourned; but the Radicals issued the Wade-Davis Manifesto, declaring that reconstruction was up to Congress, and saw to it that the principles of the manifesto were incorporated into the Republican presidential platform of 1864. Lincoln was forced to concede that the Wade-Davis system was "one very proper plan" for reconstruction. And, in March 1865 he bowed to pressure and signed into law an act creating the Freedmen's Bureau—a federal agency designed to serve as a sort of guardian for southern blacks and thus a radical departure from American constitutional tradition.

When Andrew Johnson became president after Lincoln's assassination in April 1865, Congress was out of session, and Johnson tried to implement his own program of reconstruction before Congress met again in December. To that end, he issued two proclamations. The first granted a blanket pardon to all rebels who would take a loyalty oath and recognize abolition; high-ranking Confederates and persons with more than $20,000 of property were excepted from the general amnesty, but they were invited to apply for special pardons. In the second proclamation Johnson appointed a temporary governor for North Carolina to supervise the election of a state constitutional convention, in which all pardoned persons could participate. When the constitution was adopted and a government under it was formed, the state was to be readmitted on terms that gave it full control over its internal affairs. After some criticism, Johnson stiffened the qualifications somewhat, requiring also the repudiation of war debts, renunciation of secession, and ratification of the Thirteenth Amendment. In the next few months Johnson repeated the recognition of the four states Lincoln had recognized, and before the end of the year he readmitted, under the modified North Carolina Plan, all the other southern states except Texas.

Southerners promptly began to act in ways that were sure to bring the wrath of Radical Republicans upon them. In campaigns for state offices, candidates proudly described themselves as "late of the Confederate army" and won. The former Confederate states elected their former vice president, four ex-generals and five ex-colonels of the rebel army, and six cabinet officers and fifty-eight congressmen from the rebel government. Blacks were generally not allowed to vote. Georgia and the Carolinas would not repudiate Confederate debts or renounce secession, and Mississippi accepted the abolition of slavery only after the Johnson administration exerted strong pressure on the state. Moreover, the newly reestablished southern state legislatures passed laws severely limiting the civil rights of the freedmen, in some cases directly copying the Black Codes that had restricted the movement and behavior of slaves and free blacks before the war.

When Congress reconvened it set out to undo Johnson's version of reconstruction and its by-products. On December 4, 1865, the members appointed a Joint Committee of Fifteen, headed by the Radical leaders Thaddeus Stevens and Charles Sumner. Nominally, this committee's function was to pass on the credentials of southern congressmen, but actually it was designed to direct the congressional program of reconstruction. Within a month the committee had drafted and Congress had adopted resolutions declaring that the former Confederate states had no legal status. They were not to become legal entities until they had provided full civil rights for blacks and deprived rebels of such rights. In February 1866 the committee had drafted and Congress had passed a bill that, in effect, repealed the Black Codes, extended and enlarged the powers of the Freedmen's Bureau, and authorized the bureau to use military force against southern whites. Johnson vetoed the bill on the ground that the federal courts could adequately protect the rights of blacks, and Radical leaders could not muster enough votes to override the veto. Early in April Congress passed the Civil Rights Act, declaring all persons born in the United States (except Indians) to be citizens with full civil and legal rights and authorizing the use of the army to enforce and protect those rights. Johnson vetoed the measure, but this time Congress overrode the veto. Then it passed, and repassed over presidential veto, a new Freedmen's Bureau Act. It also amended the Judiciary

Act in a way that would prevent Johnson from appointing Supreme Court justices should vacancies occur.

All this was beginning to amount to a constitutional revolution, for these measures extended the powers of the federal government far beyond any existing precedent, and they clearly tended to subordinate the executive and judicial branches to the legislative. To give sanction to what it had done, Congress passed another constitutional amendment. The Fourteenth Amendment (as it turned out to be) forbade former Confederate and wartime southern state officials from holding office in the national government, confirmed Union war debts and repudiated Confederate debts, prohibited the payment of compensation for freed slaves, and attempted to guarantee blacks the right to vote by reducing congressional representation in proportion to restrictions on voting rights. In addition, the amendment gave citizenship to all persons born or naturalized in the United States, guaranteed them equal protection of the laws, and prohibited states from depriving any citizen of life, liberty, or property without due process of law. Finally, and of most immediate importance, Congress was authorized to pass any laws necessary to enforce the amendment. (The ratifications by southern states were counted even though they were held to have no legal existence. Indeed, they were forced to ratify as a condition of readmission. By that means the Fourteenth Amendment was, in July 1868, declared to be adopted.)

Meanwhile, in 1866 the differences between president and Congress were deepening. President Johnson was sure that he was acting in accordance with every constitutional principle that had prevailed during his lifetime but was uncertain as to how much popular support there was for his position. The Radicals were confident of the morality of their action, contemptuous of constitutional scruples, and not especially concerned about popular opinion; but they needed the support of politicians who were highly sensitive to popular feelings, and so they too looked for public confirmation of their position. Accordingly, the congressional elections of 1866 were a testing ground in the contest between Congress and president. Johnson took the unprecedented step of going on a speaking tour in behalf of congressional candidates who supported his stand, but the elections brought little change in the makeup of Congress. Republicans still controlled the House by a majority of about three to one and the Senate by about four to one.

Radical leaders interpreted the elections as a virtual mandate to destroy the presidency. In January 1867 Congress called the new Congress into special session to meet in March, immediately upon the end of the old one—a flagrant defiance of constitutional custom. In February it passed, over Johnson's veto, the first of a series of Reconstruction acts, dividing the South into five military districts, providing for their rule by military governors, giving all adult males (including blacks but excluding former rebels) the right to vote, and requiring adherence to the Fourteenth Amendment. On March 2 it passed the Military Appropriations Act, declaring that presidential military orders could be carried out only with the approval of General of the Armies U. S. Grant, and the Tenure of Office Act, providing that government officials appointed with Senate approval could not be fired or replaced without Senate approval.

That left the incoming Congress little more to do to the presidency besides destroy the president himself, and it set out to do just that. In June 1867 the House Judiciary Committee considered impeaching Johnson but, finding that he had violated neither the Constitution nor the laws, voted five to four against impeachment. But then Johnson decided to test the constitutionality of the Tenure of Office Act by removing Secretary of War Edwin Stanton from office. The Radicals, instead of taking the matter to court, impeached Johnson early in 1868. When the president was tried in the Senate, they fell one vote short of obtaining conviction; during Johnson's remaining few months in office, however, he was utterly lacking in power. For the time being, Congress was the supreme law of the land.

Radical reconstruction gradually came to an end. Civilian government was restored in seven states in 1868, but a coalition of blacks, northern "carpetbaggers," and southern "scalawags" dominated government there, and the same was true of the other southern states as military government ended. To ensure the continuation of such arrangements, the Fifteenth Amendment, guaranteeing black voting rights, was proposed in 1869 and adopted early the next year, and under its authority Congress passed the Force Act of 1870, imposing severe penalties on anyone convicted of using bribery, force, or intimidation to prevent any citizen from voting. Despite that, southern "redeemers" gradually regained control, partly through terrorism, and partly through other means. Conservatives won control of Virginia, North Carolina, Tennessee, and Georgia between 1869 and 1871, and of four more southern states in 1874 and 1875. By 1876 only Florida, Louisiana, and South Carolina remained under Radical control. The next year they were "redeemed," and all remaining federal troops occupying the South had been removed.

In Congress Radicals continued to be dominant, but by 1870 their enthusiasm for punishing the South and protecting the freedmen had largely given way to corruption. The new president, U. S. Grant, had no interest in expanding the duties of his office, and soon his administration began to be rocked by a succession of scandals. For those reasons, the executive and legislative branches all but stopped exercising the vastly expanded powers they had taken on themselves during and after the war. As a result, the Supreme Court obtained the opportunity to re-exert its authority, and it took it.

RECONSTRUCTION: THE COURT

At first the Court moved a bit too boldly for its own good: In *Ex parte Milligan* (4 Wallace 2) it stirred up a great deal of opposition by substantially reversing the decision it had rendered in the *Vallandigham* case, regarding trials by military commissions. Lambdin P. Milligan was an officer in a Confederate paramilitary organization that operated in Indiana during the war. In 1864 he was captured and, under the authority of the 1862 presidential suspension of habeas corpus and the 1863 Habeas Corpus Act, tried by a military commission and sentenced to be hanged. Lincoln held up his execution for several months, during which time a civilian grand jury met and failed to indict him. Two weeks after Lincoln was killed, Johnson ordered the execution of Milligan's death sentence. But the Habeas Corpus Act provided that, when a grand jury met after a prisoner was taken and ended its session without indicting, it was the duty of the federal courts to order his release; and on that ground Milligan appealed to the circuit court for a writ of habeas corpus. The circuit court judges were divided, and they requested instructions from the Supreme Court.

The Supreme Court gave its ruling in July 1866. Justice David Davis, giving the opinion, in effect apologized for the *Vallandigham* decision. "During the late wicked rebellion," he wrote, "the temper of the times did not allow that calmness in deliberation...necessary to a correct conclusion of a purely judicial question." Now that the public safety was assured, however, the question could be discussed and decided "without passion." It was essential to the safety of any government, Davis declared, that there should be a power to suspend habeas corpus, but that did not mean that martial law could be proclaimed over the whole country. "Martial law cannot arise from a threatened invasion," but only from actual and present necessity, which had not been the case in Indiana. "Martial rule can never exist where the courts are open and in the proper and unobstructed exercise of their jurisdiction." The Court was unanimous in deciding that Milligan's trial by a military commission was unconstitutional and that he be released. It was divided five to four on a related question, the majority holding that Congress could never authorize trial by military commissions in such circumstances, the minority maintaining that it could do so in extreme cases. The split was significant, for the decision implied that the Court might question the constitutionality of the continuance of military government in the South.

The Radicals in Congress denounced the decision, and Thaddeus Stevens described it as more despicable than the *Dred Scott* decision, but the Court was undaunted—for a time. Early in 1867 it brought more denunciations upon itself in rendering its decisions in the *Test Oath* cases, *Cummings* v. *Missouri* (4 Wallace 277) and *Ex parte Garland* (4 Wallace 333). The first arose under a state law, the second under an act of Congress, but they were heard and decided together. A Missouri law required that to vote, hold office, or engage in various professions, a person must take an oath attesting that he was and always had been loyal to the United States. Cummings, a Roman Catholic priest, was indicted and convicted of preaching and teaching without taking the oath. The federal law required attorneys to swear that they had never borne arms against the United States or otherwise be barred from practice in federal courts. A. H. Garland, a lawyer and Confederate veteran who had received a presidential pardon, sought to be admitted to practice before the Supreme Court and contended that the law preventing his being admitted was unconstitutional. In both cases Justice Stephen J. Field, who would remain on the Court and be of great influence for many years, abandoned the other four Lincoln appointees and joined the four pre-Lincoln justices in holding the acts unconstitutional. Both acts were held to be ex post facto laws (making something a crime retroactively) and bills of attainder (laws declaring individuals guilty without trials), and thus prohibited by Article I, Section 9 of the Constitution. Again, congressional Radicals expressed their displeasure with the decisions.

Three months later, in April 1867, the Court handed down two important decisions that were more to the Radicals' liking, but only because of unusual circumstances about the way the suits were brought. The Reconstruction Acts of March 1867 were challenged by Mississippi and Georgia shortly after their passage. Mississippi attorneys, acting on behalf of the state, requested the Court's permission to seek an injunction against Andrew Johnson and the district military commander, restraining them from executing and enforcing the acts. Both Johnson and Attorney General Henry Stanbery thought the acts were unconstitutional, but the attorney general, on the president's instructions, argued against Mississippi's motion. The Court, he contended, should refuse the request both because it made the president a defendant and because it sought to restrain him from performing his constitutional duty to enforce the laws.

Chief Justice Chase in *Mississippi* v. *Johnson* (4 Wallace 475) gave the opinion for a unanimous Court. The opinion, for the most part, followed the attorney general's argument almost word for word, but it also went further. Chase distinguished between "ministerial" and "executive" duties. Ministerial duties were those routinely prescribed by law, such as issuing a commission—as had been the situation in *Marbury* v. *Madison*—and were subject to court orders. Executive duties involved political discretion and were beyond the Court's authority, even if the law involved was alleged to be unconstitutional. In addition, Mississippi's request called upon the Court to take an unprecedented, "absurd and excessive" action. In a series of hypothetical questions, Chase described what would happen if the Court agreed. If it served the injunction on the president, he would either refuse to heed it, in which case the Court could do nothing to enforce its order; or he would obey it, in which case he would be open to impeachment for failing to execute an act of Congress. And if he were impeached for obeying a Court order, the Court could not protect him by issuing an injunction to prevent the Senate from following its constitutional role in impeachments. As Chase said, "these questions answer themselves."

The Georgia suit was more nearly reasonable: It sought an injunction against Secretary of War Edwin Stanton, General Grant, and the commander of the Third Military District. *Georgia* v. *Stanton* (6 Wallace 50) was actually a dual case, for after *Mississippi* v. *Johnson* the Court allowed Mississippi to alter its bill to apply to Stanton and the military men. Attorney General Stanbery argued that the suits involved a political question and were therefore best left to the political branches of government. Lawyers for Georgia contended that Congress had no power to annihilate a state and its government and to deprive its citizens of legal and political rights. Eight of the nine judges (the number having been reduced again) agreed to refuse jurisdiction on the ground that only political questions were involved as the suit had been presented. For a question to be judicially determined, the majority opinion stated, "the rights in danger...must be rights of persons or property, not merely political rights, which do not belong to the jurisdiction of a court."

That was a strong hint that if a suit were brought on the basis of an issue of property rights, the Court would consider the constitutionality of the Reconstruction Acts. Mississippi's attorneys picked up the hint and filed a motion, asking to amend their bill to make property rights the central issue. But one justice—the old Democrat Robert Grier, who almost certainly would have voted with those who favored the amended motion—was absent, and the others split four to four, and so the motion was lost.

During the remainder of 1867, as the contest between President Johnson and the Radicals was moving to a climax and the government was veering toward total legislative supremacy, rumors began to circulate that early in 1868 the Court would, in a pending case, rule the Reconstruction Acts unconstitutional. The case was *ex parte McCardle* (6 Wallace 318) and involved a question of purely private rights. William H. McCardle, a newspaper editor in Vicksburg, Mississippi, was arrested under the Reconstruction Acts and held for trial by a military commission. He applied for a writ of habeas corpus in the federal Circuit Court in Mississippi, which refused his petition. But a recently enacted revision of the Judiciary Act, passed for the protection of federal officials and loyal citizens in the South, defined the right of appeal to the Supreme Court in such broad terms as to cover the McCardle case, and the Court decided unanimously that it had jurisdiction.

It heard the substantive arguments in the case in March 1868, just before the impeachment trial of President Johnson got under way. In that highly charged atmosphere, Congress wanted no interference by the judiciary. For the first time, Congress exercised its constitutional power to pass an act altering the Judiciary Act so as to remove the Court's jurisdiction. Deciding that it was imprudent "to run a race with Congress," the Court announced a postponement of the McCardle case until its next term, when it would hear new arguments on the question of jurisdiction. When *Ex parte McCardle* was reheard early in 1869 (7 Wallace 506), the Court had no option but to agree that Congress had full power under Article III, Section 2 to abolish its jurisdiction in the case.

And so the Supreme Court did not, just yet, rule on the constitutionality of the Reconstruction Acts; but it did, in a decision rendered on the same day as the final determination of the *McCardle* case, give a ruling that undermined the constitutional foundations of the Radical position. *Texas* v. *White* (7 Wallace 700) arose from the sale by Texas officials during the war of some United States government bonds that had been held in the state treasury. After the war the state sued for the recovery of the bonds, and the Supreme Court upheld its claim. Because secession was not possible, the Court declared, the Confederate state government had no legal existence and its acts were invalid. The Constitution, Chief Justice Chase said in the opinion, "looks to an indestructible Union, composed of indestructible states."

Finally, toward the end of 1869, the Court handed down a decision that ran directly counter to the Reconstruction Acts, though it did not explicitly declare them unconstitutional. A Mississippian named Edward Yerger was tried by a military commission for killing an army officer. When Yerger applied for a writ of habeas corpus, the Court accepted jurisdiction on a special ground. The 1868 act removing jurisdiction in the McCardle case had applied only to appeals arising under the Judiciary Act (Habeas Corpus Act) of 1867; it was silent on the subject of direct petitions for writ of habeas corpus, which had been provided for by the original Judiciary Act of 1789. The Court accordingly agreed, in October 1869, that it would hear Yerger's case. Radical Republicans responded with three different bills, one abolishing the Court's appellate jurisdiction in all cases involving habeas corpus, one denying the Court authority to review "political questions" including all cases arising under the Reconstruction Acts, and one entirely abolishing judicial review of acts of Congress. All failed, however, for the Radicals no longer had absolute control of Congress; and in *Ex parte Yerger* (8 Wallace 85), the Court overturned the decision of the military commission and ordered Yerger released.

Thus by 1870 the Court was acting as boldly and vigorously as ever. It demonstrated its newly recovered self-confidence most dramatically in a series of cases decided toward the end of the Reconstruction period, in which it curtailed the scope of the Fourteenth and Fifteenth amendments. The first cases were the so-called *Slaughterhouse* cases (16 Wallace 36). In 1869 the carpetbagger government of Louisiana passed an act that confined the slaughtering of livestock for New Orleans and a large surrounding area to a single location and the buildings of a single corporation. The butchers in the area brought suits protesting that the act, which, in effect, deprived them of their livelihoods, was a violation of the Fourteenth Amendment's prohibition against state laws that "abridge the privileges or immunities of citizens of the United States."

The Supreme Court, in 1873, decided against the butchers by a five-to-four vote. Justice Samuel F. Miller, in the majority opinion, declared that the general aim of all three Civil War amendments was the same: to free the slaves, to secure and firmly establish that freedom, and to protect the freedmen from oppression by whites. The main purpose of the first section of the Fourteenth Amendment, which contains the privileges and immunities clause, was to establish Negro citizenship—a provision made necessary by the *Dred Scott* decision, which had never been reversed. But, said Miller, the section made a clear distinction between citizenship of the United States and citizenship of a state, and thus between the "privileges and immunities" that derived from each. The clause prohibited states from abridging rights arising from citizenship of the United States, but it did not forbid them from abridging rights arising from state citizenship. The great mass of civil rights derived from state citizenship. Those deriving from national citizenship and common to all were such things as the right to go to the seat of government, transact business with the government, seek its protection, have free access to the seaports, and demand federal protection of one's life, liberty, and property when on the high seas. The right to engage in a particular occupation, such as being a butcher, was derived from state citizenship and thus not protected by the Fourteenth Amendment.

Counsel for the butchers raised two other points, both of which Miller dismissed. The amendment prohibits states from depriving any person of life, liberty, or property without due process of law, but Miller rejected the butchers' argument that the Louisiana law violated due process. It also forbids the states to deny anyone the "equal protection of the laws," but Miller ruled that the clause was intended solely for securing the rights of Negroes.

The dissenting opinions of Justices Stephen Field, Noah Swayne, and Joseph Bradley were important as indicators of the direction in which interpretation of the Fourteenth Amendment would go in the future. The privileges-and-immunities clause, Field wrote, referred to inalienable rights, derived from the Creator, which "belong to the citizens of all free governments. Clearly among these must be placed the right to pursue a lawful employment in a lawful manner." Bradley agreed with Field and added that the due-process and equal-protection clauses were general, not specific to blacks, and were applicable in the present case. Swayne said, in effect, that the Fourteenth Amendment extended the Bill of Rights to apply to the states: "By the Constitution, as it stood before the war, ample protection was given against oppression by the Union, but little was given against wrong and oppression by the states. That want was intended to be supplied by this amendment."

The Court would, in future, reflect the division in the *Slaughterhouse* cases. In keeping with the views of the dissenters, the scope of the equal-protection and due-process clauses would be greatly expanded during the next generation. In keeping with the views of the majority, the interpretation of the privileges-and-immunities clause would remain narrow for another eighty years. Just after the *Slaughterhouse* decision, for instance, the Court held in *Bradwell* v. *Illinois* (16 Wallace 130) that a state could prevent a female citizen of the United States from practicing law. The next year, in *Bartemeyer* v. *Iowa* (18 Wallace 129), it held that a law depriving a man of the right to sell liquor was no violation of the privileges-and-immunities clause. In 1875 the Court unanimously ruled, in *Minor* v. *Happersett* (21 Wallace 162), that the clause did not give women citizens of the United States the right to vote.

As it was narrowly defining the rights of whites under the amendment, the Court was simultaneously curtailing the power of Congress to legislate to protect the rights of blacks. The Enforcement Act of 1870, designed to enforce the Fourteenth and Fifteenth amendments, provided among other things punishment for conspiracy to use force or intimidation to deprive any person of any right derived from the Constitution or federal laws. The act was presumably justified by the last section of the Fourteenth Amendment, which gives Congress power to pass "appropriate" enforcement legislation, but that presumption was denied in a case that arose in Louisiana. In 1873, after a massacre of blacks, several people were indicted under the 1870 act. When the case reached the Supreme Court in 1876, as *United States* v. *Cruikshank* (92 U.S. 542), the Court held that the amendment authorized Congress only *to prevent the states from interfering* with the rights in question and not to legislate generally to protect those rights. The authorization "does not extend to the passage of laws for the suppression of ordinary crime within the states. This would be to clothe Congress with power to pass laws for the general preservation of social order in every state. The enforcement of the guaranty does not require or authorize Congress to perform the duty which...it requires the state to perform."

During the same term, the Court, in *United States* v. *Reese* (92 U.S. 214), rendered a similar ruling in regard to the enforcement clause of the Fifteenth Amendment. Two Kentucky election inspectors were indicted under the Enforcement Act for refusing to receive and count the vote of a Negro citizen. Again the Court ruled that the act went too far. "The Fifteenth Amendment does not confer the right of suffrage upon anyone," it merely prohibits states or the United States from discriminating, in matters of voting rights, "on account of race, color, or previous condition of servitude." The "appropriate legislation" authorized by the amendment must therefore be directed against the actions of states and not, as the Enforcement Act was directed, against the actions of individuals. As Congress had gone beyond its legitimate sphere, it was the duty of the Court to "annul its encroachments upon the reserved power of the States and the people."

CIVIL WAR AND RECONSTRUCTION: THE CONSTITUTIONAL OUTCOME

There was a supreme irony in this course of affairs. For sixty years after the election of Thomas Jefferson to the presidency, American constitutional history had been marked primarily by two developments, the general (though not unqualified) acceptance of a states' rights interpretation of the Constitution and the emergence of a powerful (though not unchallenged) federal judiciary. Extremism in regard to both was involved in the triggering of a destructive Civil War and an almost equally destructive period of Reconstruction, during which the powers of the national government were temporarily expanded beyond all precedent and the Supreme Court was temporarily in eclipse. And yet, when it was all over, when the reunited nation celebrated its centennial in 1876, states' rights doctrine prevailed and so did the Supreme Court.

QUESTIONS
FOR DISCUSSION

1. Were Radicals consistent in constitutional theory? How did they accept ratification of the Thirteenth, Fourteenth, and Fifteenth amendments by states that were not legal entities?

2. How does the preamble to the Confederate Constitution compare with the preamble to the United States Constitution?

3. In the Thirteenth Amendment, what does "involuntary" mean? Would it apply to the modern draft? If Congress declares war through the votes of your representatives, does that constitute consent? How would it apply to the Vietnamese War?

4. What does "servitude" mean? Can a state require welfare recipients to do public-service work in exchange for their benefits?

5. During the Second World War, Americans of Japanese descent were interned in camps without charges, trials, or recourse to habeas corpus. What parallels are there to Civil War actions? If you were a lawyer representing a Japanese-American, what cases could you use as precedents?

RECOMMENDED
READINGS

MICHAEL LES BENEDICT, *The Impeachment and Trial of Andrew Johnson* (New York: Norton, 1973).

MAXWELL BLOOMFIELD, *American Lawyers in a Changing Society, 1776–1876* (Cambridge: Harvard University Press, 1976).

HAROLD M. HYMAN, *A More Perfect Union: The Impact of the Civil War and Reconstruction on the Constitution* (New York: Knopf, 1973).

STANLEY I. KUTLER, *Judicial Power and Reconstruction Politics* (Chicago: University of Chicago Press, 1968).

PHILLIP S. PALUDAN, *A Covenant with Death: The Constitution, Law, and Equality in the Civil War Era* (Urbana: University of Illinois Press, 1975).

6
THE CONSTITUTION IN THE AGE OF INDUSTRIALIZATION

*T*he Constitution survived intact through the Civil War and Radical Reconstruction, but even before the end of those ordeals, new strains were emerging. The United States was becoming a place that the Founding Fathers would scarcely have recognized. The South, once proud and prosperous, was reduced to an impoverished backwater region, almost entirely outside the mainstream of American life. Westward expansion continued at an accelerated pace until, by the end of the century, the country encompassed more than three million square miles and consisted of forty-five states. The population likewise grew at an accelerated pace: By the time of the Civil War it had already increased nearly tenfold since the adoption of the Constitution, and it grew as much in the next three decades as it had in the preceding seven. Moreover, the population changed qualitatively in two important ways. First, it changed ethnically. Until the 1870s the overwhelming majority of the American people were Protestant Christians who had originated in the British Isles, where constitutional, legal, and political traditions were closely akin to those in America. During the next forty years immigrants arrived at an average rate of six hundred thousand a year, and most of the new immigrants were Catholics or Jews from southern and eastern Europe who had no experience with anything resembling Anglo-American government. Second, the population became progressively more urban, especially in the Northeast. Villages of two or three thousand people became cities of two or three hundred thousand, and cities of two or three hundred thousand became super-cities of two or three million. With this change came another, the transformation of the population from one of self-employed farmers and independent businessmen to one of people who worked for someone else.

Increasingly, that someone was not a person but a corporation, and the work itself was done with the aid of machines. Corporations emerged as the best available means for providing the capital, durability, and flexibility necessary to develop and use certain technological innovations that, together, radically altered man's relationship with his environment and brought about an unprecedented improvement in material standards of living. One measure of the impact of these developments is economic growth. Production of coal, iron, and steel increased as much as 2,000 percent, and railroad freight, carried at steadily cheaper rates, increased from 8 billion ton-miles in 1870 to 150 billion in 1900. Another measure is the use of "prime movers," or sources of power. At the time of the Civil War the total power of all prime movers in the country was about 13 million horsepower, and two-thirds of it was animal power; by 1900 the total had quadrupled and four-fifths of the power was being generated by steam engines.

Changes of such scale and quality produced, along with material benefits, disruptions of almost every aspect of American life. Work became geared to the clock rather than to the seasons; men who once labored in the earth, growing things, now toiled in a factory, operating machines that made parts of larger things. People in New England ate fresh meat that was slaughtered in Kansas and transported in refrigerated cars so cheaply that local farmers and butchers were driven out of business. Speculators in Chicago bought carloads of North Dakota wheat by wire and sold it by wire in Liverpool, England, without ever seeing the grain. Local elites the nation over—country squires and small-town merchants, bankers, manufacturers, and lawyers—suddenly found their traditional status and authority undermined, for what local consumers gained from the emergence of corporate giants like United States Steel and Sears Roebuck, the local ironmonger and storekeeper lost in proportion.

And the times were turbulent. Eight years of postwar boom were followed by a nationwide financial collapse in 1873. In the deep depression that ensued, violence, political radicalism, and corruption were widespread; the presidential election of 1876 was stolen by the Republicans after the Democrats had won it. Prosperity and stability returned in the 1880s, only to be followed by another depression in the 1890s, along with a new wave of radicalism, both rural and urban, and more domestic violence than the country had known except during the Civil War.

Government at every level was overwhelmed by it all: The American system of divided sovereignty simply could not keep pace with the times. To the extent that government did adapt to keep up with the changes, the adaptation was largely the work of the Supreme Court, adjusting the Constitution to fit the new circumstances on a case by case basis. Critics of the Court, then and later, charged that the justices were rewriting the Constitution to bring it into accord with the laissez-faire philosophy of big business—the idea that government should leave the economy alone and let it run itself. The charge is unfair. It was and, under Anglo-American jurisprudence, always has been a legitimate function of the courts to interpret the law, as applied to individual cases, so as to keep it abreast of changing realities. As for philosophy, the Court sought not to curtail government power but to keep it lawful, and that is what constitutional government is all about.

IN THE MATTER OF RACE

Though most of the significant constitutional issues of the late nineteenth century arose from changing economic realities, one major problem, that of race relations, stemmed mainly from other sources. There was, to be sure, an economic dimension to the racial problem. In the new circumstances the freedmen, along with most southern whites, failed as farmers and lapsed into the virtual peonage of sharecropping, a system whereby landowners and suppliers took two-thirds of what the croppers produced. But the sources of the problem lay deeper. During Radical Reconstruction the freedmen—uprooted, landless, and trained for slavery rather than for the responsibilities of citizenship—did not know how to comport themselves among the whites in whose midst they were suddenly thrust as political equals. Most whites, in turn, had experienced only limited personal relations with blacks, for nearly four-fifths of the whites had neither owned slaves nor had much contact with plantation life. The white plain folk strongly resented the new black presence, and that resentment was heightened by the activities of the blacks' temporary protectors (and exploiters), the federal army, the Freedmen's Bureaus, and the carpetbagger and scalawag state governments. As local control gradually returned in the South, no small number of southern whites were accordingly determined to put the Negro "in his place" and to make sure he stayed there.

To some extent, the Supreme Court helped pave the way. In 1875 Congress had passed a new Civil Rights Act prohibiting racial discrimination in the selection of juries and forbidding segregation in inns, taverns, transportation facilities, and other public accommodations. In 1880 the Supreme Court ruled that a West Virginia law barring blacks from jury service violated both the Civil Rights Act and the equal-protection clause of the Fourteenth Amendment, and the next year it struck down a similar statute in Delaware. But in the meantime it effectively nullified the practical application of these decisions by ruling in *Virginia* v. *Rives* (100 U.S. 303) that the absence of blacks from a jury trial did not necessarily mean that blacks were being deliberately excluded.

Thenceforth, white local officials could exclude blacks from jury service simply by making up jury panel lists that "coincidentally" included no blacks.

The public accommodations portions of the Civil Rights Act were challenged in five separate suits, which the Court reviewed together in 1883 as the *Civil Rights* cases (109 U.S. 3). The decision, consistent with those in the *Slaughterhouse* cases and *United States* v. *Cruickshank*, was that, though the Fourteenth Amendment forbade discriminatory acts by states—the language is unmistakable—it made no reference to discriminatory acts by individuals. As the Civil Rights Act did prohibit discrimination by individuals and individually owned businesses, it exceeded the authority granted to Congress by the enforcement clause of the amendment and was therefore unconstitutional.

But the civil rights of the freedmen were not truly in danger so long as blacks retained the right to vote, and in protecting that right the Supreme Court held firm by extending federal authority. It will be recalled that in the 1842 case involving the Fugitive Slave Act, *Prigg* v. *Pennsylvania*, the Court had declared that the federal government could not compel state officials to enforce federal laws. In 1880 the Court partially reversed that earlier decision. An 1871 Civil Rights Act required state election officials to enforce both state and federal laws when supervising elections at which both state and federal officers were chosen and prohibited racial discrimination at the polls. The 1880 decision, in *Ex parte Siebold* (100 U.S. 371), upheld the constitutionality of the act, not on the ground of the Fifteenth Amendment but on the ground that Article I, Section 4 of the Constitution empowers Congress to regulate congressional elections. That left open the possibility of disfranchisement of blacks by intimidation—when bands of horsemen showed up at southern polling places and announced to no one in particular, "the hanging starts in fifteen minutes, boys," few blacks were disposed to stay around long enough to ask whom they had in mind. But the Court upheld efforts to curtail that, too. In *Ex parte Yarbrough* (110 U.S. 651) it ruled that the Ku Klux Klan Act, making it a crime for private individuals to interfere with the right of an American citizen to vote in federal elections and authorizing the use of the army to enforce the act, was likewise legitimized by Article I, Section 4.

The security of the black's voting rights, however, as well as his other rights, depended as a practical matter upon informal political arrangements rather than upon constitutional law. Upper-class southern whites—former plantation masters and new-rich capitalists—saw to it that blacks got fair treatment, and in exchange blacks generally voted as the upper-class whites required. There were some exceptions, and they were tolerated. Hence, for example, at least one black man was elected to every Congress but one until after the turn of the century, and in presidential elections blacks voted for the party of Lincoln. But otherwise, a silent bargain was struck. Blacks would vote in state and local elections as upper-class whites should decide, and in return they would be ensured legal rights and economic opportunities equal to those accorded whites in the same circumstances. The arrangement was like that prevailing between big-city political bosses and immigrants in the North.

Then, in the late 1880s, blacks began to be pushed into making a choice between the lesser of evils. Poor white farmers, growing steadily poorer as the economic revolution continued, began to organize politically to try to better their condition, and they both invited and demanded the support of poor blacks. If the blacks joined the poor whites, they faced the possibility that their upper-class white benefactors would disfranchise them and the poor whites as well, which is what happened in several southern states with the enactment of poll-tax requirements for voting (entirely constitutional and upheld by the Supreme Court). If blacks refused to side with white radicals and the radicals came to power anyway, it was overwhelmingly likely that the white radicals would find constitutional ways of depriving the blacks of the vote. That happened in several southern states, too. Mississippi started the process by adopting, in 1890, the "grandfather clause," restricting the vote to persons whose ancestors had been eligible to vote in 1866. The Supreme Court ultimately declared that particular form of disfranchisement unconstitutional, but southern radicals came up with other means. The most common were literacy tests—which, though sometimes administered by people who were themselves scarcely literate, were theoretically legitimate and, as a practical matter, outside the range of control of the federal courts. And thus, between the late 1880s and the early years of the twentieth century, black voting declined from a level comparable to that of whites to almost zero. By 1910 blacks were allowed to vote only in western Tennessee, eastern Texas, and a scattering of other places.

Hand in hand with disfranchisement came social segregation by law, as sanctioned by the "separate but equal" doctrine. The pivotal case approving that doctrine, *Plessy* v. *Ferguson* (163 U.S. 537), arose under an 1890 Louisiana statute requiring all railway companies carrying passengers in the state to provide separate coaches for whites and blacks and prohibiting members of either race from sitting in the coaches reserved for the other. Plessy, an octaroon, was assigned a train seat with blacks, insisted upon sitting with whites, and was arrested. In his defense Plessy took two distinct positions, that he was not a member of the "colored race" and that the act was in violation of the Thirteenth and Fourteenth amendments. When the Supreme Court decided the case in 1896 it rejected both contentions with only one justice dissenting.

The majority opinion, written by Henry B. Brown of Michigan, took for granted that a man with "seven eighths Caucasian and one eighth African blood" was legally a Negro, and it disregarded the claim that the statute violated the Thirteenth Amendment. Then it considered at length whether the law was compatible with the Fourteenth Amendment. The object of the amendment, Brown said, was "to enforce the absolute equality of the two races before the law, but in the nature of things it could not have been intended to abolish distinctions based upon color, or to enforce social, as distinguished from political equality, or a commingling of the two races upon terms unsatisfactory to either." Citing an 1849 Massachusetts case, he pointed out that segregation in public schools had long been the accepted practice even in states "where the political rights of the colored race have been longest and most earnestly enforced." He also pointed out that Congress had established segregation in the schools of the District of Columbia. The measure of the acceptability of a segregation law was whether it was in accordance with "the established usages, customs and traditions of the people." If racial segregation did accord with those usages, it was as reasonable as segregation of public facilities by sex or age. It was fallacious to assume that "enforced separation of the races stamps the colored race with a badge of inferiority. If this be so, it is not by reason of anything found in the act, but solely because the colored race chooses to put that construction upon it." If blacks should regain control of a state legislature and enact the same law, no whites would assume they were being placed in an inferior position. It was also fallacious to assume that "social prejudices may be overcome by legislation.... If the two races are to meet upon terms of social equality, it must be the result of natural affinities, a mutual appreciation of each other's merits and a voluntary consent of individuals." Legislative efforts to force social integration "can only result in accentuating the difficulties of the present situation."

In subsequent cases the Court extended the doctrine considerably further. *Cumming* v. *County Board of Education* (175 U.S. 528) dealt with the problem of a poor school district in which not enough money would be available to operate an elementary school for blacks if funds were used to maintain a high school for the few blacks who would attend. No black high school was established, but a white one was. A black who sued to be admitted to the white high school was turned down by the Court, even though it was a matter of separate and nonexistent rather than separate but equal. That was in 1899. Nine years later, in *Berea College* v. *Kentucky* (211 U.S. 45), the Court upheld a state law prohibiting private schools from educating blacks and whites together.

Segregation thus became the norm throughout the country,

and the United States adopted a caste system—despite the Thirteenth, Fourteenth, and Fifteenth amendments.

ECONOMIC REGULATION: THE STATES

While the Fourteenth Amendment was passing into disuse in regard to the civil rights of freedmen, it was evolving into a potent check upon the economic regulatory activities of the states. The state governments' powers to promote, regulate, prohibit, or otherwise control economic activity were of three broad descriptions: taxation, eminent domain, and the police power. Prior to the Civil War, the only constitutional restraints upon the exercise of those powers were contained in Article I, Section 10, most notably the contract clause and the restrictions on the kinds of taxes that could be levied. As the Court's interpretation of the Fourteenth Amendment was developed during the late nineteenth and early twentieth centuries, the due-process clause became another, and sometimes more significant, restraint.

Cases involving the states' taxing powers stemmed mainly from promotional and developmental activities. During the postwar boom many state and local governments, especially in the South and the trans-Mississippi West, granted large subsidies to attract railroads and industries. The granting of special privileges for such purposes was a practice of long standing, but the awarding of cash subsidies—financed by the selling of municipal and state bonds—had never been done on such a grand scale. During the post-1873 depression, hundreds of localities repudiated their bonds, and litigation arose over whether they could constitutionally do so. Because the suits usually involved bondholders in one state and local governments in another, they could be heard in the federal courts; and about three hundred reached the Supreme Court. For the most part, the Court upheld the claims of the bondholders on the basis of the contract clause, but in certain important particulars it whittled away at the extreme sanctity-of-contracts doctrines originally established by the Marshall Court.

The selling of bonds involved the pledging of future taxes, and thus the legitimacy of bond issues depended upon whether those taxes were to be levied for legitimate purposes. The state courts in Wisconsin and Michigan supported the repudiation of municipalities on the ground that their bonds had been issued to subsidize private corporations, whereas taxes could properly be levied only for general public purposes. In a succession of cases the Supreme Court overruled the state courts, holding that railroads were "public highways" even when built, owned, and operated by private persons for profit, and thus that taxes levied to subsidize them were for "public use." On the other hand, the Court ruled in several cases that pledging taxes for the support of "ordinary trades" was not legitimate, and that the contract clause did not protect bondholders in such instances. One such case, settled in 1874, was *Loan Office Association* v. *Topeka* (20 Wallace 655). The city of Topeka, Kansas, had lured the nation's biggest maker of wrought-iron bridges to the community by a campaign that included a large cash subsidy, and then repudiated the bonds it had issued to pay the subsidy. The Court held that the bondholders' contract with the city was invalid, on the ground that manufacturing was an ordinary trade and not a public service. Similarly, the Court retreated from, though it did not entirely reverse, the Marshall Court's 1812 decision (in *New Jersey* v. *Wilson*) that grants of tax immunity to corporations were protected by the contract clause. For instance, in decisions rendered in 1876 and 1877, the Court held that state legislatures could revoke all privileges and franchises not "essential to the operation of the corporation," including tax immunities, when corporations changed hands or were consolidated.

What the Court was seeking to accomplish with such decisions was to preserve effective state government by preventing legislatures from bargaining away fundamental powers, whether for corrupt motives or out of an excessive zeal for promoting corporate enterprise. It exerted the same kind of protective restraint in regard to eminent domain and the police power. The power of eminent domain—the taking of private property for public use—had long been abused by the practice of compensating owners only when property was taken and not when it was just damaged, even if the damage amounted to total destruction. In 1872, in the case of *Pumpelly* v. *Green Bay and Mississippi Canal Company* (13 Wallace 166), a landowner's property was permanently flooded by the backwater from a canal, and the Court instituted the requirement that compensation must be paid for damages.

On the other hand, the Court held that owners need not be compensated for private property that was taken through the police power—the power to protect the health, safety, welfare, and morality of the citizenry. The Court allowed the states wide latitude in the exercise of that power, holding that judicial interference was warranted only if persons in the same business were subjected to different restrictions and were thus denied the equal protection of the laws. Not even the contract clause was allowed to interfere. In a case in Alabama, an agent of a mutual-aid association was convicted of selling lottery tickets in violation of a state law, even though the association had earlier been empowered by its charter to carry on a lottery. The Supreme Court upheld the conviction despite the contract clause, and though it did so on a technicality, Justice Stephen Field in his opinion for the Court said no legislature could by contract restrain a subsequent legislature from exercising the police power "to suppress any and all practices tending to corrupt the public morals." In *Stone* v. *Mississippi* (101 U.S. 814), settled in 1880, the Court denied contract-clause protection to a lottery corporation on the specific ground that a state cannot grant away its right to exercise the police power.

This was moving a long way from the Marshall Court's sweeping protection of public contracts in *Fletcher* v. *Peck*, and in another leading decision the Court went the rest of the distance. In 1869 the extremely corrupt legislature of Illinois had granted to the Illinois Central Railroad title to all the submerged lands along the Chicago waterfront. The state subsequently tried to repossess the property, and the case reached the Supreme Court as *Illinois Central Railway Company* v. *Illinois* (146 U.S. 387). Justice Field, speaking for a narrow majority of the Court, denied the validity of the grant on the basis of a "public trust" doctrine: that the state legislatures' trinity of powers, police, taxation, and eminent domain, were held in trust for the public and were therefore inalienable.

It was in this context of trying to protect state governments from their own excesses that the Court worked out its most important doctrine regarding the regulation of business enterprise, that of substantive due process. The first step in the development of the doctrine took place in the *Granger* cases of 1877. In the late 1860s organizations of farmers known variously as the Patrons of Husbandry and The Grange were formed in many parts of the country as social, educational, and cooperative marketing groups. In the depression of the 1870s the Granges, secretly backed by eastern merchants interested in reducing railroad freight rates, went political. They gained control of the legislatures in several midwestern states and enacted laws setting railroad rates and regulating speculators in farm commodities, operators of grain elevators, and various other businessmen. In *Munn* v. *Illinois* (94 U.S. 113), the best known of the *Granger* cases, the Court reviewed the authority of states to enact such legislation. Specifically at issue was an Illinois law fixing the maximum prices charged by grain elevators in Chicago, over the companies' insistence that that amounted to taking their property without due process of law in violation of the Fourteenth Amendment. The Court, in a decision written by Chief Justice Morrison Waite, held that grain elevators, being "affected with a public interest," were subject to regulation under the state's police powers. Such regulation, including the setting of prices, had been exercised since colonial times. The due-process clause guaranteed only procedural rights, not substantive rights, and was therefore irrelevant to the case. In another of the *Granger* cases, Waite ruled that in the absence of congressional legislation the states could regulate railroads even when their operations were interstate in character.

During the decade that followed these cases, two things happened that caused the Court to change its mind. One was that the decisions proved to be out of touch with the economic changes that were taking place. The states went wild in enacting new regulations, and in the ensuing chaos it became nearly impossible for railroads and other interstate businesses to operate rationally, effectively, and at a profit. The other thing that happened was that five of the nine justices who participated in the *Granger* cases died or retired by the early 1880s and were replaced by lawyers who were attuned to the new economic realities and believed strongly that corporations were valuable servants of the public interest.

As a result, the Court began to alter its positions. Two cases decided in 1886 indicated the new direction. One case involved California laws that imposed different rates of taxation on the property of railroad corporations and the property of individuals. Counsel for the railroad, following an argument advanced earlier by the corporation lawyer and former senator Roscoe Conkling, contended that the word "person" in the due-process and equal-protection clauses of the Fourteenth Amendment (which Conkling had helped write) had been chosen to extend the amendment's benefits to artificial legal persons, that is, corporations. In *Santa Clara County* v. *Southern Pacific Railroad Company* (118 U.S. 394), the Court held that a corporation was a person under the meaning of the amendment. In the *Wabash* case (118 U.S. 557), an Illinois law prohibiting railroads from charging lower rates for long interstate shipments than for short intrastate shipments was declared unconstitutional on the ground that the state law was an effort to regulate interstate commerce.

In the 1890s the Court began to reconsider the states' powers to establish rates. First, it declared unconstitutional a Minnesota statute that gave a state railroad and warehouse commission power to fix rates and forbade appealing the commission's rulings to the courts. Denial of recourse to the courts was held to be, in substance, deprivation of property without due process of law. Four years later the Court held, in a case concerning a Texas commission, that rates must be reasonable and that it was a proper function of the courts to judge whether they were reasonable or not. Finally, in *Smyth* v. *Ames* (169 U.S. 466), settled in 1898, the rate-setting power of the states was more or less reduced to a formula. The power extended to all businesses affected with the public interest, but the rates must be sufficient to allow a "fair return" on the "fair value" of the investment in producing the goods or services.

The outcome of this judicial groping was to liberate large-scale interstate corporations from the restraining hand of state governments. In these circumstances, big business thrived and, not coincidentally, so did the country. But politicians were already beginning to plunge the national government into the regulatory void.

ECONOMIC REGULATION: THE FEDERAL GOVERNMENT

The constitutional questions arising from federal regulation were much less complex than those arising from state and local regulation. There was, after all, only one federal government as opposed to thousands of state and local governments, and it was a relatively small operation. Despite its growth during the Civil War, it continued to employ only about a fifth as many people and spend a fifth as much money as state and local governments. Moreover, apart from the levying of protective tariffs and the granting of land subsidies for the building of transcontinental railroads, the federal government had little to do with running the economy during the first two decades after the war.

The nearest thing to an exception concerned federal monetary and tax policies, and the Supreme Court seemed entirely unable to make up its mind on either. One issue was disposed of simply: A federal tax designed to drive state-chartered banks out of business was upheld by the Court in 1869. More characteristic were the *Legal Tender* cases (8 Wallace 603 and 12 Wallace 457). Congress had passed two acts making it legal to pay debts in paper money even if contracts called for payment in gold; in 1870, by a five-to-three margin, the Court declared those acts unconstitutional, but the next year, by an identical margin, it ruled that they were constitutional. The federal income tax, which Congress levied for the first time during the war, underwent a similar judicial history. In 1871 the Court held that the tax could not be collected from state employees, but it did not challenge the tax itself. Ten years later it specifically upheld the constitutionality of the tax; but then, in 1895, it declared federal income taxes unconstitutional. That decision stuck until it was voided by the adoption of the Sixteenth Amendment in 1913.

The first federal regulatory agency, the Interstate Commerce Commission, was established by an act of Congress in 1887 in response to the *Wabash* decision of the year before. The act prohibited a variety of pricing practices, required that rates be published, and stated that charges for rail transportation in interstate commerce must be "reasonable and just." Enforcement was entrusted to a five-member commission, which was empowered to hear complaints, investigate railroad companies' account books, and compel the testimony of witnesses. It was not specifically authorized to fix rates, but it could issue "cease and desist" orders, enforceable in the courts, against companies that violated the law. On paper, then, the ICC was a major constitutional innovation, for it was the first permanent federal agency to which Congress delegated broad powers that were partly legislative, partly executive, and partly judicial.

The Supreme Court liked the innovation not at all. It never declared any part of the act unconstitutional, but in a succession of interpretive opinions, rendered over the course of a dozen years, it reduced the commission to impotence. It denied the commission the power to fix rates on the ground that rate making was a legislative function that could not constitutionally be delegated to an executive agency; and it seriously curtailed the commission's investigatory powers by refusing to accept its findings as final, as that would be an encroachment upon the powers of the judiciary. As a result of such decisions, the ICC became little more than a statistics-gathering agency, and it remained so until Congress began to revitalize it in 1906.

Meanwhile, Congress had taken another fling at regulation by passing one of the most questionable pieces of legislation in its history, the Sherman Antitrust Act of 1890. The act declares illegal, and makes punishable by a fine up to $5,000 and imprisonment up to one year, "every contract, combination in the form of a trust or otherwise, or conspiracy in restraint of trade" and every attempt "to monopolize any part of the trade or commerce of the several States." Except in specifying that the word "person" was to include corporations, the statute gives no hint as to the definition of any of its terms, and those terms are so general and ambiguous as to be meaningless. If its words are taken literally, the Sherman Antitrust Act outlaws virtually every form of economic activity, for every contract "restrains" trade and every commercial transaction "monopolizes" some part of the totality of trade. The English common law against restraint of trade could provide guidelines; and though there was no common law of the United States, the Sherman Act made the development of one possible by its enforcement provisions. That is, proceedings under the act were to be brought in circuit courts by federal district attorneys, and the proceedings were to be in equity—meaning court actions in cases in which neither common law nor statutory law applies, or if applied would lead to injustice. In other words, whatever its intentions, Congress gave the federal courts what amounted to a mandate to write the national antitrust law.

What is more, the aim of the law was unrealistic, for it presupposed economic conditions that had long since disappeared. The new heavy industries required huge amounts of capital and stable, predictable markets, and those could be obtained only through some form of combination, either monopoly (one company in a given industry) or oligopoly (a few companies in a given industry). The problem—and the difficulties inherent in attempts to enforce antitrust legislation—can be illustrated with the example of John D. Rockefeller's Standard Oil Company. The petroleum industry had grown rapidly after the discovery of oil in Titusville, Pennsylvania, in 1859, for kerosene, a petroleum derivative, provided a source of household lighting that was cleaner, cheaper, and safer than any that mankind had had before. For the next twenty years, however, cutthroat competition among hordes of small operators made prices and supplies wildly unstable, to the detriment of consumers and producers alike. Rockefeller, a Cleveland businessman, repeatedly tried to bring order to the business, but also repeatedly ran afoul of the law. In the 1870s he formed a "pool," whereby the business was apportioned among the leading firms, but the state of Ohio outlawed pools. In 1882 he came up with another device, the "trust": The stock of forty companies was placed in the hands of nine trustees having irrevocable powers of attorney. The trust proved satisfactory for a time, and a number of others were formed in other industries—the Cotton Oil Trust, the Whiskey Trust, the Sugar Trust, the Lead Trust. At least some of these proved beneficial to the public, but the sheer size of the combinations frightened many people (the Standard Oil Trust alone controlled $70 million of stock). The ancient American fear of monopoly was reawakened, and state after state enacted antitrust laws. Rockefeller's own trust was dissolved by Ohio in 1890. Wild competition, widespread business failure, unemployment, and uncertainty of supply followed in industry after industry. If Americans were to enjoy the fruits of technological progress, some legal form of business combination would have to be developed.

Whether it would be developed depended upon whether the Sherman Act turned out to be enforceable. The first case to reach the Supreme Court under the act, *United States* v. *E. C. Knight Company* (156 U.S. 1), settled in 1895, seriously limited its scope and effectiveness. The American Sugar Refining Company, through contracts with four other companies, controlled 94 percent of the manufacture of refined sugar in the United States. The government brought an antitrust suit, contending that this near-monopoly control of production constituted a restraint of trade. Chief Justice Melville Fuller, who had been appointed after Waite's death in 1888, delivered the Court's opinion to the contrary. The power of Congress to regulate interstate commerce was exclusive, but though "commerce" had, since the *Gibbons* v. *Ogden* case, always been held to include both trade and transportation, it had never been held to include manufacturing. "Commerce succeeds to manufacturing, and is not a part of it." It was true that control of manufacturing "might unquestionably tend to restrain external as well as domestic trade, but the restraint would be an indirect result, however inevitable." The power to regulate production, to the extent that it existed at all, was reserved exclusively to the states. If national power were extended "to all contracts and combinations in manufacture, agriculture, mining, and other productive industries, whose ultimate result may affect external commerce, comparatively little of business operations and affairs would be left for state control," and that would be the end of "our dual form of government."

The decision in the *Knight* case did not declare the Sherman Act unconstitutional, but it limited its applicability mainly to railroads. Indeed, the act was applied to railroads a few months later, in a way that surprised many people: to stop a strike by a labor union. In the summer of 1894 the workers at the Pullman car company near Chicago went out on strike, and the American Railway Union, newly formed and headed by Eugene V. Debs, refused to handle Pullman cars during the strike. Many railway workers were fired, the Railway Union struck, and soon railroad transportation from Chicago westward was at a halt and transportation in the East was threatened. City police and private detective agencies were employed in an effort to break the strike, but Illinois Governor John P. Altgeld, sympathetic to the workers, called out the state militia to preserve order and protect the strikers. Postmaster General Richard Olney then sought an injunction against the union on the ground that the strike prevented the delivery of the United States mails. Instead, the federal circuit court in Chicago issued the injunction on the ground that the strike was a combination in restraint of trade, in violation of the Sherman Act. President Grover Cleveland sent in two thousand army troops to enforce the injunction, and the nation's transportation system was soon back in operation.

Debs, however, attempted to keep the strike going, and he was arrested for contempt of court. He then applied to the Supreme Court for a writ of habeas corpus, maintaining that the injunction he had disobeyed was illegal, because the handling of strikes was properly an executive, not a judicial, function. The Court heard the case as *In re Debs* (158 U.S. 564) and announced its decision in May 1895. The opinion upheld the injunction but went beyond the Sherman Act. The injunction could have been sustained on the ground that the strike interfered with the mails, wrote Justice David Brewer, but the Court chose instead to answer Debs' contention and assert its own broad powers in the matter. "Every government, entrusted by the very terms of its being with powers and duties to be exercised and discharged for the general welfare, has a right to apply to its own Courts for any proper assistance."

Most people approved of the vigor with which the strike was ended, for radicalism and labor violence were common during the depression of the 1890s, and labor unions were generally regarded with hostility. Yet many found the incident unsettling, for if the regulation of manufacturing was outside the scope of federal authority, so was the breaking of strikes.

THE EXPANSION OF FEDERAL REGULATION

The effect of these first Sherman Antitrust Act decisions was to set off a flurry of activity on a variety of levels. The Court itself, during the next few years, rendered two decisions overturning business combinations in violation of the act, one involving railroads and one involving the interstate marketing of steel pipe. Of more immediate importance was the stimulus the *Knight* ruling gave to business consolidations. A new and effective legal means of consolidation had just been devised: New Jersey and Delaware passed laws legalizing the ownership of one corporation by another, which was previously prohibited in every state, and the "holding company," as a corporation that owned other corporations was called, became the main instrument in a great wave of consolidations that took place in the decade after 1895. At the time of the *Knight* decision, there were only a dozen important industrial combinations in America and their total capitalization was about half a billion dollars. By 1904 there were 318 industrial combinations, representing the merger of 5,300 separate plants with a total capitalization of more than $7 billion. Lest this sum seem not especially large by today's standards, it should be remembered that the total amount of taxes collected by the federal government in 1904 was $541 *million*. Truly, the age of big business had dawned.

Coincidentally, the president of the United States at the time was Theodore Roosevelt, who had moved up from the vice presidency when President William McKinley was assassinated in 1901. Roosevelt, an aggressive and energetic man, believed that the United States could adjust to the new economic realities only by strengthening the power of the federal government, especially the executive branch. "There inheres in the Presidency," he observed, "more power than in any other office in any great republic or constitutional monarchy of modern times. . . . I believe in a strong executive; I believe in power." As for the gigantic new industrial combinations, Roosevelt recognized their necessity: "Business cannot be successfully conducted in accordance with the practices and theories of sixty years ago unless we abolish steam, electricity, big cities, and, in short, not only all the modern business and modern industrial conditions, but all the modern conditions of our civilization." But, in his view, the combinations could be guaranteed to serve the public interest only if they were regulated by the federal government. He urged Congress to amend the Sherman Act so that it would "forbid only the kind of combination which does harm to the general public," would permit federal licensing of corporations, and would provide "supervisory power to the Government over these big concerns engaged in interstate business." Federal control should be exercised for the benefit and prosperity of big business "no less than for the protection of investors and of the general public." Most big-business men desired the same thing, for the alternative—state regulation—was certain to be erratic and inefficient and likely to be radical.

Six months after he took office, Roosevelt instructed Attorney

General Philander Knox to institute an antitrust action against the Northern Securities Company. That was a bold and shrewd political move, well calculated to attract attention to the president, for the Sherman Act specified that federal district attorneys should institute antitrust proceedings "under the direction of the Attorney-General." The choice of targets was likewise bold and shrewd. Northern Securities was well known, for it had been formed as a holding company in 1901 as part of the settlement of a much-publicized battle for control of the railroads of the Northwest. It was readily identifiable in the public mind as an evil monopoly, because most people believed, mistakenly, that it was a pet creation of the powerful investment banker J. P. Morgan and that it held together a great consolidated railroad system. It could be dissolved with a minimum of destruction to the financial community, and the government's case was so prepared that if it should win, none of the financiers involved would suffer any loss and they might even make a good deal of money out of losing the case (as it turned out, they did). That they were not displeased with the suit is attested to by their large contributions to Roosevelt's reelection campaign funds.

And yet, even though it was rather in the nature of a political publicity stunt, the case was important in the evolution of federal regulation. When the case was decided in 1904, the Court ruled, five to four, in favor of the government's position and ordered the dissolution of the company; but there was some uncertainty about the decision. Previously, in trying to make sense of the vague language of the Sherman Act, a majority of the justices had agreed that the intention of the act could not have been to prohibit every combination in restraint of trade, and they had loosely formulated the notion that only "unreasonable" combinations were banned. The majority opinion in the *Northern Securities* case (193 U.S. 406) was written by Justice John M. Harlan, who believed the act prohibited *all* combinations, reasonable or unreasonable, as did three other justices. Justice Brewer, who believed otherwise, nonetheless voted with the majority in this instance because he believed that Northern Securities was an unreasonable combination. In other words, despite the decision, a majority of the justices still held to the reasonableness concept. Yet that concept was as abstract as the language of the Sherman Act itself and would require other decisions in other cases before it could be fully worked out.

Maturity of the "rule of reason" doctrine would come later, under Roosevelt's successor. Meanwhile, of the forty-three other antitrust actions brought by the Roosevelt administration, only one resulted in a major victory for the government and a significant ruling by the Court. The assistant to the attorney general in charge of antitrust work (whose office was created by Congress in 1903) instituted suit against the so-called Beef Trust, a group of great meat-packing houses in Chicago. The combination had taken place in local stockyards, all the animals involved were for the moment at rest there, and the sales were local transactions; but the prosecution contended that the activity was interstate commerce nonetheless. Justice Oliver Wendell Holmes, Jr., though usually critical of the Sherman Act, wrote the opinion for a unanimous Court, sustaining the government's case and ordering the dissolution of the combination. In *Swift and Company* v. *United States* (196 U.S. 375), Holmes broadened the traditional definition of interstate commerce by advancing the doctrine of the "current of commerce." Commerce, he said, was not a technical legal concept but a practical one. When cattle are sold in one state for shipment and sale in another, "and when this is a typical, constantly recurring course, the current thus existing is a current of commerce among the states, and the purchase of cattle is a part and incident of such commerce." That pronouncement by no means overruled the decision in the *Knight* case, but it considerably expanded the prospective field of antitrust actions.

One other major antitrust decision was rendered during the Roosevelt years, though the action was brought by a private company rather than by the government. Workers in a hat factory in Danbury, Connecticut, went out on strike in an effort to gain recognition of their union, and the United Hatters Unions instituted a nationwide boycott of the company's hats. The company responded with a civil suit charging the unions with conspiracy to restrain trade, in violation of the Sherman Act. In the *Debs* case the circuit court had issued the labor injunction under the Sherman Act; the Supreme Court had given its decision on other grounds. Now, in *Loewe* v. *Lawler* (208 U.S. 274), the Court dealt specifically with the applicability of the act in labor disputes. The defendant unions had argued that because they themselves were not engaged in interstate commerce the Court had no jurisdiction. Chief Justice Fuller, in the opinion, rejected the contention; pointing out that several unsuccessful attempts had been made to exempt organizations of farmers and workers when the act was under discussion in Congress, he concluded that the legislators intended to prohibit "combinations of labor, as well as of capital."

As the Court was slowly putting teeth into the antitrust act, Congress was moving rapidly to exert both its power over interstate commerce and its taxing powers. It passed an act forbidding the transportation of lottery tickets from state to state and levied taxes on oleomargarine—not for revenue and the pretended reason that margarine was dangerous to health but actually to improve the competitive position of dairying. These acts laid claim, in effect, to the existence of federal police power, a radical new idea. When the Supreme Court upheld the constitutionality of the acts in 1903 and 1904, the door was opened for a vast expansion of the regulatory activities of the federal government.

Two major acts designed to regulate business in the interest of public health were passed in 1906. The Pure Food and Drug Act prohibited the production, interstate transportation, or sale of impure or fraudulently labeled food and drugs and established the Food and Drug Administration to enforce the act. It resulted from several years of efforts by a dedicated scientist in the Department of Agriculture and lobbyists for various businesses that expected to profit from the legislation. The Meat Inspection Act had a more colorful background. For years the big packinghouses in Chicago had been lobbying for rigorous federal inspection of meat shipped in interstate commerce for two self-interested reasons: to help the sale of American meat in foreign markets and to strike at the domestic competition of three hundred or so small packers who supplied half the American market, often sold impure meat, and could not afford to meet high sanitation standards. The efforts were in vain. Then, during the winter of 1905–06, the big packers came under widespread public disfavor, partly because of the publication of Upton Sinclair's book *The Jungle*, which contained descriptions of nauseating conditions in the stockyards, and partly because the packers evaded on a technicality the injunction that had been issued against them in the antitrust action. Congress reacted to the popular clamor by passing the Meat Inspection Act to "punish" the packers, thus giving them just what they wanted.

Still a third regulatory measure was adopted in 1906. For some time, various groups of manufacturers, farmers, and merchants had been agitating to have the Interstate Commerce Commission revitalized. The Elkins Act of 1903, prohibiting rebates of freight charges, was billed as a step toward stronger railroad regulation; in fact, however, it was drafted by railroad attorneys and made no effective changes. Then President Roosevelt came out strongly in favor of a new regulatory law, and the Hepburn Act of 1906 was the result. The act increased the membership of the ICC from five to seven, extended its jurisdiction to oil pipelines, sleeping cars, ferries, and other carriers, curtailed the issuing of passes by railroads, and prohibited railroads from carrying commodities they or their affiliates produced, except materials used in railway construction. Most important, the act gave the commission power to establish maximum rates and to require uniform methods of accounting. To ensure the constitutionality of the act, the right to appeal rate decisions to the courts was specifically provided for, though rates were to be binding while review was pending.

The Hepburn Act had two important weaknesses. The first was that the act did not permit the commission to determine the value of the property of the railroads. Because the Court had ruled that regulated rates must yield a fair return on the value of the investment, the roads could challenge ICC rates by claiming that their capital investments were almost any amount they pleased. The other weakness was that the kind of regulation contemplated by the act made sense only in regard to railroads that operated as monopolies in the territories they served. For the others—for example, for the half-dozen lines that competed for freight over essentially the same territory from Chicago to the Eastern Seaboard—it would have been reasonable either to merge them into monopolies and regulate them as such or to allow them to continue in unrestrained competition. It was quite unreasonable to insist that they remain as fierce competitors but to regulate them as if they were monopolies. Both weaknesses would hamper the effective functioning of the commission as well as the railroads.

Clearly, to be effective in assuming the regulatory functions of the states, Congress had a great deal to learn.

QUESTIONS
FOR DISCUSSION

1. What does the ruling in *Plessy* v. *Ferguson* reveal about the Court's attitudes toward the nature of society and the role of government in it? Is the reasoning consistent with the decision in the *Cumming* case?

2. How was the police power of government protected and expanded on both state and federal levels? How is the police power used today?

3. How did decisions in business cases affect the balance of federal/state relations? What was the impact of the innovation of federal regulatory agencies?

4. What could "restraint of trade" include under the Sherman Act? If you sell your car to your next-door neighbor, are you restraining trade by excluding the possibility of purchase by the girl down the street? If you invent and patent a solar-powered car and become the only producer of it, are you violating the Sherman Act by monopolizing the market?

5. How did Theodore Roosevelt view the constitutional powers of the presidency? Does the modern presidency relfect an enlargement of his vision?

RECOMMENDED
READINGS

RICHARD MAXWELL BROWN, *Strain of Violence: Historical Studies of American Violence and Vigilantism* (New York: Oxford University Press, 1975).

ALFRED D. CHANDLER, JR., "The Beginnings of 'Big Business' in American Industry," *Business History Review* 33 (1959); William R. Doezema, "Railroad Management and the Interplay of Federal and State Regulation," ibid. 50 (1976).

TONY A. FREYER, *Forums of Order: The Federal Courts and Business in American History* (Greenwich, Conn.: JAI Press, 1979).

JAMES WILLARD HURST, *Law and Social Order in the United States* (Ithaca: Cornell University Press, 1977).

CHARLES McCURDY, "Justice Field and the Jurisprudence of Government-Business Relations," in Lawrence M. Friedman and Harry Scheiber, eds., *American Law and the Constitutional Order: Historical Perspectives* (Cambridge: Harvard University Press, 1978).

MARY CORNELIA PORTER, "That Commerce Shall Be Free: A New Look at the Old Laissez-Faire Court," *The Supreme Court Review* (1976), 135–159.

7
FOUNDATIONS OF A CONSTITUTIONAL REVOLUTION: 1910–1937

*D*espite the technological revolution and the sweeping economic and social changes that came with it, the Constitution continued to be, until 1910 or thereabouts, much what it had been a century earlier. It still provided a mixed "republican" form of government, with sovereignty divided by the federal system and the separation of powers. Government had grown greatly in size and in the complexity and variety of its functions, yet it had no central administration that affected the daily lives of ordinary citizens. Growing numbers, however, were convinced that the system was obsolete, that government was not adequately responsive to the will of the people, and that it was grossly inefficient. During the next quarter of a century major overhauls were made to remedy these supposed defects. As a result, the system of checks and balances and the very idea of limited government underwent a great deal of erosion.

Broadly speaking, the changes were in two opposite, or at least not entirely compatible, directions. One was toward greater democratization and nationalization—toward a powerful central government that was, in Lincoln's famous phrase, of the people, by the people, and for the people. That was not what the Founding Fathers had had in mind; their aim had been to create a diverse system that would protect the people from one another and from government itself. The other direction was away from democracy, toward government by specially trained and qualified experts. That was not what the Founding Fathers had had in mind, either.

Much of the democratizing and nationalizing was done through constitutional amendments. State after state adopted amendments providing for popular referendums on legislation, for giving voters the right to remove elected officials before the expiration of their terms, for nominating candidates in primary elections, and even for allowing voters to enact laws without the intervention of the legislatures. All told, nearly two thousand amendments to state constitutions were adopted between 1910 and 1930. On the national level, the Constitution was amended six times. The Sixteenth Amendment, proposed in 1909 and declared ratified in 1913, authorized the collection of federal income taxes. That source of revenue greatly increased the potential power of the national government. Moreover, at the time of its adoption it was thought to have a democratizing effect as well, for it was expected, rather naively, that income taxes would be levied to "soak the rich" and drain big-business corporations for the benefit of the common man, that they would never be collected from ordinary individuals. The Seventeenth Amendment (proposed 1912, ratified 1913) provided for the election of senators by popular vote rather than by the state legislatures, and the Nineteenth (proposed 1919, adopted 1920) broadened the suffrage by giving women the right to vote. The Eighteenth (proposed 1917, adopted 1919) increased federal power by prohibiting the manufacture, sale, or transportation of intoxicating liquor, but it was repealed in 1933 by the Twenty-first Amendment. The Twentieth (proposed 1932, adopted 1933) was another democratizing step, for it shortened the period between the election of federal officials and the time they took office, and

thus made the expression of the popular will more nearly immediate.

Democratization and nationalization also came about through
the efforts of vigorous and popular presidents. Theodore Roosevelt had restored to the presidency more prestige than it had
had since Jefferson's time, and he had popularized the idea that
the office was the one truly democratic branch of the national
government, as it was the only one elected (albeit indirectly) by
all the people. Woodrow Wilson, the first president to speak of the
United States as a democracy—his predecessors had always referred to it as a republic—likewise contributed to the democratization and increased power of the presidency. He initiated the
practice, common ever since, of drawing up entire legislative programs and assuming responsibility with the voters for the laws
passed by Congress during his administration; and under his leadership, during World War I, the national government exerted far
broader powers than it had ever exercised before. Warren G.
Harding and Calvin Coolidge temporarily reversed the trend, but
Herbert Hoover energized the office anew and Franklin Roosevelt
became the most powerful and popular president in the nation's
history.

The growth of government by non-elected specialists, though
contrary to the increase of democracy, was part of the same movement. "Progressive" reformers sought to oust corrupt political
bosses who controlled many state and local governments and,
through them, the national party machinery. Democratization was
one means to this end; for example, choosing nominees in primary
elections rather than in conventions of boss-picked delegates gave
progressive candidates greater chances of being elected to public
office. Once they gained control of a state, they undermined the
bosses still further by enacting civil-service laws. These reduced
political patronage by providing that government employees be
appointed on the basis of competitive examinations instead of
political influence and by prohibiting the firing of most of them
except for incompetence or dishonesty. Gradually, federal gov-

ernment employees were also brought under civil service. Thus, of the roughly 240,000 civilian employees of the federal government when Theodore Roosevelt took office in 1901, four-fifths were either elected or appointed directly by elected officials and were subject to firing after every election. Of the more than 600,000 such employees when Franklin Roosevelt took office in 1933, three-quarters held their jobs by virtue of civil-service examinations and retained them no matter what the will of the voters.

The increase in the number of appointed administrators was accompanied by an increase in regulatory activities. Virtually every state established commissions to regulate public utilities, banks, insurance companies, and other industries "affected with a public interest," and most created agencies to enforce public-health measures and passed laws establishing safety standards in mines and factories. On the national level, Congress enacted a succession of statutes that expanded federal regulation beyond railroads and "trusts" into control over conservation of natural resources, banking, agricultural commodities, and radio broadcasting. Moreover, Congress increasingly entrusted administrative functions to special agencies. Sometimes this was done by creating new executive departments, as with the Department of Commerce and Labor (established 1903, separated into two departments 1913); sometimes by setting up special divisions in older departments, as with the Bureau of Forestry under the Interior Department (1905); and sometimes by establishing independent agencies such as the Federal Trade Commission (1914) and the Federal Tariff Commission (1916, 1922).

The multiplication of administrative bureaus brought about a host of constitutional problems. One concerned the specialization of evidence. Judges, trained in the law, could scarcely be expected to have an expert's understanding of the technical, accounting, and financial data upon which a case involving, say, electric utility rates would depend. Accordingly, though the courts clung jealously to their power to review the decisions of regulatory commissions, they increasingly found it necessary—beginning with an *Interstate Commerce Commission* case in 1910—to accept the factual findings of the commissions' experts at face value. Related to this problem was another: The new administrative agencies, though usually contained within the executive branch, exercised legislative and judicial as well as executive powers. The federal courts had repeatedly held to the sound constitutional doctrine that the powers of government could not be delegated by one branch to another. To cope with this difficulty, the Supreme Court developed the doctrine of "quasi-legislative" and "quasi-judicial" powers. For instance, in 1911 it upheld an act granting the secretary of agriculture power to make rules, enforceable by criminal proceedings, for the regulation of forest reserves; and in 1928 it upheld a tariff act that gave the Tariff Commission power to raise or lower duties within a certain range. In both cases, the Court held that the acts had not delegated pure legislative power to the executive branch but had merely given it "administrative discretion" as to the details of the law.*

All this amounted to the beginning of a constitutional revolution through the emergence of a fourth branch of government. Within the framework of that process, fundamental constitutional issues arose in three broad areas: economic regulation, the conduct of foreign relations, and civil rights. But an even greater challenge, a wholesale challenge to traditional constitutional government, was just around the corner: Franklin Roosevelt's New Deal.

ECONOMIC REGULATION

Between 1907 and 1914 most states established public utility commissions based upon the principle of the "natural monopoly"—that such businesses as intrastate railroads, electric and gas companies, and waterworks require so much capital as to make com-

---

*After the 1930s the Court increasingly permitted the delegation of powers to administrative agencies. The leading case was *Fahey* v. *Malonee* (322 U.S. 245), decided in 1946.

petition impractical—and, upon the Supreme Court's doctrine in *Smyth* v. *Ames*, that regulated industries are entitled to a reasonable rate of return on their capital investments. The laws establishing these commissions resulted from the joint efforts of the regulated industries, civic groups, and legislators, and by and large they effectively promoted the interests of the companies and the public alike. Similar commissions, the product of similar efforts, were established for regulating the insurance business, again with advantageous results. Commissions established to regulate manufacturing and mining, on the other hand, were fewer and less successful.

For the most part, the states' efforts to control manufacturing and mining were directed toward improving the working conditions of employees in those industries, who numbered perhaps a fifth of all economically active people in the country. The big new manufacturing combinations—International Harvester, Standard Oil, U.S. Steel, General Electric, and others—were pioneers in the field of improving working conditions, for their managers recognized that voluntary welfare capitalism, as it was called, made for more efficient, productive, and loyal work forces. And because big-business men also recognized, as clearly as labor organizers and radicals, that intolerable working and safety conditions were breeding grounds for unionism and radicalism, they worked for the passage of laws regulating factory conditions and establishing industrial commissions to enforce them.

The Supreme Court, however, stood in the way, at least for a time. The leading case in the matter was *Lochner* v. *New York* (198 U.S. 45), which concerned a New York law limiting workers in bakeries to a maximum of sixty hours a week, a standard that was convenient for big mechanized bakers but impossible for the small bakers to meet. Though the Court had previously upheld a Utah statute limiting miners to an eight-hour day on the ground that it was a health measure and thus a valid exercise of the police power, it declared the New York law unconstitutional. The reasoning of the majority (against which Justice Oliver Wendell Holmes objected in a famous dissenting opinion) was that the

New York statute interfered with the right to freedom of contract between employers and employees and thus deprived both of due process of law. Several other cases were decided on the same basis.

Then, in 1908, came a breakthrough. The state of Oregon had passed an act that prohibited employers from requiring females to work more than ten hours a day. Louis D. Brandeis, a Boston lawyer who was hired by the state to defend the act, shrewdly perceived that the implication of the *Lochner* decision was that the Court would uphold such legislation if it could be convinced that public health—or any other legitimate object of the police power—was genuinely at stake. Accordingly, instead of building his case upon legal precedents, he presented what came to be known as the Brandeis brief: a massive compilation of sociological, economic, and medical data designed to show that "woman's physical structure and the performance of maternal functions place her at a disadvantage in the struggle for subsistence." Convinced by the novel argument, the Court ruled in *Muller v. Oregon* (208 U.S. 412) that the law was constitutional. The Court held that "the physical well-being of woman becomes an object of public interest and care in order to preserve the strength and vigor of the race." It justified its protective action on the ground that "history discloses the fact that woman had always been dependent upon man.... Legislation designed for her protection may be sustained.... It is impossible to close one's eyes to the fact that she looks to her brother and depends upon him." As other states began to frame and defend their regulatory statutes more carefully, in keeping with the Brandeis brief approach, most of them passed the test of constitutionality.

But in the 1920s the Court imposed a new barrier: It held that state laws regulating wages, hours, or working conditions were valid only in regard to businesses affected with a public interest, and it defined such businesses narrowly. A growing number of the justices dissented from that position as the decade wore on, however, and by the early 1930s the Court was holding that states could define the public interest as they saw fit.

Meanwhile, the interplay between legislatures and courts had produced a body of law regarding workers who were injured or killed on the job. The liability of employers to compensate such workers or their families was limited by two old principles of common law: the "fellow-servant rule" and the doctrine of "contributory negligence," which exempted employers if it could be shown that the accident arose from the negligence of another employee or the worker himself. In 1906 Congress passed an act requiring railroads and other common carriers to pay compensation for injuries or accidental death of their employees irrespective of the common-law rules. The Supreme Court declared the act unconstitutional in 1908, but only on the ground that it extended to intrastate as well as interstate railroads. Congress promptly repassed the act, carefully limiting it to employees directly engaged in interstate commerce, and in 1912 the Court upheld the revised statute. It also upheld the Workmen's Compensation Act passed by Wisconsin in 1911, and more than half the states soon adopted similar laws.

In ruling upon regulatory activities of the national government, the Court tended to follow a pattern opposite to that which it followed with the states. That is, with the states the Court was fairly strict in regard to regulation of business as such and relatively lenient in regard to regulation of working conditions, whereas with congressional acts it was the other way around. The justices' approval of federal regulation first began to surface in 1911. President William Howard Taft had appalled the business community in 1910 by instituting the first of a series of sixty-five antitrust suits against corporate giants. In 1911 the Supreme Court, following the "rule of reason," concluded that American Tobacco Company and Standard Oil, among others, were combinations engaged in "unreasonable" restraint of trade and ordered their dissolution. Though the decisions were generally popular, the application of the rule of reason stirred up a great deal of criticism. Justice Harlan, in a biting dissent, attacked the rule as amounting to "judicial legislation," and many another critic echoed that charge. And yet, given the muddled quality of the Sherman Antitrust Act, the Court had little choice in the matter.

In 1914 Congress clarified the Sherman Act with the passage of two statutes, the Clayton Antitrust Act and the Federal Trade Commission Act. The Clayton Act, in effect, gave congressional confirmation to interpretations the Court had placed on the Sherman Act. For instance, the new law forbade price discrimination and contracts that prohibited one party from doing business with the competitors of the other, both of which practices the Court had decided were unreasonable restraints of trade. It also exempted labor unions from most of the restrictions it placed on businesses, prompting Samuel Gompers, president of the American Federation of Labor, to hail the act (prematurely, it turned out) as the "Magna Carta of Labor." The Federal Trade Commission Act established the FTC, gave it power to investigate all interstate businesses except railroads and banks (which were regulated by the ICC and the newly created Federal Reserve Board, respectively), and authorized it to issue "cease and desist" orders to any that were engaged in unfair practices. Between the two acts, what constituted an unfair practice was defined in reasonably clear, if not entirely specific, terms.

The purpose of the acts was not to punish wrongdoers but, in the spirit of the presidential administration of Woodrow Wilson, to prevent wrongdoing. This was to be accomplished partly through publicity: The FTC was authorized to investigate businesses, to require annual and special financial reports from corporations, and to publicize its findings. Partly it was to be done through voluntarism: Wilson believed that most people, businessmen included, would do the right thing without being coerced by government, provided they were taught to and allowed to and provided they were policed by informed public opinion. Accordingly, under his administration the FTC and the attorney general began an educational program to show corporations how to operate within the limits of the antitrust laws. Any interested corporation was invited to send its lawyers to Washington for free advice from FTC staff members and Justice Department lawyers. Among others, American Telephone and Telegraph, the New Haven Railroad, and the Ford Motor Company took advantage of this "free antitrust insurance." The arrangements actually gave the federal government a more effective voice in regulating corporations than it would have had simply by prosecuting them in antitrust suits, and the policy was continued through the 1920s and the early 1930s.

Railroad regulation was expanded by a succession of congressional enactments: the Mann-Elkins Act of 1910, the Physical Valuations Act of 1913, the Adamson Eight-Hour Act of 1917, the Railroad Control Act of 1918, and the Transportation Act of 1920. The Supreme Court upheld all this legislation, and railroads thus became the first industry to be brought thoroughly under the control of the federal government. Not coincidentally, they became the first industry to be destroyed, in the long run, by an excess of regulation.

The Court was equally permissive in upholding federal regulation of trading in grain, of meat-packing, and of the new radio broadcasting industry, but it was considerably less so in dealing with social legislation passed by Congress. In 1916 Congress enacted a child-labor law, prohibiting the shipment in interstate commerce of products manufactured by the labor of children. Though the Court had previously upheld federal laws prohibiting interstate transportation of lottery tickets, adulterated food, and prostitutes, and would in 1925 uphold a law forbidding interstate transportation of stolen automobiles, in 1918 it struck down the child-labor law. The test of the constitutionality of such laws, the majority opinion said, was whether products being shipped were of themselves harmful. A year later Congress tried again by passing a high tax on goods produced by child labor; in 1922 the Court struck that one down, too. Meanwhile, in 1921 the Court ruled that secondary boycotts by labor unions could still be stopped by injunctions despite the exemption granted by the Clayton Act. Then in 1923, in *Adkins* v. *Children's Hospital* (261 U.S. 525), the Court struck down a law establishing a minimum wage for women in the District of Columbia as a violation of freedom of contract and as depriving employers of property without due process of law.

Reformers and advocates of increased government power over the economy were generally critical of the Court's decisions in these areas. Some of their charges were justified. It is true that the Court was exercising more power than ever before, and that by the late 1920s it had taken on a certain arrogance about its power. In 1904 Edward D. White, then an associate justice and later chief justice, had said modestly that the Court never declared a statute unconstitutional on the ground that it was "unwise or unjust," for that would be an "act of judicial usurpation"; Charles Evans Hughes, who became chief justice in 1930, wrote that "the Constitution is what the judges say it is." It is also true that, in rendering a decision on the basis of sociological evidence in the *Muller* case and afterward, the justices were setting a dangerous precedent, for sociological perceptions and values change from one generation to another and are hardly the stuff of which stable constitutional institutions are made. Finally, in introducing the rule of reason into its antitrust decisions, it was in fact legislating, as Justice Harlan charged.

But when all is said and done, it must be admitted that the Court was doing its duty. Its only alternative course of action would have been to leave the Constitution to the mercy of unbridled democracy and/or executive power, and these were precisely the forces it had been designed to check.

FOREIGN AFFAIRS

Though the constitutional problems arising from economic change were serious, they were not nearly so serious as those arising from the emergence of the United States as a world power. Overseas involvements, which began in earnest with the Spanish-American War of 1898, were simply not contemplated by the Constitution; and when they began, it was generally, if vaguely, assumed that the federal government had whatever powers were necessary to manage them. That attitude is illustrated by three Supreme Court decisions spaced over a third of a century. The first, *Downes* v. *Bidwell* (182 U.S. 244), rendered in 1901, concerned the territorial possessions acquired from Spain as a result of the war. The question was whether full constitutional rights extended to the inhabitants of those areas; the Court, almost with a shrug of the shoulders, declared that it was entirely up to Congress. The second decision, handed down in 1920, involved the treaty-making power. Earlier, the Court had declared unconstitutional an act regulating the killing of migratory birds. Congress repassed the act after a migratory bird treaty had been negotiated with Canada. In *Missouri* v. *Holland* (252 U.S. 416), the Court upheld the statute, holding that a treaty could give the federal government powers it did not otherwise possess. The third decision, delivered in 1936, established the doctrine of inherent powers: In *United States* v. *Curtiss-Wright Export Corporation* (299 U.S. 304), the Court declared that the president has wide-ranging powers in dealing with foreign nations and that those powers do not require as their basis an act of Congress.

The gravest strains upon the Constitution arose during World War I: It was almost true, as one congressman said, that in time of war the Constitution was suspended. President Wilson could not see anything or do anything halfway; he believed war was evil, but when it must be resorted to it required "force to the utmost, force without stint or limit." Accordingly, he conducted the war in an unheard-of fashion, by drafting young men into the army and pouring them into Europe, first by the hundreds of thousands and then by the millions, until no European with eyes to see could doubt that he would continue, if necessary, until the very last American was under arms in Europe.

At home, he believed, the war required that civilians devote their total energies to the work of destruction and that "conformity would be the only virtue . . . and every man who refused to conform would have to pay the penalty." Mobilization at home took place in two broad areas, the organization of the economy for war production and the indoctrination of the people in what was officially described as a "proper war spirit." The results of efforts in the first area, though significant, were not what had been intended. The results of efforts in the second area were tragic.

The organization of the economy was turned over to five great agencies, one each for shipping, food, fuel, transportation, and industry. The War Shipping Board was created before the United States entered the war and was headed by a committee. The policing of the production, distribution, and consumption of food and fuel was authorized by the Lever Act of August 10, 1917; Herbert Hoover, the future president, headed the Food Administration, and Harry Garfield, son of the former president, directed the Fuel Administration. As for transportation, the original plan called for the coordination of the railroads through boards of volunteers and company cooperation, but that approach proved inadequate to cope with the enormous traffic generated by the war, and late in 1917 the railroads almost ceased to function. Accordingly, Wilson acted under assumed emergency powers and without congressional authorization to seize control of the railroads and place them under direct government operation. Congress subsequently sanctioned the action and established the Railroad Administration. Finally, control of industry was vested in the War Industries Board, headed by the Wall Street speculator Bernard Baruch.

The federal government proved to be no more effective at running the economy than it had been at regulating it. For example, the War Shipping Board, given an appropriation of hundreds of millions of dollars and orders to build a fleet of merchant ships, constructed four huge shipyards but did not launch its first vessel until the week after the war ended. Again, there was the distribution of war contracts. In its haste to convert the economy to war, the government placed most of its orders for war materials in the East, with the result that eastern factories were overworked and understaffed, whereas plants in the Middle West, lacking war contracts and curtailed by restrictions on nonwar production, were idle. Early in 1918 Baruch's War Production Board began a large-scale reallocation of war contracts, but by the time war production was efficient the war was over. As a result, the American army in Europe was abundantly equipped with such supplies as American factories had already been producing for the Allied armies but was almost totally lacking in supplies the economy had to produce from scratch. For instance, the army had twenty million rounds of artillery ammunition but had to borrow French guns to be able to fire them.

The long-range effects of economic mobilization were as immense as the immediate results were ineffectual. Hoover's efforts brought hundreds of thousands of acres of marginal and sub-marginal lands into production, with the consequence that farm surpluses and rural depression plagued the country throughout the otherwise prosperous 1920s; in addition, within a dozen years fantastically large areas had been converted into dust bowls, their soil eroded and depleted. Garfield's efforts set off a consolidation movement among operators of soft-coal mines and resulted in the mechanization of many mines and the closing of scores of others that did not lend themselves to mechanization. Tens of thousands of miners were thrown out of work and vast pockets of poverty resulted throughout southern Appalachia. The Railroad Adminis-tration's efforts led to the passage of the Transportation Act of 1920, which reversed thirty years of government policy by re-quiring the ICC to encourage, rather than prevent, the consoli-dation of railroads and the pooling of their operations. Baruch's doings brought about a drastic standardization of production and set off a new wave of business consolidations, thus resulting in an enormous increase in the wealth and power of the great cor-porations.

The second broad aspect of the wartime domestic program—the mobilization of public opinion—was carried out with awesome effectiveness. The legal foundations were laid in two acts. The Espionage Act of 1917 provided maximum penalties of a $10,000 fine and twenty years' imprisonment for statements or actions promoting insubordination, disloyalty, disunity, or interference with the conduct of the draft. The Sedition Act of 1918 provided the same penalties for writing, printing, or uttering profane or abusive language about the government, the Constitution, the flag, or the armed forces, or tending to curtail production. More than a thou-sand persons were imprisoned under these acts. "Enemy aliens," people from Germany and Austria-Hungary who had not yet be-come citizens, were persecuted on a large scale. Under a presi-dential proclamation issued in April 1917, several thousand enemy aliens were arrested and detained for the duration of the war in what would later be called concentration camps.

Yet these were trivial affairs compared to the work of the legally established propaganda and vigilante agencies, the Committee on Public Information and the State Councils of Defense. The Committee on Public Information, under the zealous direction of former newspaperman George Creel, engaged ministers, college professors, novelists, and people from all other walks of life to write and distribute hate literature, falsify both history and current news, harangue audiences, and expose everybody to a continuous barrage of propaganda designed to promote enthusiasm for the war and hatred of the enemy. The State Councils of Defense, in addition to helping finance the war by selling billions of dollars' worth of Liberty Bonds, organized networks of vigilance committees to investigate and spy upon the inhabitants of every neighborhood in the country. Much of what they did was vicious but petty. Store windows of German-American shopkeepers were broken, and sometimes the owners were stoned or tarred and feathered; most high schools and colleges stopped teaching German, and favorable references to Germany were removed from history books; the name of sauerkraut was changed to liberty cabbage, and frankfurters became known as liberty sausages. But much of it was not at all petty. In the month of July 1918, for example, vigilance committees in Chicago alone seized and searched 150,000 men, detained 20,000 of them in jails and warehouses, and triumphantly announced that fourteen of the men thus abused were draft dodgers. For nineteen months the nation was governed by controlled hysteria, by government-sponsored mob action, by totalitarian democracy.

IN THE MATTER OF CIVIL LIBERTIES

Most of the government's war measures went unchallenged in the courts, and those that were challenged were either approved or not declared unconstitutional until the war was safely over. The constitutionality of the military draft was contested in a number of cases, but the Supreme Court declared that compulsory military service was sanctioned by the law of nations as well as the Constitution; it contemptuously dismissed the claim that such service was "involuntary servitude" under the meaning of the Thirteenth Amendment. In *Northern Pacific Railway Company* v. *North Dakota*, among other cases, the seizure of the railroads was challenged, but the Court upheld the seizure as justified by the government's constitutional powers to conduct a war. A portion of the Lever Act was declared unconstitutional, but not until 1921.

The violations of civil liberties under the Espionage and Sedition acts ran squarely into the First Amendment: "Congress shall make no law...abridging the freedom of speech, or of the press." In *Schenk* v. *United States* (249 U.S. 47), decided in 1919, the Supreme Court coped with the problem in regard to the Espionage Act. A group of socialists were convicted of mailing leaflets urging draftees to refuse to serve. Speaking for a unanimous court, Justice Holmes upheld the act with the "clear and present danger" doctrine. In ordinary times, Holmes wrote, the circulation of the leaflet would have been protected by the First Amendment. "But the character of every act depends upon the circumstances in which it is done....The most stringent protection of free speech would not protect a man in falsely shouting fire in a theatre and causing a panic....The question in every case is whether the words used are used in such circumstances and are of such a nature as to create a clear and present danger."

By formulating the clear and present danger doctrine instead of following the First Amendment literally—"Congress shall pass *no* law"—the Court opened a can of worms as troublesome as the rule of reason had been. In 1919 it applied the doctrine to the Sedition Act and found itself divided. *Abrams* v. *United States* (250 U.S. 616) arose from the publication of communist pamphlets criticizing the president for sending troops to help suppress the Russian Revolution and urging workers in American munitions plants to go on strike in support of their Russian "comrades." A majority of the Court voted to uphold the convictions of the persons responsible, but two justices, Holmes and Wilson's recent apointee Louis Brandeis, registered vigorous dissent. Holmes said that "nobody can suppose that the surreptitious publishing of a silly leaflet by an unknown man, without more, would present any immediate danger." Congress could not "forbid all effort to change the mind of the country"; only an emergency warranted any interference with free speech.

The problem did not go away with the end of the war. The vigilante atmosphere created during the war took the form, afterward, of the Great Red Scare. Radicalism, strikes, and violence swept over Europe and America, and fear of communist revolution became widespread. Hoping to exploit that fear as a means of winning the presidency in 1920, Attorney General A. Mitchell Palmer launched a series of raids on radical organizations, mainly those of Italian anarchists and Jewish socialists. Palmer's predecessor had already arrested and deported 249 radicals, and on January 20, 1920, Palmer's agents rounded up thousands of radicals and suspected radicals in thirty-three cities from coast to coast. He formally arrested more than 5,000, turned about a third over to state governments for prosecution, and deported 556. In the turbulence, blacks too were attacked: Lynchings increased and race riots occurred in twenty-five localities across the nation. Congress passed laws restricting immigration; states passed laws restricting left-wing activities.

In these circumstances the Supreme Court was faced with a succession of cases, the cumulative effects of which were to increase civil liberties and to establish the Court as their guardian. The earliest important such case was that of *Gitlow* v. *New York* (268 U.S. 652), settled in 1925. Benjamin Gitlow, a radical socialist, was convicted under an old New York criminal anarchy law of publishing tracts advocating the violent overthrow of government. In considering the constitutionality of the statute, the Court declared for the first time that "freedom of speech and of the press—which are protected by the First Amendment from abridgment by Congress—are among the fundamental personal rights and 'liberties' protected by the due-process clause of the Fourteenth Amendment from impairment by the states." That was an abrupt shift from the position the Court had held since the *Slaugh-terhouse* cases of 1873, and it marked the first application of the doctrine of substantive due process to non-economic matters. Even so, the opinion went on, the right of free speech was not absolute, and the New York law was constitutional in regard to Gitlow. "The state cannot reasonably be required to measure the danger from every such utterance in the nice balance of a jeweler's scale. A single revolutionary spark may kindle a fire that, smoldering for a time, may burst into a sweeping and destructive conflagration."

In at least four other cases decided during the 1920s, the Court repeated its expression of the doctrine that the Fourteenth Amendment extended the First to include the states. One of these involved a California communist and resulted in a ruling essentially the same as in the *Gitlow* case. The others involved state laws restricting teachers and what could be taught in parochial and other private schools and resulted in overturning the statutes. The Court was divided on most of these cases.

Then in 1931, not long after Charles Evans Hughes became chief justice, the Court handed down two landmark decisions on free speech and freedom of the press. A young communist was convicted under the California "red-flag law," which banned the displaying of a red flag as a symbol of anarchism or communism. Her case came to the Court as *Stromberg* v. *California* (283 U.S. 359). Hughes, writing the opinion, held that the statute was too broad in scope to be constitutional. "Opportunity for free political discussion to the end that government may be responsive to the will of the people," he wrote, "is a fundamental principle of our constitutional system. A statute which ... is so vague and indefinite as to permit the punishment of the fair use of this opportunity is repugnant to the guaranty of liberty contained in the Fourteenth Amendment."

The other case, *Near* v. *Minnesota* (283 U.S. 697), involved a Minnesota statute authorizing the permanent suppression, as a public nuisance, of any newspaper or magazine publishing malicious, scandalous, or defamatory material. The act might have been challenged as a bill of attainder, for it was actually aimed at one particular highly abusive newspaper editor; but a newspaper publishers' association and the *Chicago Tribune*, fearing censorship for all newspapers should the act stand, came to the defense of the editor and insisted that he contest the act on free-press grounds. The Court, in a five-to-four decision, overturned the statute on the ground that a single violation of the act would have resulted in permanent suspension of a periodical irrespective of its content thereafter.

THE CHALLENGE OF THE NEW DEAL

Reformers generally applauded these decisions, and for a time the justices had the unaccustomed experience of being popular. The cheering soon stopped, however, for the Court was called upon to defend the Constitution against the wholesale reforms instituted by the New Deal.

When Franklin Roosevelt became president in 1933, the country was in a great depression. Nearly two-fifths of all corporate businesses had failed since the stock market crash of 1929, the banking system lay in ruins, and a quarter of the working-age population was unemployed. There was no unemployment compensation and the capacity of private charities to aid the needy was limited. Yet none of these conditions explains the massive array of federal programs established to combat the depression. The nation had weathered numerous recessions and six major depressions in its history, and no one had ever seriously proposed that the federal government should intervene on a grand scale: It was expected that the economy would heal itself. It always had. The federal government intervened this time on the scale it did for a host of minor reasons and two major ones. The major reasons were that momentum and precedent for federal intervention into the workings of the economy had been building for three decades and that a large number of people in government, including President Roosevelt, had been exhilarated by the experience of running the economy during World War I. They were convinced that the country could be mobilized to fight a depression as well as to fight a war.

The New Deal's measures were vigorous, indeed, and the administration's view was that the Constitution could again be virtually suspended. The federal government greatly expanded its policing and regulatory activities in the areas in which it had been engaged previously. It moved into new areas of regulation such as the selling of corporate stocks. It provided relief for the unemployed. It promoted labor unions, provided job-hunting services, and passed minimum-wage laws. It went into business on its own by creating the Tennessee Valley Authority to generate and sell electric power. It attempted to control manufacturing through the National Industrial Recovery Administration, or NRA, and to control farm production through the Agricultural Adjustment Administration, or AAA. (Justice James McReynolds, a Wilson appointee from Tennessee, threatened to resign in protest against the multiplication of "alphabet agencies" when his own office in the new Supreme Court building was assigned a letter rather than a number.)

At first it appeared that the Supreme Court justices might sit idly by or act as rubber stamps as Congress and the president enacted radical anti-depression measures and state governments passed similar laws. In 1934 it rendered decisions, in two cases arising under state laws, suggesting that the justices, like other people in government, regarded the Constitution as suspended. In one, a New York case, the Court held that the "public interest" was whatever legislatures declared it to be. The other arose from a Minnesota statute postponing the payment of mortgages; though the act was directly contrary to the contract clause, the Court upheld it as an emergency measure.

But those decisions were deceptive. Of the nine justices, four—McReynolds, Pierce Butler, George Sutherland, and Willis Van Devanter—were uncompromising constitutional conservatives. Only three justices—Brandeis, Benjamin Cardozo, and Harland Fiske Stone—were sympathetic to the New Deal, and Brandeis' sympathy was tempered by an extreme hostility toward bigness in any form. Chief Justice Hughes and Justice Owen J. Roberts were "swing" members of the Court, but they generally sided with the conservatives.

The first indications that the Court was likely to cause trouble came during the winter of 1934–35. The National Industrial Recovery Act had provided that representatives from each industry should draw up "codes of fair practices" governing production, labor relations, pricing, and the like; when these were approved by the president, the codes took on the force of law. Many were hastily and sloppily drawn, and they were repeatedly revised without informing the industries involved. When the petroleum code was revised, for instance, someone forgot to include the enforcement provisions of the original, and one man was arrested, indicted, and temporarily jailed under a law that did not exist. Counsel for the government had intended to use that suit to test the constitutionality of the NRA, but the case was dropped when the blunder was discovered. Another case involving the petroleum code, *Panama Refining Company* v. *Ryan* (293 U.S. 388), reached the Supreme Court in February 1935. The justices agreed, eight to one (Cardozo alone dissenting), that the code was an unconstitutional delegation of legislative power.

That did not undermine the entire NRA, however, for it struck down only one clumsily drawn code, which Congress could and quickly did revise. Moreover, the Court upheld, a few days later, the controversial "gold-clause" actions of the New Deal. Partly through executive proclamation and partly through congressional legislation, the dollar had been devalued to fifty-nine cents, private possession of gold was prohibited, and both public and private debts were made payable in the depreciated paper money even if contracts stipulated payment in gold. In three related cases the Court sustained these actions, but only on technicalities and only by a five-to-four vote. Justice McReynolds, after reading the dissenting opinion he had written for himself and the three other conservatives, said: "As for the Constitution, it does not seem too much to say that it is gone."

But it was not to go without a struggle. In May 1935 the Court struck down four New Deal measures. It declared Roosevelt's removal of an FTC member unconstitutional, invalidated the Federal Farm Bankruptcy Act of 1934 and the Railroad Retirement Act of 1934, and struck a devastating blow by demolishing the NRA. The latter decision was rendered in *Schechter Poultry Corporation* v. *United States* (295 U.S. 495), better known as the "sick chicken case." The live-poultry code applied only to New York City and vicinity, and regulated hours, wages, working conditions, marketing practices, and other aspects of the industry. The defendant was arrested and convicted on a charge of killing and marketing chickens in ways that violated the code, and he appealed on two grounds. One was that he was engaged exclusively in intrastate commerce and was thus outside the reach of congressional legislation. The other was that Section 3 of the NRA act, authorizing the regulation of industry through the fair practice codes, was unconstitutional because it went beyond the principle of administrative discretion and allowed the president to legislate. In a unanimous decision, the Court agreed with both contentions, and the NRA was destroyed.

During the 1935–36 term the Court continued to strike down New Deal legislation. In *United States* v. *Butler* (297 U.S. 1), by a six-to-three vote, it overturned most of the Agricultural Adjustment Act. The act had established a complex system of subsidies for farmers as a means of controlling prices and production. A central feature of the system was a processing tax, which in the *Butler* case was held to be unconstitutional. The levying of taxes for purposes other than revenue was legitimate, the Court said, but only if those purposes were themselves within the range of federal powers. Regulating and controlling agricultural production was "beyond the powers delegated to the federal government," and thus the tax amounted to "the expropriation of money from one group for the benefit of another," which was palpably unconstitutional.

And there were others. In *Carter* v. *Carter Coal Company* (298 U.S. 238) the Court rejected an argument attempting to justify, on the basis of the general welfare and commerce clauses, an act regulating coal mining and fixing coal prices. It struck down the Municipal Bankruptcy Act of 1934 and reasserted its power to review the factual findings of administrative agencies. For good measure, it reaffirmed its earlier position and declared unconstitutional a New York minimum-wage law. In only one decision did the Court uphold a major New Deal measure during this term. In *Ashwander* v. *Tennessee Valley Authority* (297 U.S. 288), the Court ruled (with only McReynolds in dissent) that the TVA's Wilson dam had been built for national defense and the improvement of navigation, both of which were legitimate exercises of federal power. The government could constitutionally sell any electricity that was "incidentally" generated at that dam.

The TVA decision was politically important as a defense of the Court against its critics. President Roosevelt and others, infuriated by the succession of adverse decisions, had charged that the Court was deliberately sabotaging the entire New Deal in the interest of a reactionary economic philosophy; by upholding the TVA, the one truly socialistic aspect of the New Deal, the Court discredited the charge. But that did not stop the administration's hostility toward what Roosevelt called the "nine old men" from "the horse-and-buggy age."

Upon being reelected by a record majority in 1936, Roosevelt proposed a controversial court-packing plan, which combined bribery with coercion. All Supreme Court justices over the age of seventy (which included the four conservatives) would be permitted to retire with comfortable pensions. Those who chose not to take advantage of this generosity could not be forced to do so, but for each who did not retire within six months after reaching the age of seventy, the president would be authorized to appoint an additional justice. The plan was hotly debated throughout the spring of 1937 and appeared headed for passage. It was the 1860s all over again: If the Court were to save itself as a functioning part of constitutional government, it would have to retreat.

It did not retreat, it surrendered. First, Justice Van Devanter announced that he would retire at the end of the term. That stopped the passage of the court-packing plan, for it meant that Roosevelt could shift the majority with a new appointment within a year. More significantly, Justice Roberts, who had fairly consistently voted with the four conservatives, shifted sides and gave supporters of New Deal measures a five-to-four majority.

In three decisions rendered during the remainder of the term, the Court reversed long-standing precedents—and, in so doing, all but abolished the constitutional limitations on the powers of Congress. In the first case, *West Coast Hotel Company* v. *Parrish* (300 U.S. 379), the Court upheld a Washington state minimum-wage law and overturned the doctrine of freedom of contract. "What is this freedom?" Hughes asked in the majority opinion. "The Constitution does not speak of freedom of contract. It speaks of liberty and prohibits the deprivation of liberty without due process of law." Neglecting the fact that in both the Fifth and the Fourteenth amendments the phraseology is "life, liberty, or property," and that property was what was at stake in minimum-wage legislation, Hughes added that "in prohibiting that deprivation the Constitution does not recognize an absolute and uncontrolled liberty." Though the case involved a state statute, by implication the decision sanctioned federal minimum-wage legislation as well. (In little more than a year, the first federal minimum-wage law would be forthcoming.)

In the second case, *National Labor Relations Board* v. *Jones and Laughlin Steel Corporation* (301 U.S. 1), the Court stretched the commerce clause beyond recognition. The NLRB had been created by the Wagner-Connery Act of 1935. The board was empowered to supervise unionization, and the act not only authorized collective bargaining but, by the procedures it established, virtually guaranteed unionization in the industries it covered. Jones and Laughlin, charged with unfair labor practices in violation of the act at its plant in Aliquippa, Pennsylvania, maintained that it was engaged in manufacturing, not commerce, and that its operations were entirely intrastate in character. Dismissing these arguments and the Court's own precedents, the majority held that "congressional authority to protect interstate commerce from burdens and obstructions is not limited to transactions which can be deemed to be an essential part of a 'flow' of interstate and foreign commerce." The authority, it was now held, extends to intrastate production, if that activity might directly or even indirectly affect interstate commerce. Labor strife at the Jones and Laughlin plant could have such an effect, and so it was within the scope of congressional authority.

In the third case, *Helvering* v. *Davis* (301 U.S. 619), the majority found a source of congressional power in a clause of the Constitution that had been designed as a limitation on that power. Article I, Section 8 confined the taxing and spending power by restricting taxation to purposes of the common defense and general welfare—meaning that taxes could not be levied for narrow, local, or individual purposes. Now, however, the Court's majority upheld the Social Security Act of 1935 on the ground that the general-welfare clause was a positive grant of power; and it declared that determining what promoted the general welfare was left to the discretion of Congress.

The Court, in sum, had stepped out of the way, and it would stay out of the way for more than a generation. The only remaining restraints upon Congress and the president were democracy and bureaucracy—neither of which is to be found in the Constitution.

QUESTIONS FOR DISCUSSION

1. How does the "Brandeis brief" reflect the attitudes of its time? How would a lawyer for the National Organization for Women argue the case? Would the Supreme Court today use such reasoning? What reasoning might it use?

2. Was Justice Hughes correct in regard to the modern Court? Is the Constitution what the Court says it is?

3. Is the Constitution an effective control on government in time of war? Is the "clear and present danger" doctrine compatible with the language of the First Amendment?

4. Constitutionally, what was new about the New Deal?

5. How can protection of the "public interest" be balanced with protection of private rights to life, liberty, and property? Must one be sacrificed for the other? What lines would you draw? What lines did the Founding Fathers draw?

RECOMMENDED READINGS

PAUL CONKIN, *The New Deal* (New York: Crowell, 1967).

WILLIAM E. LEUCHTENBURG, "The Origins of Franklin D. Roosevelt's 'Court-Packing' Plan," *The Supreme Court Review* (1966), 347–400; Charles A. Lofgren, "Missouri v. Holland in Historical Perspective," ibid. (1975), 77–122; Frank R. Strong, "Fifty Years of 'Clear and Present Danger': From Schenck to Brandenburg—and Beyond," ibid. (1969), 41–80.

ROBERT K. MURRAY, *Red Scare: A Study in National Hysteria, 1919–1920* (Minneapolis: University of Minnesota Press, 1955).

GEORGE J. STIGLER, *The Citizen and the State: Essays on Regulation* (Chicago: University of Chicago Press, 1975).

ALAN STONE, *Economic Regulation and the Public Interest: The Federal Trade Commission in Theory and Practice* (Ithaca: Cornell University Press, 1977).

8
CONSTITUTIONAL REVOLUTION: 1937–1957

*G*overnment in America was swiftly revolutionized after 1937. The balance between federal and state powers, having shifted back and forth within a fairly narrow range for a century and a half, now swung decisively toward the national government. Inside the national government, power flowed away from the Court to Congress and from Congress to the executive branch. On all levels, government grew greatly in size and enormously in the scope of its functions. Americans learned to look to government for solutions to problems previously regarded as private affairs, and no activity seemed too small or too large—nor beyond what was proper and possible—for the government to tackle.

But such matters are relative, and how big the changes appear depends upon the perspective. The Founding Fathers would have regarded them as tyrannical; but compared with the revolutions in Communist Russia, Fascist Italy, and Nazi Germany, they were the essence of moderation, and even in comparison with France and Britain the United States remained relatively decentralized. To Americans at the time, the changes seemed the logical culmination of trends that had been in motion since the turn of the century. And, though many people thought them deplorable, a broad consensus approved them as a trade-off—as the exchange of some liberty for a large measure of social and economic security. It remained to be seen whether, in the long run, the bargain would prove advantageous—and if not, whether it would be renegotiable.

THE NEW DEAL COURT

Perpetuation of the Supreme Court's 1937 shift of positions was ensured by a change in personnel. In less than two years, three of the four solid conservatives—Van Devanter, Sutherland, and Butler—had retired or died. In their places Roosevelt appointed Hugo Black of Alabama, Stanley Reed of Kentucky, and Frank Murphy of Michigan, all of whom were ardent New Dealers. Cardozo and Brandeis also died; they were replaced by the Harvard law professor Felix Frankfurter and the former Yale professor William O. Douglas, who shared all of their predecessors' enthusiasm for social reform and none of their aversion to bigness. By 1941, Roosevelt had appointed seven justices.

The constitutional philosophy of the New Deal Court was that of judicial restraint: the belief that the courts should yield to the elected branches of government in all cases except those involving gross and unmistakable violations of the Constitution. Frankfurter expressed the philosophy well. "As a member of this Court," he said, "I am not justified in writing my private notions of policy into the Constitution, no matter how deeply I may cherish them or how mischievous I may deem their disregard.... It can never be emphasized too much that one's opinion about the wisdom or evil of a law should be excluded altogether when one is doing one's duty on the bench."

That attitude had prevailed on the Court before, of course,

depending largely upon the vigor of the other two branches of the federal government. Throughout American history the Court had been restrained when there was a strong and aggressive president and when the president and Congress were members of the same party and were working harmoniously. So it was during the presidencies of Jefferson, Lincoln, and Wilson. When the president was weak or he and Congress were at cross-purposes—as during the 1850s, the late nineteenth century, and the 1920s—the Court tended to reexert and expand its authority.

It should also be pointed out that the Court's modesty and self-restraint was in part a sham, that underneath the new fear of president and Congress lay a goodly portion of the old arrogance. This was particularly visible when the justices were dealing with someone—such as public utility companies—out of favor with federal authorities. There was, for instance, the 1944 case of *Federal Power Commission* v. *Hope Natural Gas Company* (320 U.S. 584). The FPC had established rates that did not permit the company a fair return on its investment and were, in fact, confiscatory. On the basis of the doctrine of *Smyth* v. *Ames*, the company appealed to the courts. Contemptuous of the company's claim that it had a right to earn a reasonable profit and of the commonsense proposition that if it could not earn profits it could not survive to serve the public, the Court cast *Smyth* v. *Ames* aside. Justice Douglas, for the Court, said that "the fixing of prices, like other applications of the police power, may reduce the value of the property which is being regulated. But the fact that the value is reduced does not mean that the regulation is invalid."

In any event, the Court approved virtually all the economic-reform and social-welfare legislation enacted by the state legislatures as well as by Congress during the two decades after 1937, even though that entailed overturning precedents established by every previous Court. The informal rule of judicial decision making had always been that of *stare decisis*, let the decision stand. Though the Court had not invariably followed that rule, it had been extremely cautious about departing from precedent. Now, caution was almost gone. In 1938 the Court upheld the NLRB in a case of a business whose activities were unrelated to interstate commerce, thus overturning the "stream of commerce" doctrine. It also upheld a federal minimum-wage law, overturning the *Adkins* decision, and a new child-labor law, overturning several decisions of the 1920s and opinions in the *Schechter* and *Carter* cases. In 1939 it upheld a new Agricultural Adjustment Act, reversing *United States* v. *Butler*. In 1942 it substantially abolished the distinction between intrastate and interstate commerce by declaring that a farmer who raised grain to feed livestock that he consumed on his own property was subject to regulation as interstate commerce. So, according to another decision, were the elevator operator and janitor in an office building in which a few of the tenants were engaged in interstate business. Along the way, the Court eroded the concept of substantive due process as applied to property rights; and, while justifying its labor decisions on the ground that strikes would interfere with the flow of interstate commerce, it simultaneously held that the power to regulate commerce included the power to stop it altogether.

Two New Deal measures of dubious constitutionality never received the Court's official sanction because they were never given a hearing. In one of the gold-clause cases, *Nortz* v. *United States* (294 U.S. 317), the Court had held that the repudiation of gold-repayment requirements in federal government bonds was unconstitutional, but nevertheless ruled against the claimant, by a five-to-four decision, because he personally had lost nothing by devaluation and was thus not entitled to sue. The door that was left open for a suit that would undo the government's devaluation scheme was closed by Congress: It passed a law depriving the federal courts of jurisdiction in such matters. The other subject on which the Court never gave its explicit approval was the TVA. In the *Ashwander* case, it had sanctioned the building of the first dam, which had been started during World War I, and it had held that the government could sell electric power generated at the dam; but it did not pass upon the constitutionality of the building of a complete government-owned power system. On two occasions investor-owned electric companies attempted to obtain a direct ruling, but both times the Court dodged the issue by dismissing the suits on technical grounds—which suggests that even the New Deal justices entertained some doubts about TVA's constitutionality.

The Court did not, after 1937, declare a single significant action of the federal government unconstitutional as long as Roosevelt was president, and it did so only twice during the presidency of his successor, Harry S Truman. The first such ruling took a great deal of courage, even though the violation of the Constitution was clear. During World War II the House Un-American Activities Committee became incensed over the discovery that there were a number of Communists in the federal bureaucracy (though it did not, as yet, have any idea how big the problem was). In 1943, at the recommendation of the chairman of the committee, Congress included in an appropriations bill a clause that after a certain date no salaries should be paid to three suspected Communists on the federal payroll. That was obviously a bill of attainder—a legislative act decreeing punishment without a trial in court—and was therefore prohibited by Article I, Section 9 of the Constitution. In 1946, in the case of *United States* v. *Lovett* (328 U.S. 303), the Court ruled unanimously that the provision was unconstitutional.

The other negative decision concerned presidential action. In 1952 the United Steelworkers union called a nationwide strike. President Truman, believing the strike would seriously impair the conduct of the Korean War, instructed Secretary of Commerce Charles Sawyer to take possession of the steel mills and operate them in the name of the United States government. The companies sought and obtained an injunction prohibiting Sawyer from executing the president's order, and in *Youngstown Sheet and Tube Company* v. *Sawyer* (343 U.S. 579) the Court declared the seizure unconstitutional in a six-to-three decision. All six justices in the majority wrote separate opinions justifying their votes; but there was general agreement that the president's action was invalid only because it had not been authorized by an act of Congress.

And that was the essence of judicial restraint as practiced by the New Deal Court. A third of the justices held that the president could do anything he chose to regard as being in the national interest. The other two-thirds held that he could do so with the approval of Congress. None held that the Fifth Amendment, forbidding the taking of property for public use without just compensation and due process of law, forbade the taking of property for public use without just compensation and due process of law.

THE MUSHROOMING OF GOVERNMENT

Being thus freed from constitutional limitations on the scope of its powers, the federal government expanded apace. Much of the expansion was along lines laid out before; hence the FTC, the ICC, the Food and Drug Administration, and other federal agencies increased the number and variety of their functions. Some new agencies duplicated forms of regulation already being exercised by the states—for example, the Securities and Exchange Commission and the Federal Power Commission. Two important functions, those represented by the Social Security Board and the National Labor Relations Board, have already been mentioned. Apart from these various increases in federal authority, qualitative changes in three broad areas were the most important enduring developments of the period: subsidies, relations with big business, and government ownership and operation of business enterprise.

Subsidies, of course, were nothing new. State and local governments had long subsidized business by granting special privileges, tax exemptions, and even cash awards. The federal government had subsidized manufacturing through the protective tariff and had subsidized the building of the trans-Mississippi railroad system through grants of millions of acres of land. But the subsidies granted during and after the New Deal differed both in purpose and in size from what had gone before. Earlier subsidies had been given almost exclusively for economic development; now they were awarded to effect social reforms or to redistribute wealth. They sometimes took the form of direct grants, as with some of the farm programs and the food-stamp program initiated in 1938. More commonly, they took the form of tax exemptions and low-interest loans, as with housing for the poor, the Rural Electrification Administration, the Small Business Administration, and measures to end farm tenantry.

The increase in the size of subsidies was related to the development of what has been called the "crash-program mentality": the notion that there is no problem so large or so complex that it cannot be solved quickly if the federal government invests a few billion dollars in it. That approach to problems began with the REA (1935) and the National Housing Act (1937), but it received its greatest impetus during the war with defense production and the atomic-bomb project. During the late 1940s crash programs produced scores of thousands of low-income public-housing developments, in the early 1950s came a crash program of interstate highway building, in the late 1950s a crash program in education. Each such program increased the power of the federal government by making individuals, businesses, state and local governments, and schools dependent upon continued federal appropriations.

Relations with big business evolved in a similar direction, though that was not the New Deal's intention. During his second term, Roosevelt revived the antitrust laws with a vengeance, assigning a special prosecutor to bring suits seeking the dissolution of General Electric, Alcoa, DuPont, General Motors, A&P, and a host of other corporate giants. Before these suits could be brought to a conclusion, however, World War II began and the administration recognized that the United States could not win the war without the productive capacity of its great corporations. The actions were therefore suspended and mammoth war-production contracts were awarded. Simultaneously, the government supervised production through a War Production Board and a War Labor Relations Board, controlled wages and prices, rationed food and fuel, imposed excess-profits taxes, and set ceilings on corporate salaries and earnings by raising the maximum income-tax rate to 91 percent. Shortly after the war these controls were dropped and defense production declined sharply, but things did not return to "normal." The beginnings of the Cold War in 1947 and the Korean War in 1950 brought about a permanent war economy in which a number of huge companies produced exclusively or almost exclusively military hardware, and most sizable producers of nonmilitary goods derived an appreciable portion of their revenues— say, 10 to 20 percent—from sales to government. Those sales could mean the difference between profit and loss, and thus government and big business became interdependent. On the one hand, the government could not break up GE or Westinghouse or even let them suffer excessively from foreign competition, because it needed the special electrical equipment that only they could produce. On the other, it could force most industries to follow the president's bidding, without the need for legislation or lawsuits, simply by threatening to withdraw as a consumer of the industry's products.

The third major innovation was the movement of the federal government into direct ownership and operation of economic enterprises on a large scale. During the war the Reconstruction Finance Corporation (originally created in 1932 to help save businesses from collapse during the depression) was at the center of a New Deal plan to shift control of production from private industry to the federal government. In 1940 the RFC was authorized to buy, lease, or build plants in any way it saw fit, and during the next five years it built plants costing $8 billion, which was more than a third as much as the total corporate investment in heavy industry. By that means the government came to own 96 percent of the country's synthetic-rubber industry, 90 percent of its magnesium-metal industry, 71 percent of its aircraft manufacturing, 58 percent of its aluminum manufacturing, and dominant interests in the shipping, machine-tool, and various lesser industries.

After the war some of these plants were sold to private industry, but during Harry Truman's Fair Deal, expansion into new areas was quietly but rapidly begun. By 1950 the federal government had become the nation's (if not the world's) largest banker, insurer, utility operator, shipper, trucker, landlord, and tenant. Republicans denounced what they knew of this development as "creeping socialism," and when Dwight David Eisenhower became president in 1953 he ordered the closing down of government establishments that competed with the economic activities of private citizens. It took three years just to determine how many there were (26,000) and where they were and what they were doing. It was learned that the federal bureaucracy had employed existing laws, left over from the depression and the war, to cause the government to become the nation's largest owner and operator of bakeries, dry-cleaning establishments, plant nurseries, livestock farms, shoe-repair shops, and ice-cream plants, and also to become a large-scale producer of rum, false teeth, eyeglasses, fertilizer, and other items. Becoming involved in all these activities had taken an investment of 26 billion tax-derived dollars and incidentally resulted in the wiping out of thousands of tax-paying small-business men.

And, of course, as rapidly as small-business men were wiped out, new federal agencies were established to finance and protect more small-business men. By these and similar means, government agencies multiplied like rabbits, performing overlapping, competing, and mutually contradictory functions. No less than seventy-four different federal agencies were regulating the energy supply, more than twenty were regulating water power, and whole legions had a hand in regulating transportation. So confused was Congress that, during a single session, it passed acts authorizing and appropriating money for two different agencies to build a dam on the same site. (The agencies settled the jurisdictional difference, involving hundreds of millions of dollars, by flipping a coin.) The situation was becoming what President Eisenhower eloquently described as "a mess."

And yet it would be inaccurate to overrate either the confusion in or the growth of the federal government up through the 1950s. Brainless as many bureaucrats were, most were at least reasonably intelligent and devoted to public service, and a generation of experience had taught governmental regulatory agencies prudence, restraint, and moderation. In other words, despite its growth, the government was functioning, and it was functioning tolerably well. Moreover, the growth itself had not been as great as most people believed. Total nonmilitary spending by the federal government increased sevenfold between 1932 and 1952, but if inflation and the interest on the public debt engendered by World War II are allowed for, the actual expenditures for nonmilitary functions had little more than doubled. As a percentage of gross national product, nonmilitary federal expenditures were the same when Eisenhower took over the presidency as they had been when Hoover left it—5.5 percent—and they remained around that level through the 1950s. The number of civilian federal employees quadrupled between 1932 and 1952, from 605,000 to 2.6 million, but two-thirds of the increase was in the Defense and Post Office departments; and the Eisenhower administration reduced the number of employees by more than 200,000. (Nor had the federal government swallowed up the state and local governments. They spent nearly twice as much as the federal government did in both 1932 and 1952, and in the 1950s they had nearly twice as many employees.)

In short, though the federal government affected the lives of ordinary Americans more than ever before, it was at worst a nuisance and it provided a wide range of services for which most citizens were grateful. And, in spite of the constitutional revolution, most citizens continued to enjoy a greater measure of personal freedom than did the inhabitants of almost any other nation on earth.

THE PROBLEM OF CIVIL LIBERTIES

It will be noticed that the comment about freedom refers to "most citizens," not all. The Supreme Court's drift toward expanding the rights protected by the Fourteenth Amendment came to a halt in 1937 with the case of *Palko* v. *Connecticut* (302 U.S. 319). Palko was a man convicted of second-degree murder, whereupon the prosecution, on appeal to a higher state court, obtained a new trial on a first-degree charge. Though that was a clear case of double jeopardy, the Court upheld the conviction on the ground that the due-process clause of the Fourteenth Amendment did not automatically extend the Bill of Rights to the states. Rather, it guaranteed only those rights that are "implicit in the concept of ordered liberty," such as freedom of speech, and those principles of justice that are "so rooted in the traditions and conscience of our people as to be ranked as fundamental." From that point until the late 1950s, the Court repeatedly upheld restrictions on civil liberties.

The grossest violations of the Bill of Rights occurred during World War II. There were on the Pacific Coast about 115,000 persons of Japanese descent, of whom about 70,000 were American citizens. Immediately after the attack on Pearl Harbor, California Attorney General Earl Warren began to round up these people as spies, using as his legal pretext the doctrine of "constructive treason." They had not been observed in the commission of sabotage or other illegal activity, but because spies always try to appear innocent, their innocent behavior was proof of their guilt. In March 1942 President Roosevelt took over. He established, by executive order, a War Relocation Authority to gather up all Japanese-Americans on the Pacific Coast and ship them to "Relocation Centers," where most of them were detained for nearly four years. They were never convicted, nor tried, nor even charged with violating any law. Their "crime" was their race.

Three major cases challenging these actions reached the Supreme Court. In the first, *Hirabayashi* v. *United States* (320 U.S. 81), the court dodged the question of the constitutionality of the relocation order. Before the order was issued, the army had imposed a curfew and the defendant had violated it. The justices upheld the curfew without ruling on the presidental order but indicated, in seven different opinions, that they abhorred the whole policy. The constitutionality of the main order was finally upheld late in 1944 in *Korematsu* v. *United States* (323 U.S. 214). Justice Black, for the majority, held that it had not been possible to separate the loyal from the disloyal and pointed out that "five thousand

American citizens of Japanese ancestry refused to swear unqualified allegiance to the United States and to renounce allegiance to the Japanese Emperor, and several thousand evacuees
requested repatriation to Japan." In upholding the order, he said,
"we are not unmindful of the hardships imposed by it upon a large
group of American citizens.... But hardships are a part of war."
Justices Roberts, Murphy, and Jackson vigorously dissented;
Murphy called the order a "legalization of racism," and Roberts
said it was a case "of convicting a citizen as punishment for not
submitting to imprisonment in a concentration camp, solely because of his ancestry." In the third case, *Ex parte Endo* (323 U.S.
283), decided the same day as the *Korematsu* case, the Court
released by writ of habeas corpus a Japanese-American girl who,
after being held in a camp, had had her loyalty clearly established.
She was the only one freed.

The Cold War likewise brought a curtailment of the civil liberties of some Americans, though not on so large a scale. The
Taft-Hartley Act of 1947, designed to check the excessive power
labor unions had achieved under the Wagner Act, also contained
a provision requiring union officials to take an oath that they were
not Communists. The notoriously Communist-dominated com-
munications union refused to comply and challenged the provision
in the courts on the grounds that it violated the First Amendment
guarantees of free speech and assembly and that it amounted to
a bill of attainder. The Court ruled otherwise in *American Com-
munications Association* v. *Douds* (339 U.S. 382), decided in
1950. The Wagner Act, said the majority opinion, had promoted
unionization in the interest of removing impairments, in the form
of labor strife, to the flow of interstate commerce. The Taft-Hartley
Act was designed to restrain unions for the same end, the elimi-
nation of Communist leadership being aimed specifically at the
threat of "political strikes." The right to be a Communist was not
at issue; what was at issue was whether the government, from
whose support union power derived, could deny its support to
Communists. Five of the six justices who participated in the de-

cision (three disqualified themselves for various reasons) agreed that it could.

By the time the decision was rendered, the Cold War had become a shooting war in Korea and it had come to light that Communists had occupied a number of influential posts in the federal government, that some had engaged in damaging espionage including the theft of atomic secrets, and that they were numerous in various labor unions and universities. Politicians and the people understandably responded with an intense fear of, and hostility toward, members of the Communist Party and its "front organizations." In that atmosphere, the first major trial of party leaders took place. The Smith Act of 1940 had made it unlawful to "advocate, abet, advise, or teach" the violent overthrow of any government of the United States and had prohibited publishing materials, organizing groups, or engaging in conspiracy to commit those acts. In 1948 the Justice Department obtained under the Smith Act indictments against the eleven top officials of the Communist Party. They were found guilty in the federal District Court in New York City and began their appeals. The circuit court made its decision in 1950; the Supreme Court gave its in 1951, in *Dennis v. United States* (341 U.S. 494).

The decisions resulted in a new doctrine to replace the "clear and present danger" rule. Circuit Court Judge Learned Hand formulated what was called the "sliding scale" rule for sedition cases: The greater the potential effects of the evil, the more the courts should discount the remoteness of the possibility of its coming about. The Supreme Court agreed with Hand. It was not at all likely that American Communists could succeed in their ultimate aim, but the results would be horrible if they did. "The Court must ask whether the gravity of the evil, discounted by its improbability, justifies such invasion of free speech as is necessary to avoid the evil."

Meanwhile, Congress had passed the McCarran Internal Security Act of 1950, declaring that the "world Communist conspiracy" sought to establish a dictatorship in America, and thus that

American Communists constituted a "clear and present danger." Communist and Communist-front organizations were required to register with a Subversive Activities Control Board; any who failed to register could be ordered to do so, after hearings, by the board. The act also made it unlawful to conspire to establish a totalitarian dictatorship in the United States and placed severe limitations upon the immigration of aliens with Communist connections. Finally, at the urging of old New Dealers who feared being accused of "softness on Communism," the act provided that the president could at any time declare an "internal security emergency," during which anyone who "probably will conspire with others to engage in acts of espionage and sabotage" could be held in one of the detention camps created by the act. The Communist Party refused to register, and there ensued a fifteen-year court battle over the constitutionality of the McCarran Act (it was finally declared invalid by the Warren Court in 1965).

In 1951, after Senator Joseph McCarthy had shocked the country with a succession of revelations and charges regarding Communists in government, President Truman instituted a strenuous new loyalty program. Truman regarded McCarthy's charges as a "red herring" and had early in 1947 established a comprehensive loyalty review system, which brought about 7,000 resignations and 560 removals; but McCarthy's charges were, at the least, politically damaging. The new program provided that it was unnecessary to prove disloyalty. An employee could now be discharged if there was a "reasonable doubt as to the loyalty of the person involved to the Government of the United States." During the next two years nearly 200 more federal employees were fired under this program.

Even so, Communism in government was a major issue in the presidential election of 1952, and when Eisenhower took office he was pledged to root out the remaining security risks. Soon after his presidency began, he issued an executive order revising the loyalty program. The criterion for discharge now became a finding that the individual's employment "may not be clearly consistent with the interests of national security." The standards for measuring security risks included drug addiction, homosexuality or other sexual perversions, refusal to testify before authorized bodies on grounds of possible self-incrimination, and conspiracy or acts of treason, sabotage, or disclosure of classified information.

The most spectacular and controversial anti-Communist activities were those of the House Un-American Activities Committee and Senator McCarthy's Permanent Subcommittee on Investigations. Radicals called before these committees sometimes declined to testify on First Amendment grounds, in which case they were likely to be jailed for contempt of Congress; sometimes they "took the Fifth," refusing to testify lest they incriminate themselves, in which case their reputations were smeared and they were likely to lose their jobs. Yet for a long time no one challenged the committees on the one ground on which, in accordance with Supreme Court rulings, they might have been successful. The investigative powers of Congress had been established and clarified in a series of decisions back in the 1920s, especially in the cases of *McGrain* v. *Daugherty* (273 U.S. 135) and *Sinclair* v. *United States* (279 U.S. 263). The powers were broad, said the Court, but they were subject to two sets of limitations: Witnesses must be given procedural rights as if before a court of law, and Congress could conduct investigations only for the purpose of obtaining the information necessary for enacting legitimate legislation. The anti-Communist committees of the 1950s were scrupulously careful in regard to procedures but not at all so in regard to legislative intent. Abandoning all pretense that their inquiries were to gather information for legislative purposes, they repeatedly declared that their function was one of publicity, to expose to the American people the seriousness of the Communist threat.

Some legislation did result, indirectly. State and local governments joined businesses, universities, and vigilante groups to purge the nation of Communists and their sympathizers. A member of the Texas legislature proposed the legalization of the wearing of six-shooters as a means of cleaning out the "reds" and "pinkos"; but the legislature settled for requiring every man, woman, and child who was connected in any way with a state-supported school or other institution to sign an oath testifying to his loyalty and swearing that he had never been a Communist. Many states required loyalty oaths of public employees, as did a considerable number of colleges; the motion-picture industry developed blacklists, prohibiting employment to persons with past or present Communist associations; other businesses, even in the least sensitive of industries, developed security and loyalty systems more strict than those of the federal government.

As the anti-Communist fever mounted, former Communist sympathizers disavowed all connection with the party, and liberal reformers, who likewise came under suspicion, joined in the turnaround. Lifelong friends were disowned, longtime associations were denied. The most outspoken of the liberals in Congress, Senator Hubert H. Humphrey, set out to prove that liberals were more anti-Communist than anybody. In 1954 he proposed that American Communists be declared criminals and that they be put in concentration camps. Others in the Senate, including John F. Kennedy, rushed to claim co-authorship of the proposal. President Eisenhower strongly opposed the measure, partly because it would enable Communists to avoid registering under the McCarran Act on the ground that doing so would be self-incrimination in violation of the Fifth Amendment. In the end, the Communist Party was declared illegal, but party membership itself was not made a crime. In that form, Humphrey's bill was passed as the Communist Control Act of 1954.

All this was going rather far. It is true that the vast majority of Americans suffered no loss of rights or liberties as a result of anti-Communism. But there was a peril inherent in the crusade against Communism: It demonstrated that, in the absence of a working system of constitutional restraints, popular opinion is a danger to individual rights, not a protector of them. Senator McCarthy became the most feared man in Washington precisely because he had the enthusiastic support of the American people.

Only after McCarthy fell into disrepute (which happened in several steps between 1954 and his death in 1957) did the Supreme Court show any renewed enthusiasm for the Bill of Rights. Until then it tended to sustain not only persecution of radicals but also state legislation curtailing picketing, demonstrating, and pamphleteering by nonradicals. Then in 1956 it reversed a pair of state actions against Communists, and in 1957 it made two important decisions limiting federal anti-Communist activity. In *Yates* v. *United States* (354 U.S. 298), concerning the conviction of many "second-string" Communists under the Smith Act, the Court abandoned the sliding-scale doctrine employed in the *Dennis* case and imposed standards that made Smith Act convictions all but impossible. The majority opinion distinguished between advocacy of subversive action, which could be prosecuted, and advocacy of subversive doctrine, which could not. The essential distinction, said Justice Harlan for the majority, "is that those to whom advocacy is addressed must be urged to *do* something, now or in the future, rather than merely believe in something." In *Watkins* v. *United States* (354 U.S. 178) the Court reversed a contempt conviction resulting from a hearing before the House Un-American Activities Committee. A witness had finally refused to answer certain questions on the ground that they were not relevant to proper legislative functions, and the Court, repeating the decisions in the *Daugherty* and *Sinclair* cases, upheld his right to do so. The majority opinion declared that the investigatory power of Congress is broad but not unlimited: Congress was not "a law enforcement or trial agency," and it had "no general authority to expose the private affairs of individuals without justification in terms of the function of Congress."

The Court soon backed away from these decisions, however, and for the next five years it again tended to support a restrictive position in regard to civil liberties. Then it would veer sharply into the civil-libertarian camp, with extremely disruptive social consequences.

NEGRO RIGHTS RECONSIDERED

The Supreme Court had already set major social changes in motion in the one area in which, from the appointment of the New

Deal justices onward, it had been both activist and a champion of civil rights—the legal and constitutional status of American blacks. Segregation, disfranchisement, and other forms of legal discrimination against blacks had concerned most white Americans very little during the late nineteenth century, for more than 90 percent of the blacks then lived in the rural South. They began to migrate northward in increasing numbers during and after World War I, however, and by World War II nearly 3 million of the nation's 12.8 million blacks lived in the North, mainly in cities. They were discriminated against there, too—particularly in housing, education, and employment—but in the North they had at least one advantage, they constituted an important voting bloc. In 1936 and thereafter the New Deal set out to try to win their votes away from the Republican Party of Lincoln, to which they were traditionally loyal, and though not much was actually done, improvement of the lot of the Negro became vaguely part of the spirit of the New Deal. That, combined with reaction against the extreme racism of Nazi Germany, made the New Deal Supreme Court sensitive on the subject.

Its first important case concerning the rights of Negroes came up in 1938 and involved the "separate but equal" doctrine. The state of Missouri had provided segregated schools up through college, but rather than go to the expense of establishing separate graduate and professional schools for blacks, it provided subsidies for qualified Missouri blacks to attend unsegregated schools in neighboring states. Lloyd Gaines, a graduate of an all-black college, sought to be admitted to the University of Missouri Law School. When he was denied admission, he obtained the support of the National Association for the Advancement of Colored People and went to court. The Supreme Court, in *Missouri ex rel Gaines* v. *Canada* (305 U.S. 337), declared that the Missouri law deprived Gaines of the equal protection of the laws and was therefore in violation of the Fourteenth Amendment. Subsequently, the state established a law school for blacks.

It was more than a decade before the Court again considered the question of segregated educational facilities, but in the meantime it handed down an important decision concerning voting rights. One of the devices for depriving blacks of the vote was the all-white primary. Because the South was solidly Democratic, securing the Democratic nomination amounted to being elected, and blacks could be effectively disfranchised by preventing them from voting in the primaries. The Court had declared their exclusion unconstitutional if done by state action, but in the 1930s the state of Texas avoided this ruling by leaving the matter to Democratic Party officials. The Democratic State Convention adopted a resolution declaring the party to be a "private group" whose membership was confined to whites. In 1935 the Court had upheld the constitutionality of this device, but in 1944, in *Smith* v. *Allright* (321 U.S. 649), it reversed that decision. The Democratic Party of Texas, it now ruled, was acting as the agent of the state because of the character of its duties in holding elections and was thus subject to the Fifteenth Amendment.

Negro voting increased in much of the South after this decision, but the whites in the Deep South still resisted. South Carolina, to avoid the net of the *Smith* decision, abolished all its laws and constitutional provisions regarding the Democratic Party, thus making it legally nonexistent. Despite that effort, a federal district judge ruled in 1947 that the Democratic primaries still effectively controlled the choice of candidates in South Carolina and that exclusion of blacks from them was thus de facto state action in violation of the Fourteenth and Fifteenth amendments. The circuit court upheld that ruling, and the Supreme Court, in *Rice* v. *Elmore* (333 U.S. 875), bestowed its approval by refusing to review the case. Poll taxes and literacy tests, however, still stood as barriers to Negro voting rights.

In 1948 the Court turned again to education. In *Sipuel* v. *Oklahoma* (322 U.S. 631) it ordered Oklahoma to provide a law school for a Negro woman, in a situation much like that of the *Gaines* case; and, significantly, it emphasized that separate but equal required genuine equality. Then in 1950, in cases involving Texas and Oklahoma, it moved just short of ruling that separation was inherently unequal. The Texas case turned around the efforts of a black Houston mail carrier, Herman Sweatt, to obtain admission to the University of Texas Law School. To avoid admitting him, the state set up a law school that in most respects was equal to the one at the university. He was given a separate building in downtown Austin, about a mile from campus; he was provided a library that duplicated the university's law library; and he was taught the same courses as the regular students by the university's professors, but on a one-to-one basis. The Oklahoma case arose from the efforts of the state to provide separate but equal graduate-school education at the University of Oklahoma. In keeping with state law, the university admitted a black graduate student, G. W. McLaurin, but required that he sit in a designated place, apart from white students, in the library, in classrooms, and in the cafeteria. He received precisely the same instruction as whites; he was simply not allowed to be physically near them.

Both men sued, and the Court ruled on both cases—*Sweatt v. Painter* (339 U.S. 629) and *McLaurin* v. *Oklahoma State Regents* (339 U.S. 637)—on June 5, 1950. Declaring the arrangements to be unequal because they deprived Sweatt and McLaurin of educational exchange with fellow students and other intangible advantages enjoyed by whites, the Court ordered the admission of the two men as regular students in the white schools. Yet it did not go all the way and overturn the separate but equal doctrine. The decisions were encouraging to the NAACP lawyers who handled the case, however, as was another 1950 decision: *Henderson v. United States* (339 U.S. 816), which struck down compulsory racial segregation on interstate railroad trains.

Accordingly, the NAACP lawyers, headed by Thurgood Marshall, believed the time might be ripe for challenging *Plessy* v. *Ferguson* at the most fundamental of levels, the public schools. On the other hand, southern states were energetically building new all-black schools and colleges and rapidly upgrading their quality. An all-out challenge to *Plessy*, if it failed, would jeopardize the gains southern blacks were thus making. If it succeeded, southern whites were almost certain to stop improving black education and also to resist desegregation, which could be to the disadvantage of black children for a number of years. Either way, the children would lose for a time. Balancing the prospects of short-term losses against long-term gains, the NAACP decided to go for desegregation. In September 1950 suits challenging segregation were begun in five carefully selected places: one each in South Carolina, Virginia, Delaware, the District of Columbia, and Kansas.

The Kansas case involved the efforts of Oliver Brown to enroll his daughter Linda in an all-white elementary school in Topeka. When he was refused, he filed suit in the federal district court, which found that the black school Linda could attend was equal in quality to the white school from which she was excluded and followed *Plessy* v. *Ferguson* in ruling against her. The NAACP lost in South Carolina and Virginia as well, and won only a limited victory in Delaware. In June 1952 the Supreme Court agreed to review the decisions, but in October it postponed argument until December to await the outcome of the District of Columbia case—which also went against the NAACP. During the arguments in December, counsel for the NAACP argued that segregation denied Negroes equal protection of the laws in violation of the Fourteenth Amendment and that separation of the races in public schools was inherently unequal treatment of blacks. In an appendix that was to become famous, the NAACP presented the opinion of various sociologists and social psychologists that segregation was harmful to members of both races, causing irreparable damage to their development as well-adjusted citizens. Counsel for the opposition, including the distinguished constitutional lawyer John W. Davis (representing South Carolina), held to the traditional doctrines as expressed by the Court itself in the *Plessy* v. *Ferguson* opinion. In conference after the arguments, five justices leaned toward upholding segregation, four toward overthrowing it; but they were only "leaning," some on each side being uncertain. Chief Justice Fred M. Vinson was particularly impressed by the fact that in 1868, when the Fourteenth Amendment was passed, Congress had segregated the schools of the District of Columbia and no one doubted the constitutionality of that. Accordingly, after six months of indecision, the Court took the unusual step of re-scheduling arguments for December 1953 and of submitting a set of questions to counsel for both sides. These had mainly to do with the original meaning and intention of the authors of the Fourteenth Amendment in regard to segregation, though some dealt with certain practical aspects of desegregation.

Thurgood Marshall promptly enlisted the support of more than a hundred experts on constitutional history who gathered evidence designed to prove that the Fourteenth Amendment had been intended to ban segregation "as a last vestige of slavery." That, together with the argument of the social psychologists, was the heart of the NAACP's case during the second hearing. John W. Davis repeated his historical arguments but appealed mainly to judicial self-restraint. No judicial body, said he, had the power to declare unconstitutional on sociological or psychological grounds—regarding neither of which were judges qualified as experts—a school system that had been duly enacted by representatives of the people and had stood for three-quarters of a century.

Presiding over the Court during the re-argument was Earl Warren, appointed by Eisenhower on the death of Vinson in 1953. According to his later account, Warren could not understand how, in that day and age, one racial group could be set apart from another and denied rights shared by the other. Disregarding the historical problems that had so concerned Vinson (and disregarding, as well, his personal history as a persecutor of Japanese-Americans), Warren made up his mind on the basis of the arguments of the sociologists and psychologists—as he understood those arguments. Warren's appointment tipped the balance to five to four against segregation, and two other justices who had leaned in favor now leaned against, making the balance seven to two. But Warren, wisely perceiving the importance of solidarity in a decision of such great social significance, persuaded the remaining two justices to go along so as to make the decision unanimous.

He succeeded, and in *Brown* v. *Board of Education of Topeka* (347 U.S. 483), delivered on May 17, 1954, the Court handed down its decision declaring public-school segregation unconstitutional. In a brief opinion for the unanimous Court, Warren concluded "that in the field of public education the doctrine 'separate but equal' has no place. Separate educational facilities are inherently unequal." Therefore, plaintiffs in the Brown case, the other four cases, "and others similarly situated" were deprived of equal protection by segregation laws, and all such laws were declared unconstitutional.

That marked the beginning of the end of the legally enforced caste system of racial separation in the United States. Given the spirit of the Constitution and the ideals that Americans professed to hold dear, there was no other way the Court could have ruled. From that perspective, the decision was a monumental step toward the ideal of social justice, and Chief Justice Warren's role in bringing about unanimity was a monumental act of statesmanship.

Despite the merits of the decision, however, the method by which it was reached had some unfortunate implications. First, in declaring that the original intention of the Fourteenth Amendment in regard to segregation was irrelevant and in overturning a huge body of statutory law on the basis of the opinion of sociologists and psychologists, Warren was substituting social science for the Constitution and laws as the basis of a legal decision. To do that was to cast judicial restraint to the winds and to engage in judicial legislation on a grand scale. Legislative power is constitutionally vested in the elected representatives of the people, and to the extent that those representatives had spoken unambiguously on the subject, they had spoken against the position taken by the Court.

Second, the decision violated one of the Court's basic principles. The Court had repeatedly struck down actions of presidents, Congress, and the states when those actions were so vague or general or sweeping that, given the complexities of American life, there could be no certainty or even confidence as to what the law was. In declaring an end to all school segregation, the Court overlooked or disregarded the fact that segregation came in many and complex forms, different in many and complex ways from direct segregation by statute. In other words, the *Brown* decision was, by the standards that the Court applied to congressional and state enactments, "bad law"; and it was certain to necessitate a great deal more judicial legislation before it could be made into "good law."

Third, and most tragic, despite its equalizing aim, the decision rested upon a racist assumption. The arguments of the social scientists had maintained, for the most part, that segregation was detrimental to children of both races. Warren, however, was moved by only one part of the argument. He cited with approval the following passage from a lower-court opinion: "Segregation of white and colored children in public schools has a detrimental effect upon the colored children. The impact is greater when it has the sanction of the law; for the policy of separating the races is usually interpreted as denoting the inferiority of the negro group. A sense of inferiority affects the motivation of the child to learn. Segregation with the sanction of law, therefore, had a tendency to retard the educational and mental development of negro children." "Deprivation" of association with whites in education, Warren concluded, "may affect their hearts and minds in a way unlikely ever to be undone." He left unsaid the corollary—that it was not disadvantageous to whites to be deprived of blacks in their classrooms—but the assumption ran through the entire opinion.

THE BRICKER AMENDMENT

One other major constitutional issue arose during the 1950s. Constitutional conservatives had long been concerned about the growth of executive power and the impact of foreign relations upon domestic affairs. The adoption, in 1951, of the Twenty-second Amendment, limiting presidents to two terms, was an expression of popular uneasiness about the first of these problems. Uneasiness about the second led to a controversial proposed amendment three years later.

It will be recalled that, in the case of *Missouri* v. *Holland*

(1920), the Supreme Court had held that treaties need not be in accordance with the Constitution and could in fact give Congress power it did not otherwise possess. In *United States* v. *Curtiss-Wright* (1936) it held that the president had inherent powers in foreign affairs that required neither a treaty nor a congressional act as their basis. Roosevelt often used executive agreements as if they were treaties, and in *United States* v. *Belmont* (301 U.S. 324) and *United States* v. *Pink* (315 U.S. 203), decided in 1937 and 1942, respectively, the Supreme Court held that executive actions in foreign affairs had the status of law and could be enforced in the courts. Theoretically, the president might thus bargain away the Constitution entirely. Then, about 1950, the question arose whether the International Covenant on Human Rights being prepared by the United Nations would, by virtue of these various decisions, become a part of the "supreme law" of the United States. Several legislatures petitioned Congress for a constitutional amendment limiting the treaty-making power and executive agreements, and the American Bar Association recommended an amendment to invalidate any provision of a treaty that conflicted with the Constitution.

In February 1952 Senator John Bricker of Ohio responded to these recommendations. His proposed amendment had three sections: (1) that a treaty conflicting with the Constitution should be of no effect; (2) that treaties should become effective as internal law only through legislation that would be valid in the absence of a treaty; and (3) that Congress should have power to regulate executive agreements and that such agreements should be subject to the limitations on treaties in Section 2. At first Bricker had strong support for the amendment, but then a vigorous campaign against it was conducted on the ground that the president needed flexible powers in the modern world and could be trusted to use them wisely (the presidencies of Lyndon Baines Johnson and Richard M. Nixon lay in the future). Even so, in 1954 the Senate voted 60 to 31 in favor—only one vote short of the required constitutional majority.

The amendment lost its political support as the 1950s wore

on and as the much-trusted Eisenhower conducted foreign relations in a manner that most found acceptable. Moreover, the Supreme Court more or less ruled—in a "plurality" opinion in a pair of 1957 cases in which there was no majority opinion—that treaties are subject to being declared unconstitutional just as acts of Congress are. On that ambiguous note the subject was laid to rest, where it would remain until it exploded into public consciousness anew during the Vietnamese War.

By 1957 the constitutional revolution seemed to be over, and to most Americans it seemed to have been a whopping success. Big business was learning to live and prosper under federal regulation, big labor had been brought under a reasonable measure of control, and big government had stopped its relentless expansion. The great red scare was over, and blacks were beginning at last to enter the mainstream of American life as full-fledged citizens. At that happy time, the future seemed bright and secure.

But it was all illusion: The revolution had only begun.

QUESTIONS
FOR DISCUSSION

1. What is meant by the term "judicial restraint"? Is the Constitution more safe or less safe when judicial restraint is being exercised?

2. Were the sweeping constitutional changes after 1937 necessary to adapt our government to modern times? Is "progress" always desirable?

3. Considering that about 20 percent of the Japanese on the Pacific Coast were loyal to Japan, did the whole group constitute a "clear and present" danger? Why were neither German-Americans nor Italian-Americans interned?

4. Could the decision in *Brown* v. *Board of Education* have been reached by any other route?

5. If the Bricker amendment had been adopted would it have affected American foreign policy for better or for worse? Would the United States have become involved in the Vietnamese War? What would have been the effects on the Cold War and détente? As it was not adopted, could the Constitution be bartered away through treaty obligations?

RECOMMENDED
READINGS

HENRY J. ABRAHAM, *Freedom and the Court: Civil Rights and Liberties in the United States* (New York: Oxford University Press, 1967).

DONALD L. HOROWITZ, *The Courts and Social Policy* (Washington, D.C.: Brookings Institution, 1977).

RICHARD KLUGER, *Simple Justice* (New York: Random House, Vintage Books, 1977).

PHILIP B. KURLAND, *Politics, the Constitution, and the Warren Court* (Chicago: University of Chicago Press, 1970).

JACK W. PELTASON, *Fifty-Eight Lonely Men: Southern Federal Judges and School Desegregation* (New York: Harcourt, Brace, 1961).

9
BREAKDOWN

*B*etween the late 1950s and the early 1980s government in the United States became so big and so complex that it all but lost the ability to function. A medical term, "iatrogenic disease," illness resulting from treatment by a physician, fairly well describes what happened. Starting with the New Deal, government attempted to solve problems of a nature and magnitude that were beyond the capacities of a limited constitutional system and perhaps of any system. Some remedies worked, others did not. When they did not, the tendency was to create a new program on top of an old one, rather than to scrap the old. By the early 1960s this jerry-built machinery was beginning to produce, or aggravate, social problems of a scale previously unknown in America. Every governmental "remedy" produced a new government-caused sickness; and yet Americans had become so addicted to the habit of believing that government could cure everything that the response of the late sixties was wave after wave of crash programs. These created new problems that, in the seventies, resulted in more programs. By the time considerable numbers of people began to suspect that they were overgoverned, the reality was that, though government interfered with their lives from cradle to grave, it scarcely governed at all, in the original constitutional sense of the term. Government had ceased to be able to protect people in their lives, their liberty, and their property; and it had lost the capacity to establish justice, ensure domestic tranquility, provide for the common defense, and promote the general welfare.

OF THE PEOPLE

A central part of the problem was the emergence of an assortment of self-proclaimed spokesmen for segments of the public that demanded a right to preferred treatment—minority racial or ethnic groups, women, consumers, homosexuals, the poor, defenders of the environment, and so on. Representatives of special-interest groups, such as particular industries or professions or organized labor, had long exerted influence upon government, of course. But they had worked quietly, even secretively; and though they might assert and believe that government policies that were advantageous to them would also benefit the country, they rarely claimed more. The new spokespersons, by contrast, sought the widest possible audience for their doings, through television whenever that could be arranged, and insisted that their cause was morally superior to other considerations of policy, to the interests of the general public, and to the Constitution. What is more, government tended to respect their demands and to satisfy them, or at least to try.

It is important to understand the process by which this state of affairs came about, for the process itself helped bring on the paralysis of government. For convenience, the beginning may be dated with the promises made to blacks by the New Deal, the efforts by Truman's Fair Deal to fulfill those promises, and the culmination of the first phase of the civil-rights movement in the

Supreme Court's desegregation decision in *Brown* v. *Board of Education*. In 1955 the Court decided how the transition to desegregated schools was to be accomplished: Local school boards would draw up plans, subject to the approval and supervision of federal district judges, for desegregation "with all deliberate speed." But southern school boards, encouraged by their governors, legislators, and congressmen, dragged their feet, dodged court orders, and resorted to such means as closing the public schools and enrolling whites in supposedly "private schools." There were also intimidation and threats of violence by whites toward black parents who sought to enroll their children in white schools. As a result, desegregation inched along at a snail's pace.

On the other hand, the federal government made it clear to southern blacks, in a series of actions, that its might was pledged in their support. First, there was the Montgomery bus boycott. From December 1955 through 1956, blacks in Montgomery, Alabama, led by the Reverend Martin Luther King, Jr., boycotted city bus lines in an effort to have them "desegregated" (blacks were required to sit in the rear). The city refused to give in, despite the loss of revenues, until it was forced to do so by a federal district court order. Second, in 1957 Congress passed an act creating the Civil Rights Commission and making it a crime to try to prevent blacks from voting in federal elections. Third, and most dramatically, there was a confrontation between state and federal authority in Arkansas. Governor Orval Faubus, in defiance of a court order, used the state's National Guard to prevent nine black students from attending a white high school in Little Rock; but President Eisenhower federalized the National Guard and sent in a thousand paratroopers to escort the students to classes.

These and other federal actions, widely and sympathetically publicized by national news media, conveyed to southern blacks the message that the entire country, except for southern whites, was on their side. At the same time, however, segregation remained general throughout most of the South. In the circumstances, blacks read the message in two ways. Vast numbers of them, believing they would be welcomed, migrated to northern and Pacific Coast cities: More than 150,000 a year moved from the South to the North and West throughout the remainder of the 1950s and for two decades thereafter. Generations of living in the rural South had prepared them ill for the fast-paced, impersonal, and competitive life of the big cities, and northern piousness about their plight prepared them even less for the wall of discrimination they found in the urban ghettos. The other response to the message was an increase in activism in the South, led by three organizations: King's Southern Christian Leadership Conference (SCLC), mainly southern and black; the Congress of Racial Equality (CORE), mixed racially and sectionally; and the Student Non-Violent Coordinating Commiteee (SNCC), mainly white and mainly northern.

During the early sixties these groups engaged in steadily increasing demonstrations aimed at bringing an end to segregation. In 1960 large numbers of southern black students staged "sit-ins" and boycotts of restaurants and stores; when the stores were parts of national chains, desegregation usually followed. In 1961 and 1962 busload after busload of "freedom riders," sponsored by CORE and recruited mainly by SNCC, went to the South to challenge local segregation laws. The local citizenry responded with a great deal of outrage and some violence; local officials responded by making large-scale arrests. President John F. Kennedy and his brother Attorney General Robert Kennedy responded by giving the freedom riders moral support and the protection of federal marshals. Thus for the first time in American history the chief law-enforcement officers in the land employed the power of the federal government to support groups that engaged in overt violations of state and local laws and made calculated attacks upon peace and order. Some of the laws being violated were soon ruled unconstitutional, and others were clearly immoral; but they were laws nonetheless, and the Kennedys' actions constituted an invitation to civil disobedience and mob action as a means of affecting public policy.

Mob actions came, breeding in equal parts violence and new public policies. In 1963 blacks staged mass demonstrations throughout the country, sometimes peacefully marching, sometimes forcibly blocking construction projects, sometimes storming into the offices of mayors and governors with demands for an end to discrimination in employment. The demonstrations reached a climax on August 28, when two hundred thousand people of both races marched on Washington in support of a new civil-rights bill. Yet at the end of the year the bill had not been passed, and as 1964 began, no more than 2 percent of the black children in the Deep South were attending integrated public schools. That summer the demonstrations turned into riots, as they did during each of the next three years. Several were killed, hundreds were injured, and property worth hundreds of millions of dollars was stolen or burned. That got results: Congress responded with sweeping Civil Rights acts in 1964, 1965, and 1968.

Race riots had run their course by 1968; they were replaced by mass demonstrations of college students protesting the Vietnam War. The nation was hopelessly and stupidly enmeshed in that bloody conflict, just as it had been hopelessly and stupidly enmeshed in the system of race relations; and once again only mob action forced change. But along the way, radical students, black and white, became increasingly arrogant and self-righteous, viewing themselves as pure and seeing nothing but hypocrisy and evil in adult American life ("don't trust anyone over thirty"). They began to talk of revolution and to seize campus after campus; hapless administrators yielded to their every demand, no matter how extravagant. All one needed to do to bring any American institution to its knees, it seemed, was to organize a crowd, hurl accusations, and demand retribution.

The politics of confrontation came abruptly to a halt on May 4, 1970, when a mob of students confronted national guardsmen at Kent State University in Ohio, and the guardsmen opened fire. In seconds, four demonstrators were dead and nine were wounded. On the same day two students were killed by state police and nine were wounded after students had seized black Jackson State College in Mississippi. Suddenly, "the establishment" had flexed its muscles and young radicals had lost their appetite for revolution. Less than three weeks later the force of "the movement" was redirected into the celebration of Earth Day, whose message was that the archenemy to peace and brotherhood was neither racism nor war but pollution resulting from industrial civilization.

The politics of accusation and demand, however, did not die with the politics of confrontation. Already Ralph Nader and the consumerist movement had made their presence felt through the use of the technique, and during the early 1970s they were joined by champions of environmentalism. By the middle and late seventies crusaders for women's rights, gay rights, Indian rights, and Chicano rights had climbed on board the bandwagon. All employed the method of the original campaign for civil rights for blacks: Point angrily to a long history of oppression, real or imagined, and demand that government rectify and make compensation for the evil. Government at all levels and in all its branches just seemed unable to say no.

OF THE LEGISLATIVE BRANCH

The Civil Rights acts of the 1960s were part of a veritable orgy of major legislation that began with the presidency of Lyndon Johnson and continued into the early 1970s. Johnson was masterful at pushing bills through Congress and believed that congressional acts, especially crash programs, could accomplish virtually anything. Many of the new laws were passed upon his recommendation and were designed to help blacks, other minorities, and the poor as part of his "Great Society" program and his "war on poverty"; but Congress, infected with his spirit, turned out many more laws, especially in the areas of consumer and environmental protection. These included the Motor Vehicle Air Pollution Control Act of 1965, the National Traffic and Motor Vehicle Safety Act of 1966, and the Clean Air Act of 1970, aimed at the automotive industry alone, and two dozen similar acts aimed at industries ranging from pharmaceutical manufacturers and toy makers to coal miners and chicken processors.

In grinding out such legislation, Congress was as careless as it was hasty. The Wholesome Meat Act, for instance, effectively vested the state governments with power to control the amount of impurities allowed in intrastate meats—except that the law prohibited state standards from being higher than those required by the federal government for meats sold in interstate commerce. Michigan and several other states had already imposed purity standards higher than those of the federal government, and thus the effect of the act was to force those states to lower their standards. The various automobile acts were passed without knowledge of the effects that the "pollutants" actually had upon humans or the physical environment, and without regard for the fact that the safety and anti-pollution requirements drastically increased fuel consumption. The Endangered Species Act of 1973 required federal agencies to give "first priority" (above, say, national defense or the need for energy supplies) to a declared national policy of saving endangered species of plants or animals. No regard was shown for the fact that there are approximately 1.4 million known species of animals and 600,000 known species of plants, thousands of which become extinct every year from non-human causes.

One primary cause of such slipshod legislation was that congressmen were swamped with more work than they could do, and one primary effect was to overwork them still further in patching up what had been done badly the first time around. In the 1950s there had been seventy or eighty votes in each house per session; by the late seventies there were from six to seven hundred. In 1947 congressmen and the few dozen congressional committees employed 2,433 staff members; in 1980 there were 314 committees and subcommittees and more than 10,000 staff members. By the late seventies, 20,000 bills were being introduced and from six to eight hundred public laws were being passed each year. In 1977 a congressional committee found that the average congressman worked eleven hours a day, during which he had an average of eleven minutes free to think. More than a third of the day, he was scheduled to be in at least two places at once. Given such circumstances, it was impossible for congressmen to obtain the information and devote the thought necessary for intelligent legislation. Indeed, by 1980 many congressmen were admitting that they *read* only a fraction of the bills on which they voted.

Somewhere along the way there began to emerge a pattern by which the legislative power was exercised. Congress was fragmented into scores of "iron triangles," each of which consisted of private advocates of particular kinds of legislation, the bureaucrats in the agencies involved, and the congressional committee having jurisdiction over the subject. Each subject was so specialized that only members of the appropriate triangle understood it. Other congressmen had little option but to accept the recommendations of a given triangle; and besides, they were disposed to in exchange for support for the recommendations of their own triangles. The system was theoretically efficient, for the division of labor is inherently efficient. Its weakness lay in the quality of the input of information: The private citizens who provided that input were apt to be either special-interest groups or accuse-and-demand advocates of special causes, supplying moral certainty rather than reliable data and sound understanding.

As the triangle system proliferated, Congress steadily lost its capacity to fulfill its constitutional roles, those of setting broad national legislative policies and serving as a solemn forum wherein those policies could be fully and deliberately debated. One result, as indicated, was a legislative output so large and so poorly drafted that congressmen themselves had only the vaguest notion about what they had enacted. Another was that the new laws necessitated an enormous amount of bureaucratic rule making and judicial legislation, both of which were apt to be contrary to what Congress intended. Still another was a staggering increase in what economists call "transfer payments"—taking money from people who earn it and giving it to people who do not. Throughout the 1970s transfer payments increased half again as fast as wages and salaries, until social-welfare expenditures amounted to a quarter of the gross national income.

Finally, the system produced an astronomical increase in overall government spending and taxation. The federal budget during Jimmy Carter's first three years in office was four times as large as during Lyndon Johnson's last three, even though Johnson's were during the Vietnamese War. By 1976 Americans were paying more in taxes than they spent on food, clothing, and shelter combined; their governments were taking 42 cents out of every dollar of the national income. By 1980 that figure had risen until Americans were paying nearly as much in taxes as they spent on everything else combined.

OF THE EXECUTIVE BRANCH

If the legislative branch was getting out of control, the executive branch—the federal bureaucracy—was running amok. Four new departments and scores of new regulatory bodies were established during the sixties and seventies, but that only begins to tell the story, for regulations multiplied far more rapidly than did agencies. By the late seventies it was taking more than seventy thousand pages of small print in the *Federal Register* just to list the new rules and regulations put out each year. The rates and rulings that had been issued by the Interstate Commerce Commission alone numbered in the trillions. American corporations were required in 1976 to fill out 114 million forms; federal government agencies printed up 10 billion sheets of forms to be completed by business; the average small firm had to fill in 53, and the nation's largest corporation, General Motors, had 22,300 full-time employees filling in government forms. Merely processing all this paper work consumed roughly 5 percent of the federal budget.

The new programs were ineffectual and the new regulations were paralytic. Both kinds of results can best be shown by examples. There were, by government definition, 25 million poor people in the United States in 1976. In the preceding decade, the total yearly expenditure on social welfare had increased from $77 billion to $286 billion. If the increase of $209 billion simply had been given to the poor people, they would have received $8,000 a year apiece, or $32,000 tax-free for a family of four. In other words, every poor family in the country would have become a relatively rich family. But that is not what happened. Some of the money did go to poor people, and a great deal went as social-security payments to retirees; but the rest, as columnist M. Stanton Evans put it, went to people who were giving advice to poor people, to "social workers and counsellors and planners and social engineers and urban renewal experts and the assistant administrators to the administrative assistants who work for the federal government."

Though the paralytic effects of the regulations were most directly visible in regard to business, they fell ultimately upon the consumer. The Eli Lilly Company, for instance, developed a new drug for arthritis and asked the Food and Drug Administration for approval to market it. The FDA required an application that ran to 120,000 pages. The company was also required to report to the Environmental Protection Agency; a computer printout of 153 pages was needed just for the index, each index entry representing from 3 to 3,000 pages of reports. Such red tape greatly increased the costs of drugs and medicines and kept new ones from the public for as long as twelve years. The Southern Railway Company developed a vehicle that could haul grain at one-third less cost than could conventional boxcars; the ICC banned its use as unfair to other railroads and to truckers. The EPA required automobile manufacturers to install catalytic converters to reduce air pollution, only to find that the device added to pollution by emitting platinum and sulfur mist; the consumer had to pay for the heavy investment as well as breathe the noxious fumes. The electric-utility industry, forced by environmental regulations to abandon much of their use of coal (of which the nation's supply was virtually infinite) and attracted by the artificially low prices on interstate natural gas resulting from Federal Power Commission regulations, made a wholesale conversion from coal to natural gas. When the gas supply began to dry up because, though it was abundant, producers could not profitably sell it at the regulated prices, the Department of Energy recommended a multibillion dollar subsidy to enable electric companies to reconvert to coal-burning generators. And the energy crisis was not the only dislocation caused by contradictory and self-defeating regulations. By 1980 the railroads were long since practically defunct, the steel and automobile industries were in grave trouble, and the entire economy stood on an uncertain footing.

Meanwhile, the presidency itself, which had once been described, accurately, as the most powerful office in the free world, had lost much of its potency. In part the weakened condition of the presidency resulted from the increasingly cumbersome nature of the bureaucracy. As early as the presidencies of Eisenhower and Kennedy, chief executives were finding that their orders were likely to get bogged down somewhere in the middle ranges of the civil service and never be implemented. When Jimmy Carter became president he was appalled at the overgrown and unwieldy machinery of government and was determined to do some large-scale streamlining, starting with cuts in the White House staff. The apparatus was bewildering as well as unmanageable, however, and soon Carter was taking on staff members by the score, finding them necessary just to keep up with what was happening.

Equally significant was the deliberate weakening of the presidency in response to the excesses of Lyndon Johnson and Richard Nixon. That was in keeping with a pattern in American history. Andrew Jackson and Abraham Lincoln, for example, had been followed by a succession of nobodies, most of them one-term presidents who rarely exerted even the full constitutional powers of the office, and a similar reaction followed the "strong" presidencies of Theodore Roosevelt and Woodrow Wilson. But the excesses of Johnson and Nixon—beginning with Johnson's venturing full-scale into a long and futile war without a congressional declaration of war and reaching a climax in Nixon's "cover-up" of the Watergate scandal—were different. It was not so much that their offenses were graver, perhaps, as that both men were extremely unpopular and their misdeeds were mercilessly exposed by the news media.

For practical purposes, both men were forced from office, but only Nixon's ouster involved constitutional questions. During the 1972 presidential election campaign, agents of the Committee to Re-elect the President were caught burglarizing the Democratic National Committee offices in the Watergate Building in Washington. Ultimately, forty-one people were indicted for obstruction of justice and other crimes committed during the campaign, but President Nixon and his top aides claimed to have known nothing about the break-in or the subsequent attempts to cover up the involvement of high-ranking officials. In 1973 a Senate investigating committee stumbled across the discovery that most presidential conversations during the preceding two years had been recorded on tape. The Senate and a special prosecutor, appointed by Nixon himself, requested parts of the tapes to determine who was guilty and who was not, but Nixon maintained that their disclosure would violate the confidentiality of the presidency and erode the separation of powers. A complex legal battle began. In the meantime various other scandals were revealed, and Vice President Spiro Agnew resigned to escape a jail sentence for evading income taxes on bribes he had received. (He was, in accordance with the Twenty-fifth Amendment, replaced by Gerald Ford, whom Nixon appointed with the Senate's confirmation.)

The matter came to a head in 1974. The special prosecutor secured a subpoena from the federal district court ordering the president to produce the tapes. Nixon refused and took the case to the Supreme Court, contending that the special prosecutor, as an executive subordinate, had no authority to seek the order and that the tapes could be withheld as a matter of executive privilege. In July the Court rejected the president's arguments and ordered that the tapes be surrendered. In other circumstances the president might have been disposed to defy the Court as a co-equal branch of government, much as Thomas Jefferson had done during the treason trial of Aaron Burr in 1807; but on the day the

Supreme Court gave its ruling, the House Judiciary Committee began televised hearings in which both Democratic and Republican counsels urged that Nixon be impeached. He complied with the Court order on August 5, and three days later he resigned, leaving the presidency in the hands of the "caretaker," Gerald Ford.

In the wake of all this, Congress reversed a trend of more than four decades and began to curtail the powers of the president. The War Powers Resolution, for instance, required consultation with Congress for the use of the armed forces overseas; the president's authority to give military or economic aid to foreign nations was restrained; and the operations of the Central Intelligence Agency were seriously impaired. During Carter's presidency Congress began to reverse another trend, though only on a limited basis. It "deregulated" airline fares, with the result that fares dropped and flights increased, and it began to consider deregulation of many other industries.

OF THE JUDICIARY

As the legislative and executive branches of the federal government drifted out of the control of congressmen and the president, the Constitution ceased to be a fundamental law governing government. Instead, it came increasingly to be regarded as, and more or less to function as, a table of the rights of citizens, as those rights were interpreted and defined by the Supreme Court. Later we shall consider some of the implications of these changes in the meaning of the Constitution. First, however, it will be useful to survey the evolution of the Court's interpretation of the rights of Negroes and members of other minority groups.

In *Brown* v. *Board of Education* and its companion cases, the Court declared unconstitutional the denial to Negroes of "admission to schools attended by white children under laws requiring or permitting segregation according to race." The Civil Rights Act of 1964 took the same position: It authorized the attorney general to bring suits to prevent the assigning of children to schools on the basis of race. Neither the court decision nor the congressional act suggested the assigning of children to achieve "racial balance" in the schools; indeed, such assignment was in direct conflict with the language of the 1964 act. In 1966, however, the United States Court of Appeals for the Fifth District (covering the Gulf Coast states) ruled that "desegregation" meant "integration"—that the schools had a constitutional duty to "integrate," by which was meant the "racial mixing of students." The Supreme Court allowed that decision to stand, refusing to review it.

Two years later, in *Green* v. *County School Board of New Kent County* (391 U.S. 430), the Court quietly announced a radical departure from the principle of the *Brown* decision. Acting under Virginia law, the New Kent County school board had established a freedom-of-choice system under which students were allowed to choose the school they attended. After three years, seven-eighths of the black children had chosen to remain in all-black schools and all the white children had chosen to remain in white schools. The Supreme Court rejected this system on the ground that the "ultimate end to be brought about" was "a unitary, nonracial system of public education." In other words, absence of legally mandated racial segregation was not enough: Whatever the system of assigning pupils, the results must be integration.

In 1971 the Court went further: It ordered the busing of students. In Mecklenburg County, North Carolina, pupils had been assigned to the nearest school without regard to race, which resulted in about half the black pupils attending schools with whites. In *Swann* v. *Charlotte-Mecklenburg Board of Education* (402 U.S. 1) the Supreme Court upheld a district-court order requiring the busing of students to achieve a more complete racial balance. The requirement of integration was not absolute, the Court said, because "in metropolitan areas minority groups are often found concentrated in one part of the city," and thus the existence of a one-race school might sometimes be justified. The crucial question was whether segregation was the continuing effect of past discrimination, such as the "discriminatory location of school sites or distortion of school size in order to achieve or maintain an artificial racial separation." During the next four years the Court upheld citywide busing plans in various northern cities, and the requirement of proof of past discrimination gradually gave way to compulsory busing to achieve integration no matter what the causes of racial separation. Thus in twenty years the Court had fully reversed its position: In the early 1950s it had ruled that state and local governments could not use race as a factor in assigning children to schools, and in the early 1970s it was ruling that race must be the principal factor in assigning children to schools.

Meanwhile, the idea of the need for overcoming the consequences of past discrimination was spreading from integration of the public schools into other areas. There was general acceptance, in government and out, of the desirability of "compensatory treatment" of blacks, meaning measures to help them catch up to the competitive standards of society as a whole. For instance, the "head start" program initiated by the Johnson administration, giving accelerated preschool training to children from uneducated families, was widely regarded as desirable. The more active champions of blacks, however, insisted upon something in addition: suspending the competitive standards for blacks and giving them jobs and advanced educational opportunities for which they were not qualified. That approach was not at all popular, but the machinery set up by the new civil rights acts made its adoption almost certain. Several agencies were established to enforce the new laws, the most important being the Justice Department's Civil Rights Division, the Civil Rights Commission, the Office for Civil Rights in the Department of Health, Education, and Welfare, the Labor Department's Office of Federal Contract Compliance, and the Equal Employment Opportunity Commission. Both ideologically and out of concern for their own interests, the people in those agencies were disposed toward preferential treatment or, as it came to be called, "affirmative action." Too, when they surveyed area after area of American society and found that, in the more prestigious and financially rewarding areas, blacks were not represented in proportion to their percentage of the total population,

their understandable tendency was to assume that the dispro-
portion was the result of past discrimination, and their understandable urge was to require "quotas" to overcome the discrepancy.
They had a powerful weapon at their disposal without having to
resort to the courts. Universities, state and local governments, and
defense contractors received large-scale federal funding, and the
civil-rights enforcement agencies were authorized by law to withhold funding when patterns of racial discrimination were found to
exist. The problem was that affirmative action could be implemented only through racial discrimination, and racial discrimination
was positively and explicitly forbidden by the civil rights acts. On
the theory that justice was served by ignoring the law, they opted
for racial discrimination.

Three of the more important cases arising from reverse discrimination were decided between 1978 and 1980. The 1978 case,
Regents of the University of California v. *Bakke* (98 S. Ct. 2733),
concerned preferential treatment in professional training. The
medical school of the University of California at Davis, in keeping
with the kinds of policies insisted upon by the Civil Rights office
of HEW, set aside sixteen places in its entering class for minority
students. Allan Bakke, a white engineer, applied for admission
and was twice rejected in favor of minority candidates whose
qualifications were considerably inferior to his. He brought suit on
the ground that the discrimination against him violated the equal-
protection clause of the Fourteenth Amendment. The California
Supreme Court sustained his claim and ordered his admission;
the university appealed to the United States Supreme Court.

The decision was eagerly awaited by both friends and foes
of affirmative action, for it was expected that the Court would
decide upon the constitutionality of the whole approach. Instead,
the justices split three ways and avoided resolution of the constitutional issue. One group of four justices argued that the Constitution permitted racial quotas to redress continuing effects of
past discrimination and that the Civil Rights Act of 1964 did not
and could not change that. Another four justices gave their opinion
on the basis of the act alone, which prohibited the exclusion, on
grounds of race, color, or national origin, of anyone from partici-

pation in "any program of activity receiving federal financial assistance"; as the university received federal financial aid, these justices held for Bakke. The remaining justice, Lewis Powell, took an equivocal position. He held that an explicit racial quota system violated the Fourteenth Amendment, and that made it five to four in favor of Bakke's admission; but Powell left the broader question unanswered by giving as his opinion that a university may take race into account if it is one of several factors—such as seeking a diversified student body to improve the quality of student cultural interchange—and not the single decisive factor.

The 1979 case seemed even more clear-cut than the Bakke case. The Kaiser Aluminum Company, which had sizable government contracts, was under pressure from the Office of Federal Contract Compliance to increase the number of its minority employees at all levels. In response, in 1974 it reached a collective-bargaining agreement with the United Steelworkers union designed to increase the number of minority workers in the skilled crafts in its plant in Grammercy, Louisiana. Entrance into the skilled crafts was through the company's on-the-job training program. Previously, admission to the program had been based upon seniority; that was now by-passed, and entrance ratios by race were substituted. A white worker named Brian Weber was refused admission to the job-training program despite his seniority over blacks who were accepted, and the discriminatory racial basis of his non-selection was admitted by both the company and the union. Title VII of the 1964 Civil Rights Act fit his case precisely: "It shall be an unlawful employment practice for any employer, labor organization, or joint labor-management committee controlling apprenticeship or other training or retraining, including on-the-job training programs, to discriminate against any individual because of his race, color, religion, sex, or national origin." Nor was there any question of compensatory treatment for past discrimination at the plant; since its opening in 1958, the Grammercy plant had been scrupulously fair in its employment and promotion practices, irrespective of race, and no one contended otherwise. The federal district court upheld Weber, and so did the Fifth Circuit Court. The company and the union argued, on the contrary, that they were at liberty to enter into a voluntary contract in the interest of long-term "justice." In *Kaiser Aluminum and United Steelworkers* v. *Weber*, the Supreme Court agreed. The Fourteenth Amendment did not apply, because the relevant statute was federal, not state; and the federal law was simply ignored.

In 1980 the Court came down decisively in favor of affirmative action. A 1977 congressional act appropriated $4 billion to be spent in helping state and local governments finance public-works projects but required that at least 10 percent of the funds must go to contracting companies that were more than half-owned by "Negroes, Spanish-speaking, Orientals, Eskimos and Aleuts." The Court upheld the statute, in *Fullilove* v. *Klutznick*, in a six-to-three decision. Chief Justice Warren Burger, in the majority opinion, held that the Constitution gives Congress special powers to make up for the effects of past discrimination, even though the result was to punish some white contractors who had not practiced discrimination themselves. In a dissenting opinion given in a different case decided on the same day, Justice John Paul Stevens said that it would soon be necessary for the government to start spelling out who belongs to which race; and he bitterly suggested that the Nazi law defining who is a Jew might serve as a suitable model.

Despite the apparent consistency of the Court's drift, however, no one could be sure of its real intentions, for the justices reached their decisions by different lines of argument. In the week of the *Fullilove* decision, they wrote twenty-two separate opinions in four cases. They were as divided among themselves as had been the justices on the Taney Court: The judicial branch, like the legislative and executive, was confused and self-contradictory.

OF THE FEDERAL SYSTEM AND THE SEPARATION OF POWERS

The area of race relations was not the only one in which the Supreme Court substituted its own notions of social justice for those of the Constitution and the laws. Many of its decisions appeared to large numbers of Americans to be a deliberate attack upon religion, the family, the community, and ordinary standards of decency. Its decisions on religious matters, beginning in 1962, illustrate the Alice-in-Wonderland quality of its constitutional reasoning. Religion is mentioned in the Constitution in only two places: Article VI, which stipulates that "no religious Test shall ever be required as a Qualification to any Office or public Trust under the United States," and the First Amendment, which states that "Congress shall make no law respecting an establishment of religion, or prohibiting the free exercise thereof." Yet the Court held in *Engel* v. *Vitale* (370 U.S. 421) that the Constitution prohibits *local school boards* from authorizing brief nonsectarian prayers in public schools. As for the family, popular resentment of the Court's decisions turned mainly on its tolerance of sexual promiscuity and its 1973 ruling that women had a constitutional right to have abortions. (In 1980 it ruled that Congress was not *required to pay for abortions*, but it did so only by a five-to-four vote.) Regarding the community, opposition to the Court's rulings centered mainly on two kinds of decisions: busing, which undermined the concept of the neighborhood school, and criminal-procedure cases, which, to say the least, did nothing to check the enormous increase of crime in the streets. The pivotal criminal-procedure cases, *Escobedo* v. *Illinois* (378 U.S. 478) and *Miranda* v. *Arizona* (388 U.S. 436), decided in 1964 and 1966, reversed earlier decisions and held that the Fourteenth Amendment's due-process clause extended the procedural rights of the Fourth, Fifth, and Sixth amendments to apply to the states. (Those rights—"you have the right to remain silent, anything you say may be used against you, you have a right to a lawyer," and so on—became familiar to every television viewer.) Finally, in the matter of standards of decency, controversy centered on the Court's extension of the rights of free speech and free press to protect hard-core pornography.

More dangerous to constitutional government, however, were the erosion of federalism and the system of checks and balances.

Federalism was by no means defunct in form, for state and local governments were performing more functions, spending more money, and hiring more employees than ever before; but they had lost their relative independence and could no longer serve as preservers of traditional values and local preferences. Partly, their capacity to defend themselves and their citizens against federal encroachment was exhausted—as well as discredited—by the long battle over integration. But dependence also became institutionalized between 1957 and 1980 through an enormous increase in the federal funding of state and local activities. Each new program of that sort, such as federal aid to education, which began on a grand scale in 1958, or "revenue sharing," which began in 1972, was justified by its supporters as strengthening state and local governments. Each was attacked by opponents on the ground that, soon or late, the federal government would start dictating policy to the recipients. Events proved the opponents to be right: By the middle seventies, federal agencies were not only telling the recipients of their funds whom to hire, fire, admit, or promote but also directing internal policy. For instance, the Department of Health, Education, and Welfare began requiring medical schools to develop special programs in family practice medicine, irrespective of the nature of the schools and their faculties.

HEW was perhaps the worst offender in regard to federal–state relations, and not only because it was by far the biggest spender among the executive departments. Its abuses were wide-ranging. It forced schools to preserve biculturalism by conducting classes for minorities in foreign languages, including black "street talk" (a perversion of the legislation establishing the program, which was aimed at bringing minorities into the mainstream of American culture). It encouraged research in certain areas and discouraged it in others, depending upon whether the research would support its own prejudices. But its impairment of state autonomy is best illustrated by its ongoing conflict with the University of North Carolina. In the late seventies HEW decided that the existence of a program, such as home economics or nursing, at more than one of the university campuses was an unnecessary duplication reminiscent of the days of segregation, when there were duplicate campuses, duplicate rest rooms, and so on. The department ordered the university to confine its duplication to nine core areas (mathematics, the arts, the social sciences, and the like) and to confine each other program to a single campus. When the university objected, claiming that it had the right to determine the curriculum needs of its students, HEW cut off its $89 million in annual funding.

The undermining of the system of checks and balances was more direct: It came about when the Supreme Court reversed its long-standing policy of refusing to review political questions and began to order wholesale reapportionment of state legislatures and Congress. Both the Constitution and the state constitutions based legislative representation upon two different principles, place and number of inhabitants. The Senate, in which each state has two members, reflects the first principle; the House of Representatives, in which each state has a minimum of one and membership is otherwise apportioned on the basis of population, reflects both principles. Accordingly, how much an individual's vote counts in elections depends upon where he lives. After the 1960 census, for example, California had one senator for every 7,858,000 inhabitants, one representative for every 413,000, and one presidential elector for every 393,000; whereas its neighboring state of Nevada had a senator for every 147,500 inhabitants, a representative for every 285,000, and a presidential elector for every 95,000. In electing national officials, then, a Nevada voter's ballot counted from 1.4 to 53 times as much as the vote of a Californian. Similar variations existed among counties in voting for state legislatures.

The Supreme Court took its first step toward ordering reapportionment in the 1960 case of *Gomillion* v. *Lightfoot* (364 U.S. 339). An Alabama law had redrawn the boundaries of Tuskegee to place most of its blacks outside the city limits and thus deprive them of the right to vote in city elections. The Court declared the law unconstitutional, a violation of the Fifteenth Amendment, which it fairly clearly was. But it was only a short distance from that decision to judicial review of the boundaries of state and congressional legislative districts. The Court traversed that distance two years later in *Baker* v. *Carr* (369 U.S. 186). A federal district court in Tennessee, following precedent the Supreme Court had established far earlier and reconfirmed as recently as 1946, ruled against a challenge to the constitutionality of the state's legislative apportionment law. The Supreme Court, however, threw overboard both precedent and the doctrine that "political questions" are beyond the judiciary's power. Holding that disproportionate representation denied some citizens equal protection of the laws, it sent the case back to the district court for retrial "and further proceeding consistent with this opinion." In asserting its power to review political questions, the Court made no suggestions as to what it would do if a legislature refused to abide by a court order to enact a reapportionment law. Such an order was, in fact, as Justice Frankfurter had said in 1946, beyond the range of what the Court could enforce—if the legislature resisted.

As the retrial in the Baker case was pending, the federal courts were deluged with new apportionment suits brought in response to the Supreme Court's pronouncement. In 1964 the Court went the rest of the way, declaring unconstitutional the legislative apportionment systems in six states and insisting that all legislatures be reapportioned on the basis of "one person, one vote." The leading case was *Reynolds* v. *Sims* (377 U.S. 533), which struck down the Alabama apportionment system even though it was patterned precisely on the system provided in the United States Constitution. What was more, in *Wesberry* v. *Sanders* (376 U.S. 1) the Court declared unconstitutional Georgia's law defining congressional districts. In an amazing display of irrationality, the Court garbled history by asserting that Article I, Section 2, apportioning House seats among the states partly according to population, meant that the Founding Fathers intended that "as nearly as is practicable one man's vote in a congressional election is to be worth as much as another's." The opinion overlooked the fact that the same article provided the states equal representation in the Senate half of Congress, irrespective of population, and also that it provided that "Each House shall be the Judge of the Elections, Returns and Qualifications of its members." If those decisions were allowed to stand—if the Supreme Court could dictate laws to the state legislatures and deprive Congress of its constitutional power to determine the qualifications of its own members—then the doctrine of separation of powers, and with it the system of checks and balances, would become a nullity.

Congress responded swiftly but, because the two houses were divided over tactics, its response was ineffectual. The simplest solution was to pass a joint resolution depriving the federal judiciary of jurisdiction over apportionment cases, and that is the route the House took. In August 1964 it passed by a sizable margin a resolution to that effect proposed by Representative William V. Tuck of Virginia. The Senate, however, rejected the resolution by a narrow margin and, a few months later, followed its own preferred approach. Senator Everett Dirksen of Illinois offered a proposed constitutional amendment providing that the people of a state could apportion representation in one house of its legislature on the basis of geography or political subdivisions as they saw fit. The proposal was debated off and on until August 1965, when the Senate voted in favor of it, 57 yeas to 39 nays. That was seven votes short of the constitutionally required two-thirds majority, so the motion failed.

Subsequently, the Court followed the same twisted path in ordering legislative reapportionment as it followed in moving from desegregation to integration. By the middle and late seventies it was ordering reapportionment not solely on the basis of numbers but also to create legislative districts in which blacks would be in a majority. Moreover, lower federal courts began ordering legislatures to pass laws in various other fields. A judge of the middle federal district of Alabama, for example, ordered a major overhaul of the state's mental-health and prison systems, and the state meekly complied.

Ironically, it was just as this onslaught began that Richard Nixon was forced to resign the presidency. The influential *New York Times* columnist James Reston wrote on that occasion, "Dear

James Madison: It works," and he went on to praise the enduring excellence of the constitutional system of checks and balances.

In 1979 popular discontent with the Supreme Court had grown so great that a large number of congressmen believed it was time to bring the justices back to earth. Senator Jesse Helms of North Carolina introduced a resolution stripping the federal courts of jurisdiction over state laws dealing with voluntary prayer in public schools, and the Senate approved the resolution by a considerable majority. It was held up in the House Judiciary Committee for more than a year, and the efforts of Representative Philip Crane of Illinois to obtain the 218 signatures required to force it out of committee proved unsuccessful. But it seemed likely that the conservative Congress elected with Ronald Reagan in 1980 would revive the movement, and on that movement much of the future constitutional history of the United States would depend. If Congress once tasted the fruits of overturning an unpopular decision, it seemed certain that its appetite for doing so would become insatiable.

Such an event would not, of course, restore the Constitution to its pristine purity. Nor would most Americans desire a full restoration, for too many people enjoyed the advantages brought to them by the constitutional revolution that began in the 1930s. Many, indeed, regarded the Constitution—designed as it was for a simple agrarian republic—as obsolete, as unsuited to a modern technological society. And, in any event, turning the clock back all the way would be impossible, even if it were desirable.

But there was another side to the question. The United States of America was born in a revolution against big, meddlesome, arbitrary, and capricious government; and the Constitution's central purpose—whatever its other purposes—was to enshrine the ideals of that revolution in a fundamental law. As the Constitution's two-hundredth anniversary approached, the nation had witnessed the emergence of government bigger and more meddlesome, arbitrary, and capricious than any ever dreamed of by George III. If that development were not reversed, the United States would have forfeited the legitimate reason for its existence.

QUESTIONS
FOR DISCUSSION

1. How does the rise of bureaucracy change the constitutional structure of government? What constitutional problems arise in regard to bureaucracy and personal liberty? What should the role of bureaucracy be?

2. In *Fullilove* v. *Kltuznick*, Chief Justice Burger said the Constitution gives Congress powers to make up for past discrimination. What part of the Constitution do you suppose he was referring to? What are the Court's guidelines for interpreting the Constitution today?

3. Who decides what race a person is? Eleanor Holmes Norton, former chairperson of the Equal Employment Opportunity Commission, has suggested a "you're black if you say you are" principle. Would that work? Is that reasonable? Does that definition conflict with the ruling in *Plessy* v. *Ferguson* that Plessy was a Negro? Should the Constitution be color-blind?

4. Does Article I, Section 4 argue against the rulings in *Baker* v. *Carr* and *Reynolds* v. *Sims*? How does Article I, Section 5 apply?

5. Is the idea of a balance between federal and state powers viable today? What is the impact of recent trends in this area on your life? What is the future of federalism and divided sovereignty?

RECOMMENDED
READINGS

RAOUL BERGER, *Government by Judiciary: The Transformation of the Fourteenth Amendment* (Cambridge: Harvard University Press, 1977).

ALEXANDER M. BICKEL, *The Supreme Court and the Idea of Progress* (New York: Harper & Row, 1970).

RICHARD M. PIOUS, *The American Presidency* (New York: Basic Books, 1979).

THOMAS SOWELL, "Are Quotas Good for Blacks?" *Commentary*, 65 (June 1978), 39–43; and Midge Decter, "Looting and Liberal Racism," ibid., 64 (September 1977), 48–54.

LEONARD J. THEBERGE, ed., *The Judiciary in a Democratic Society* (Lexington, Mass.: Heath, 1979).

BOB WOODWARD and SCOTT ARMSTRONG, *The Brethren: Inside the Supreme Court* (New York: Simon & Schuster, 1979).

THE CONSTITUTION OF THE UNITED STATES

We the People of the United States, in Order to form a more perfect Union, establish Justice, insure domestic Tranquility, provide for the common defense, promote the general Welfare, and secure the Blessings of Liberty to ourselves and our Posterity, do ordain and establish this CONSTITUTION for the United States of America.

ARTICLE 1

SECTION 1. All legislative Powers herein granted shall be vested in a Congress of the United States, which shall consist of a Senate and House of Representatives.

SECTION 2. The House of Representatives shall be composed of Members chosen every second Year by the People of the Several States, and the Electors in each State shall have the Qualifications requisite for Electors of the most numerous Branch of the State Legislature.

No Person shall be a Representative who shall not have attained to the Age of twenty-five Years, and been seven Years a Citizen of the United States, and who shall not, when elected, be an inhabitant of that State in which he shall be chosen.

Representatives and direct Taxes shall be apportioned among the several States which may be included within this Union, according to their respective Numbers, which shall be determined by adding to the whole Number of free Persons, including those bound to Service for a Term of Years and excluding Indians not taxed, three fifths of all other Persons. The actual Enumeration shall be made within three Years after the first Meeting of the Congress of the United States, and within every subsequent Term of ten Years, in such Manner as they shall by Law direct. The Number of Representatives shall not exceed one for every thirty Thousand, but each State shall have at Least one Representative; and until such enumeration shall be made, the State of New Hampshire shall be entitled to chuse three, Massachusetts eight, Rhode-Island and Providence Plantations one, Connecticut five, New-York six, New Jersey four, Pennsylvania eight, Delaware one, Maryland six, Virginia ten, North Carolina five, South Carolina five, and Georgia three.

When vacancies happen in the Representation from any State, the Executive Authority thereof shall issue Writs of Election to fill such Vacancies.

The House of Representatives shall chuse their Speaker and other Officers; and shall have the sole Power of Impeachment.

SECTION 3. The Senate of the United States shall be composed of two Senators from each State, chosen by the Legislature thereof, for six Years; and each Senator shall have one Vote.

Immediately after they shall be assembled in Consequence of the first Election, they shall be divided as equally as may be into three Classes. The Seats of the Senators of the first Class shall be vacated at the Expiration of the second Year, of the second Class at the Expiration of the fourth Year, and of the third Class at the Expiration of the sixth Year, so that one third may be chosen every second Year; and if Vacancies happen by Resignation, or otherwise, during the Recess of the Legislature of any State, the Executive thereof may make temporary Appointments until the next Meeting of the Legislature, which shall then fill such Vacancies.

No Person shall be a Senator who shall not have attained to the Age of thirty Years, and been nine Years a Citizen of the United States, and who shall not, when elected, be an Inhabitant of that State for which he shall be chosen.

The Vice President of the United States shall be President of the Senate, but shall have no vote, unless they be equally divided.

The Senate shall chuse their other Officers, and also a President pro tempore, in the absence of the Vice President, or when he shall exercise the Office of President of the United States.

The Senate shall have the sole Power to try all Impeachments. When sitting for that purpose, they shall be on Oath or Affirmation. When the President of the United States is tried, the Chief Justice shall preside: And no person shall be convicted without the Concurrence of two thirds of the Members present.

Judgment in Cases of Impeachment shall not extend further than to removal from Office, and disqualification to hold and enjoy any Office of honor, Trust or Profit under the United States: but the Party convicted shall nevertheless be liable and subject to Indictment, Trial, Judgment and Punishment, according to Law.

SECTION 4. The Times, Places and Manner of holding Elections for Senators and Representatives, shall be prescribed in each state by the Legislature thereof; but the Congress may at any time by Law make or alter such Regulations, except as to the Places of Chusing Senators.

The Congress shall assemble at least once in every Year, and such Meeting shall be on the first Monday in December, unless they shall by Law appoint a different Day.

SECTION 5. Each House shall be the Judge of the Elections, Returns and Qualifications of its own Members, and a Majority of each shall constitute a Quorum to do Business; but a smaller Number may adjourn from day to day, and may be authorized to compel the Attendance of absent Members, in such Manner, and under such Penalties as each House may provide.

Each House may determine the Rules of its Proceedings, punish its Members for disorderly Behaviour, and, with the Concurrence of two thirds, expel a Member.

Each House shall keep a Journal of its Proceedings, and from time to time publish the same, excepting such Parts as may in their Judgment require Secrecy; and the Yeas and Nays of the Members of either House on any question shall, at the Desire of one fifth of those Present, be entered on the Journal.

Neither House, during the Session of Congress, shall, without the Consent of the other, adjourn for more than three days, nor to any other Place than that in which the two Houses shall be sitting.

SECTION 6. The Senators and Representatives shall receive a Compensation for their Services, to be ascertained by Law, and paid out of the Treasury of the United States. They shall in all Cases, except Treason, Felony, and Breach of the Peace, be privileged from Arrest during their Attendance at the Session of their respective Houses, and in going to and returning from the same; and for any Speech or Debate in either House, they shall not be questioned in any other Place.

No Senator or Representative shall, during the Time for which he was elected, be appointed to any civil Office under the Authority of the United States, which shall have been created, or the Emoluments whereof shall have been increased, during such time; and no Person holding any Office under the United States shall be a Member of either House during his continuance in Office.

SECTION 7. All Bills for raising Revenue shall originate in the House of Representatives; but the Senate may propose or concur with Amendments as on other bills.

Every Bill which shall have passed the House of Representatives and the Senate, shall, before it become a Law, be presented to the President of the United States; If he approve he shall sign it, but if not he shall return it, with his Objections, to that House in which it shall have originated, who shall enter the Objections at large on their Journal, and proceed to reconsider it. If after such Reconsideration two thirds of that House shall agree to pass the bill, it shall be sent, together with the objections, to the other House, by which it shall likewise be reconsidered, and if approved by two thirds of that House, it shall become a Law. But in all such Cases the Votes of both Houses shall be determined by Yeas and Nays, and the Names of the Persons voting for and against the Bill shall be entered on the Journal of each House respectively. If any Bill shall not be returned by the President within ten Days (Sundays excepted) after it shall have been presented to him, the Same shall be a Law, in like Manner as if he had signed it, unless the Congress by their Adjournment prevent its Return, in which Case it shall not be a Law.

Every Order, Resolution, or Vote to which the Concurrence of the Senate and House of Representatives may be necessary (except on a question of Adjournment) shall be presented to the President of the United States; and before the Same shall take Effect, shall be approved by him, or being disapproved by him, shall be repassed by two thirds of the Senate and House of Representatives, according to the Rules and Limitations prescribed in the Case of a Bill.

SECTION 8. The Congress shall have Power To lay and collect Taxes, Duties, Imposts and Excises, to pay the Debts and provide for the common Defence and general Welfare of the United States; but all Duties, Imposts and Excises shall be uniform throughout the United States;

To borrow money on the credit of the United States;

To regulate Commerce with foreign Nations, and among the several States, and with the Indian Tribes;

To establish an uniform Rule of Naturalization, and uniform Laws on the subject of Bankruptcies throughout the United States;

To coin Money, regulate the Value thereof, and of foreign Coin, and fix the Standard of Weights and Measures;

To provide for the Punishment of counterfeiting the Securities and current Coin of the United States;

To establish Post Offices and post Roads;

To promote the Progress of Science and useful Arts, by securing for limited Times to Authors and Inventors the exclusive Right to their respective Writings and Discoveries;

To constitute Tribunals inferior to the Supreme Court;

To define and punish Piracies and Felonies committed on the high Seas, and Offences against the Law of Nations;

To declare War, grant Letters of Marque and Reprisal, and make Rules concerning Captures on Land and Water;

To raise and support Armies, but no Appropriation of Money to that Use shall be for a longer Term than two Years;

To provide and maintain a Navy;

To make Rules for the Government and Regulation of the land and naval forces;

To provide for calling forth the Militia to execute the Laws of the Union, suppress Insurrections and repel Invasions;

To provide for organizing, arming, and disciplining the Militia, and for governing such Part of them as may be employed in the Service of the United States, reserving to the States respectively, the Appointment of the Officers, and the Authority of training the Militia according to the discipline prescribed by Congress;

To exercise exclusive Legislation in all Cases whatsoever, over such District (not exceeding ten Miles square) as may, by Cession of particular States, and the acceptance of Congress, become the Seat of the Government of the United States, and to exercise like Authority over all Places purchased by the Consent of the Legislature of the States in which the Same shall be, for the Erection of Forts, Magazines, Arsenals, dock-Yards, and other needful Buildings;—And

To make all Laws which shall be necessary and proper for carrying into execution the foregoing Powers, and all other Powers vested by this Constitution in the Government of the United States, or in any Department or Officer thereof.

SECTION 9. The Migration or Importation of such Persons as any of the States now existing shall think proper to admit, shall not be prohibited by the Congress prior to the Year one thousand eight hundred and eight, but a tax or duty may be imposed on such Importation, not exceeding ten dollars for each Person.

The Privilege of the Writ of Habeas Corpus shall not be suspended, unless when in Cases of Rebellion or Invasion the public Safety may require it.

No Bill of Attainder or ex post facto Law shall be passed.

No capitation, or other direct, Tax shall be laid unless in Proportion to the Census or Enumeration herein before directed to be taken.

No Tax or Duty shall be laid on Articles exported from any State.

No Preference shall be given by any Regulation of Commerce or Revenue to the Ports of one State over those of another: nor shall Vessels bound to, or from, one State, be obliged to enter, clear, or pay Duties in another.

No Money shall be drawn from the Treasury, but in Consequence of Appropriations made by Law; and a regular Statement and Account of the Receipts and Expenditures of all public Money shall be published from time to time.

No Title of Nobility shall be granted by the United States: And no Person holding any Office of Profit or Trust under them, shall, without the Consent of the Congress, accept of any present, Emolument, Office, or Title, of any kind whatever, from any King, Prince, or foreign State.

SECTION 10. No State shall enter into any Treaty, Alliance, or Confederation; grant Letters of Marque and Reprisal; coin Money; emit Bills of Credit; make any Thing but gold and silver Coin a Tender in Payment of Debts; pass any Bill of Attainder, ex post facto Law, or Law impairing the Obligation of Contracts, or grant any Title of Nobility.

No State shall, without the Consent of the Congress, lay any Imposts or Duties on Imports or Exports, except what may be absolutely necessary for executing its inspection Laws: and the net Produce of all Duties and Imposts, laid by any State on Imports or Exports, shall be for the Use of the Treasury of the United States; and all such Laws shall be subject to the Revision and Controul of the Congress.

No State shall, without the Consent of Congress, lay any duty of Tonnage, keep Troops, or Ships of War in time of Peace, enter into any Agreement or Compact with another State, or with a foreign Power, or engage in War, unless actually invaded, or in such imminent Danger as will not admit of delay.

ARTICLE II

SECTION 1. The executive Power shall be vested in a President of the United States of America. He shall hold his Office during the Term of four years, and, together with the Vice President, chosen for the same Term, be elected, as follows:

Each State shall appoint, in such Manner as the Legislature thereof may direct, a Number of Electors, equal to the whole Number of Senators and Representatives to which the State may be entitled in the Congress: but no Senator or Representative, or Person holding an Office of Trust or Profit under the United States, shall be appointed an Elector.

The Electors shall meet in their respective States, and vote by Ballot for two Persons, of whom one at least shall not be an Inhabitant of the same State with themselves. And they shall make a List of all the Persons voted for, and of the Number of Votes for each; which List they shall sign and certify, and transmit sealed to the Seat of the Government of the United States, directed to the President of the Senate. The President of the Senate shall, in the Presence of the Senate and House of Representatives, open all the Certificates, and the Votes shall then be counted. The Person having the greatest Number of Votes shall be the President, if such Number be a Majority of the whole Number of Electors appointed; and if there be more than one who have such Majority, and have an equal Number of Votes, then the House of Representatives shall immediately chuse by Ballot one of them for President; and if no Person have a Majority, then from the five highest on the List the said House shall in like Manner chuse the President. But in chusing the President, the Votes shall be taken by States, the Representation from each State having one Vote; a quorum for this Purpose shall consist of a Member or Members from two thirds of the States, and a Majority of all the States shall be necessary to a Choice. In every Case, after the Choice of the President, the Person having the greatest Number of Votes of the Electors shall be the Vice President. But if there should remain two or more who have equal votes, the Senate shall chuse from them by Ballot the Vice President.

The Congress may determine the Time of chusing the Electors, and the Day on which they shall give their Votes; which Day shall be the same throughout the United States.

No person except a natural born Citizen, or a Citizen of the United States, at the time of the Adoption of this Constitution, shall be eligible to the Office of President; neither shall any Person be eligible to that Office who shall not have attained to the Age of thirty five years, and been fourteen Years a Resident within the United States.

In Case of the Removal of the President from Office, or of his Death, Resignation, or Inability to discharge the Powers and Duties of the said Office, the same shall devolve on the Vice President, and the Congress may by Law provide for the Case of Removal, Death, Resignation, or Inability, both of the President and Vice President, declaring what Officer shall then act as President, and such Officer shall act accordingly, until the disability be removed, or a President shall be elected.

The President shall, at stated Times, receive for his Services, a Compensation, which shall neither be encreased nor diminished during the Period for which he shall have been elected, and he shall not receive within that Period any other Emolument from the United States, or any of them.

Before he enter on the execution of his Office, he shall take the following Oath or Affirmation:—"I do solemnly swear (or affirm) that I will faithfully execute the Office of President of the United States, and will to the best of my Ability, preserve, protect and defend the Constitution of the United States."

SECTION 2. The President shall be Commander in Chief of the Army and Navy of the United States, and of the Militia of the several States, when called into the actual Service of the United States; he may require the Opinion, in writing, of the principal Officer in each of the executive Departments, upon any subject relating to the Duties of their respective Offices, and he shall have Power to Grant Reprieves and Pardons for Offences against the United States, except in Cases of Impeachment.

He shall have Power, by and with the Advice and Consent of the Senate, to make Treaties, provided two thirds of the Senators present concur; and he shall nominate, and by and with the Advice and Consent of the Senate, shall appoint Ambassadors, other public Ministers and Consuls, Judges of the supreme Court, and all other Officers of the United States, whose Appointments are not herein otherwise provided for, and which shall be established by Law: but the Congress may by Law vest the Appointments of such inferior Officers, as they think proper, in the President alone, in the Courts of Law, or in the Heads of Departments.

The President shall have Power to fill up all Vacancies that may happen during the Recess of the Senate, by granting Commissions which shall expire at the End of their next Session.

SECTION 3. He shall from time to time give to the Congress Information of the State of the Union, and recommend to their Consideration such Measures as he shall judge necessary and expedient; he may, on extraordinary occasions, convene both Houses, or either of them, and in Case of Disagreement between them, with respect to the Time of Adjournment, he may adjourn them to such Time as he shall think proper; he shall receive Ambassadors and other public Ministers; he shall take Care that the Laws be faithfully executed, and shall Commission all the Officers of the United States.

SECTION 4. The President, Vice President and all civil Officers of the United States, shall be removed from Office on Impeachment for, and Conviction of, Treason, Bribery, or other high Crimes and Misdemeanors.

ARTICLE III

SECTION 1. The judicial Power of the United States, shall be vested in one supreme Court, and in such inferior Courts as the Congress may from time to time ordain and establish. The Judges, both of the supreme and inferior Courts, shall hold their Offices during good Behaviour, and shall, at stated Times, receive for their Services, a compensation, which shall not be diminished during their Continuance in Office.

SECTION 2. The judicial Power shall extend to all Cases, in Law and Equity, arising under this Constitution, the Laws of the United States, and Treaties made, or which shall be made, under their Authority;—to all Cases affecting Ambassadors, other public Ministers and Consuls;—to all cases of admiralty and maritime Jurisdiction;—to Controversies to which the United States shall be a Party;—to Controversies between two or more States;—between a State and Citizens of another State;—between Citizens of different States,—between Citizens of the same State claiming Lands under Grants of different States, and between a State, or the Citizens thereof, and foreign States, Citizens or Subjects.

In all Cases affecting Ambassadors, other public Ministers and Consuls, and those in which a State shall be Party, the supreme Court shall have original Jurisdiction. In all the other Cases before mentioned, the supreme Court shall have appellate Jurisdiction, both as to Law and Fact, with such Exceptions, and under such Regulations as the Congress shall make.

The trial of all Crimes, except in Cases of Impeachment, shall be by Jury; and such Trial shall be held in the State where the said Crimes shall have been committed; but when not committed within any State, the Trial shall be at such Place or Places as the Congress may by Law have directed.

SECTION 3. Treason against the United States, shall consist only in levying War against them, or in adhering to their Enemies, giving them Aid and Comfort. No Person shall be convicted of Treason unless on the Testimony of two Witnesses to the same overt Act, or on Confession in open Court.

The Congress shall have power to declare the Punishment of Treason, but no Attainder of Treason shall work Corruption of Blood, or Forfeiture except during the Life of the Person attainted.

ARTICLE IV

SECTION 1. Full Faith and Credit shall be given in each State to the public Acts, Records, and judicial Proceedings of every other State. And the Congress may by general Laws prescribe the

Manner in which such Acts, Records and Proceedings shall be proved, and the Effect thereof.

SECTION 2. The Citizens of each State shall be entitled to all Privileges and Immunities of Citizens in the several States.

A Person charged in any State with Treason, Felony, or other Crime, who shall flee from Justice, and be found in another State, shall on demand of the executive Authority of the State from which he fled, be delivered up, to be removed to the State having Jurisdiction of the crime.

No Person held to Service or Labour in one State, under the Laws thereof, escaping into another, shall, in Consequence of any Law or Regulation therein, be discharged from such Service or Labour, but shall be delivered up on Claim of the Party to whom such Service or Labour may be due.

SECTION 3. New States may be admitted by the Congress into this Union; but no new State shall be formed or erected within the Jurisdiction of any other State; nor any State be formed by the Junction of two or more States, or parts of States, without the Consent of the Legislatures of the States concerned as well as of the Congress.

The Congress shall have Power to dispose of and make all needful Rules and Regulations respecting the Territory or other Property belonging to the United States; and nothing in this Constitution shall be so construed as to Prejudice any Claims of the United States, or of any particular State.

SECTION 4. The United States shall guarantee to every State in this Union a Republican Form of Government, and shall protect each of them against Invasion; and on Application of the Legislature, or the Executive (when the Legislature cannot be convened) against domestic Violence.

ARTICLE V

The Congress, whenever two thirds of both Houses shall deem it necessary, shall propose Amendments to this Constitution, or, on the Application of the Legislatures of two thirds of the several States, shall call a Convention for proposing Amendments, which, in either Case, shall be valid to all Intents and Purposes, as part of this Constitution, when ratified by the Legislatures of three fourths of the several States, or by Conventions in three fourths thereof, as the one or the other Mode of Ratification may be proposed by the Congress; Provided that no Amendment which may be made prior to the Year One thousand eight hundred and eight shall in any Manner affect the first and fourth Clauses in the Ninth Section of the First Article; and that no State, without its Consent, shall be deprived of its equal Suffrage in the Senate.

ARTICLE VI

All Debts contracted and Engagements entered into, before the Adoption of this Constitution, shall be as valid against the United States under this Constitution, as under the Confederation.

This Constitution, and the Laws of the United States which shall be made in Pursuance thereof; and all Treaties made, or which shall be made, under the Authority of the United States, shall be the supreme Law of the Land; and the Judges in every State shall be bound thereby, any Thing in the Constitution or Laws of any State to the Contrary notwithstanding.

The Senators and Representatives before mentioned, and the Members of the several State Legislatures, and all executive and judicial Officers, both of the United States and of the several States, shall be bound by Oath or Affirmation to support this Constitution; but no religious Test shall ever be required as a qualification to any Office or public Trust under the United States.

ARTICLE VII

The Ratification of the Conventions of nine States shall be sufficient for the Establishment of this Constitution between the States so ratifying the same.

Done in Convention by the Unanimous Consent of the States present the Seventeenth Day of September in the Year of our Lord one thousand seven hundred and Eighty seven, and of the Independence of the United States of America the Twelfth. In Witness whereof We have hereunto subscribed our names.

Articles in Addition to, and Amendment of, the Constitution of the United States of America. Proposed by Congress, and Ratified by the Legislatures of the Several States, Pursuant to the Fifth Article of the Original Constitution.

AMENDMENT I [1791]

Congress shall make no law respecting an establishment of religion, or prohibiting the free exercise thereof; or abridging the freedom of speech, or of the press; or the right of the people peaceably to assemble, and to petition the Government for a redress of grievances.

AMENDMENT II [1791]

A well regulated Militia, being necessary to the security of a free State, the right of the poeple to keep and bear Arms shall not be infringed.

AMENDMENT III [1791]

No Soldier shall, in time of peace, be quartered in any house, without the consent of the Owner, nor in time of war, but in a manner to be prescribed by law.

AMENDMENT IV [1791]

The right of the people to be secure in their persons, houses, papers, and effects, against unreasonable searches and seizures, shall not be violated, and no Warrants shall issue, but upon probable cause, supported by Oath or affirmation, and particularly describing the place to be searched, and the persons or things to be seized.

AMENDMENT V [1791]

No person shall be held to answer for a capital, or otherwise infamous crime, unless on a presentment or indictment of a Grand Jury, except in cases arising in the land or naval forces, or in the Militia, when in actual service in time of war or public danger; nor shall any person be subject for the same offence to be twice put in jeopardy of life or limb; nor shall be compelled in any criminal case to be a witness against himself, nor be deprived of life, liberty, or property, without due process of law; nor shall private property be taken for public use, without just compensation.

AMENDMENT VI [1791]
In all criminal prosecutions, the accused shall enjoy the right to a speedy and public trial, by an impartial jury of the State and district wherein the crime shall have been committed, which district shall have been previously ascertained by law, and to be informed of the nature and cause of the accusation; to be confronted with the witnesses against him; to have compulsory process for obtaining witnesses in his favor, and to have the Assistance of Counsel for his defence.

AMENDMENT VII [1791]
In suits at common law, where the value in controversy shall exceed twenty dollars, the right of trial by jury shall be preserved, and no fact tried by a jury, shall be otherwise reexamined in any Court of the United States, than according to the rules of the common law.

AMENDMENT VIII [1791]
Excessive bail shall not be required, nor excessive fines imposed, nor cruel and unusual punishments inflicted.

AMENDMENT IX [1791]
The enumeration in the Constitution, of certain rights, shall not be construed to deny or disparage others retained by the people.

AMENDMENT X [1791]
The powers not delegated to the United States by the Constitution, nor prohibited by it to the States, are reserved to the States respectively, or to the people.

AMENDMENT XI [1798]
The Judicial power of the United States shall not be construed to extend to any suit in law or equity, commenced or prosecuted

against one of the United States by Citizens of another State, or by Citizens or Subjects of any Foreign State.

AMENDMENT XII [1804]

The Electors shall meet in their respective States, and vote by ballot for President and Vice-President, one of whom, at least, shall not be an inhabitant of the same State with themselves; they shall name in their ballots the person voted for as President, and in distinct ballots the person voted for as Vice-President, and they shall make distinct lists of all persons voted for as President, and of all persons voted for as Vice-President, and of the number of votes for each, which lists they shall sign and certify, and transmit sealed to the seat of the government of the United States, directed to the President of the Senate;—The President of the Senate shall, in the presence of the Senate and House of Representatives, open all the certificates and the votes shall then be counted;— The person having the greatest number of votes for President, shall be the President, if such number be a majority of the whole number of Electors appointed; and if no person have such majority, then from the persons having the highest numbers not exceeding three on the list of those voted for as President, the House of Representatives shall choose immediately, by ballot, the President. But in choosing the President, the votes shall be taken by states, the representation from each state having one vote; a quorum for this purpose shall consist of a member or members from two-thirds of the states, and a majority of all the states shall be necessary to a choice. And if the House of Representatives shall not choose a President whenever the right of choice shall devolve upon them, before the fourth day of March next following, then the Vice-President shall act as President, as in the case of the death or other constitutional disability of the President.—The person having the greatest number of votes as Vice-President, shall be the Vice-President, if such number be a majority of the whole number of Electors appointed, and if no person have a majority, then from the two highest numbers on the list, the Senate shall choose the Vice-President; a quorum for the purpose shall consist of two-thirds of the whole number of Senators, and a majority of the whole number shall be necessary to a choice. But no person constitutionally ineligible to the office of President shall be eligible to that of Vice-President of the United States.

AMENDMENT XIII [1865]

SECTION 1. Neither slavery nor involuntary servitude, except as a punishment for crime whereof the party shall have been duly convicted, shall exist within the United States, or any place subject to their jurisdiction.

SECTION 2. Congress shall have power to enforce this article by appropriate legislation.

AMENDMENT XIV [1868]

SECTION 1. All persons born or naturalized in the United States, and subject to the jurisdiction thereof, are citizens of the United States and of the State wherein they reside. No State shall make or enforce any law which shall abridge the privileges or immunities of citizens of the United States; nor shall any State deprive any person of life, liberty, or property, without due process of law; nor deny to any person within its jurisdiction the equal protection of the laws.

SECTION 2. Representatives shall be apportioned among the several States according to their respective numbers, counting the whole number of persons in each State, excluding Indians not taxed. But when the right to vote at any election for the choice of electors for President and Vice-President of the United States, Representatives in Congress, the Executive and Judicial officers of a State, or the members of the Legislature thereof, is denied to any of the male inhabitants of such State, being twenty-one years of age, and citizens of the United States, or in any way abridged, except for participation in rebellion, or other crime, the basis of representation therein shall be reduced in the proportion which the number of such male citizens shall bear to the whole number of male citizens twenty-one years of age in such State.

SECTION 3. No person shall be a Senator or Representative

in Congress, or elector of President and Vice-President, or hold any office, civil or military, under the United States, or under any State, who, having previously taken an oath, as a member of Congress, or as an officer of the United States, or as a member of any State legislature, or as an executive or judicial officer of any State, to support the Constitution of the United States, shall have engaged in insurrection or rebellion against the same, or given aid or comfort to the enemies thereof. But Congress may by a vote of two-thirds of each House, remove such disability.

SECTION 4. The validity of the public debt of the United States, authorized by law, including debts incurred for payment of pensions and bounties for services in suppressing insurrection or rebellion, shall not be questioned. But neither the United States nor any State shall assume or pay any debt or obligation incurred in aid of insurrection or rebellion against the United States or any claim for the loss or emancipation of any slave; but all such debts, obligations, and claims shall be held illegal and void.

SECTION 5. The Congress shall have power to enforce, by appropriate legislation, the provisions of this article.

AMENDMENT XV [1870]

SECTION 1. The right of citizens of the United States to vote shall not be denied or abridged by the United States or by any State on account of race, color, or previous condition of servitude—

SECTION 2. The Congress shall have power to enforce this article by appropriate legislation.

AMENDMENT XVI [1913]

The Congress shall have power to lay and collect taxes on incomes, from whatever source derived, without apportionment among the several States, and without regard to any census or enumeration.

AMENDMENT XVII [1913]

The Senate of the United States shall be composed of two Senators from each State, elected by the people thereof, for six years;

and each Senator shall have one vote. The electors in each State shall have the qualifications requisite for electors of the most numerous branch of the State legislature.

When vacancies happen in the representation of any State in the Senate, the executive authority of such State shall issue writs of election to fill such vacancies: *Provided,* That the legislature of any State may empower the executive thereof to make temporary appointments until the people fill the vacancies by election as the legislature may direct.

This amendment shall not be so construed as to affect the election or term of any Senator chosen before it becomes valid as part of the Constitution.

AMENDMENT XVIII [1919]

SECTION 1. After one year from the ratification of this article the manufacture, sale, or transportation of intoxicating liquors within, the importation thereof into, or the exportation thereof from the United States and all territory subject to the jurisdiction thereof for beverage purposes is hereby prohibited.

SECTION 2. The Congress and the several States shall have concurrent power to enforce this article by appropriate legislation.

SECTION 3. This article shall be inoperative unless it shall have been ratified as an amendment to the Constitution by the legislatures of the several States, as provided in the Constitution, within seven years from the date of the submission hereof to the States by Congress.

AMENDMENT XIX [1920]

The right of citizens of the United States to vote shall not be denied or abridged by the United States or by any State on account of sex.

Congress shall have power to enforce this article by appropriate legislation.

AMENDMENT XX [1933]

SECTION 1. The terms of the President and Vice-President shall end at noon on the 20th day of January, and the terms of Senators and Representatives at noon on the 3d day of January, of the years in which such terms would have ended if this article had not been ratified; and the terms of their successors shall then begin.

SECTION 2. The Congress shall assemble at least once in every year, and such meeting shall begin at noon on the 3rd day of January, unless they shall by law appoint a different day.

SECTION 3. If, at the time fixed for the beginning of the term of the President, the President elect shall have died, the Vice-President elect shall become President. If a President shall not have been chosen before the time fixed for the beginning of his term, or if the President elect shall have failed to qualify, then the Vice-President-elect shall act as President until a President shall have qualified; and the Congress may by law provide for the case wherein neither a President elect nor a Vice-President elect shall have qualified, declaring who shall then act as President, or the manner in which one who is to act shall be selected, and such person shall act accordingly until a President or Vice-President shall have qualified.

SECTION 4. The Congress may by law provide for the case of the death of any of the persons from whom the House of Representatives may choose a President whenever the right of choice shall have devolved upon them, and for the case of the death of any of the persons from whom the Senate may choose a Vice-President whenever the right of choice shall have devolved upon them.

SECTION 5. Sections 1 and 2 shall take effect on the 15th day of October following the ratification of this article.

SECTION 6. This article shall be inoperative unless it shall have been ratified as an amendment to the Constitution by the legislatures of three-fourths of the several States within seven years from the date of its submission.

AMENDMENT XXI [1933]

SECTION 1. The eighteenth article of amendment to the Constitution of the United States is hereby repealed.

SECTION 2. The transportation or importation into any State,

Territory, or possession of the United States for delivery or use therein of intoxicating liquors, in violation of the laws thereof, is hereby prohibited.

SECTION 3. This article shall be inoperative unless it shall have been ratified as an amendment to the Constitution by conventions in the several States, as provided in the Constitution, within seven years from the date of the submission hereof to the States by the Congress.

AMENDMENT XXII [1951]

SECTION 1. No person shall be elected to the office of the President more than twice, and no person who has held the office of President, or acted as President, for more than twc years of a term to which some other person was elected President shall be elected to the office of the President more than once.

But this Article shall not apply to any person holding the office of President when this Article was proposed by the Congress, and shall not prevent any person who may be holding the office of President, or acting as President, during the term within which this Article becomes operative from holding the office of President or acting as President during the remainder of such term.

SECTION 2. This article shall be inoperative unless it shall have been ratified as an amendment to the Constitution by the legislatures of three-fourths of the several States within seven years from the date of its submission to the States by the Congress.

AMENDMENT XXIII [1961]

SECTION 1. The District constituting the seat of Government of the United States shall appoint in such manner as the Congress may direct:

A number of electors of President and Vice President equal to the whole number of Senators and Representatives in Congress to which the District would be entitled if it were a State, but in no event more than the least populous State; they shall be in addition to those appointed by the States, but they shall be considered, for the purpose of the election of President and Vice President, to be electors appointed by a State; and they shall meet in the District and perform such duties as provided by the twelfth article of amendment.

SECTION 2. The Congress shall have power to enforce this article by appropriate legislation.

AMENDMENT XXIV [1964]

SECTION 1. The right of citizens of the United States to vote in any primary or other election for President or Vice President, for electors for President or Vice President, or for Senator or Representative in Congress, shall not be denied or abridged by the United States or any State by reason of failure to pay any poll tax or other tax.

SECTION 2. The Congress shall have power to enforce this article by appropriate legislation.

AMENDMENT XXV [1967]

SECTION 1. In case of the removal of the President from office or of his death or resignation, the Vice President shall become President.

SECTION 2. Whenever there is a vacancy in the office of the Vice President, the President shall nominate a Vice President who shall take office upon confirmation by a majority vote of both houses of Congress.

SECTION 3. Whenever the President transmits to the President pro tempore of the Senate and the Speaker of the House of Representatives his written declaration that he is unable to discharge the powers and duties of his office, and until he transmits to them a written declaration to the contrary, such powers and duties shall be discharged by the Vice President as Acting President.

SECTION 4. Whenever the Vice President and a majority of either the principal officers of the executive departments, or of such other body as Congress may by law provide, transmit to the President pro tempore of the Senate and the Speaker of the House of Representatives their written declaration that the President is unable to discharge the powers and duties of his office, the Vice

President shall immediately assume the powers and duties of the office as Acting President.

Thereafter, when the President transmits to the President pro tempore of the Senate and the Speaker of the House of Representatives his written declaration that no inability exists, he shall resume the powers and duties of his office unless the Vice President and a majority of either the principal officers of the executive departments, or of such other body as Congress may by law provide, transmit within four days to the President pro tempore of the Senate and the Speaker of the House of Representatives their written declaration that the President is unable to discharge the powers and duties of his office. Thereupon Congress shall decide the issue, assembling within 48 hours for that purpose if not in session. If the Congress, within 21 days after receipt of the latter written declaration, or, if Congress is not in session, within 21 days after Congress is required to assemble, determines by two-thirds vote of both houses that the President is unable to discharge the powers and duties of his office, the Vice President shall continue to discharge the same as Acting President; otherwise, the President shall resume the powers and duties of his office.

AMENDMENT XXVI [1971]

SECTION 1. The right of citizens of the United States, who are eighteen years of age or older, to vote shall not be denied or abridged by the United States or any state on account of age.

SECTION 2. The Congress shall have power to enforce this article by appropriate legislation.

JUSTICES OF THE UNITED STATES SUPREME COURT

Name (Chief Justices in italics)	Term
John Jay	1789–95
John Rutledge	1789–91
William Cushing	1789–1810
James Wilson	1789–98
John Blair	1789–96
Robert H. Harrison	1789–90
James Iredell	1790–99
Thomas Johnson	1791–93
William Paterson	1793–1806
John Rutledge	1795
Samuel Chase	1796–1811
Oliver Ellsworth	1796–1800
Bushrod Washington	1798–1829
Alfred Moore	1799–1804
John Marshall	1801–1835
William Johnson	1804–34

H. Brockholst Livingston	1806–23
Thomas Todd	1807–26
Gabriel Duval	1811–35
Joseph Story	1811–45
Smith Thompson	1823–43
Robert Trimble	1826–28
John McLean	1829–61
Henry Baldwin	1830–44
James M. Wayne	1835–67
Roger B. Taney	1836–64
Philip P. Barbour	1836–41
John Catron	1837–65
John McKinley	1837–52
Peter V. Daniel	1841–60
Samuel Nelson	1845–72
Levi Woodbury	1845–51
Robert C. Grier	1846–70
Benjamin R. Curtis	1851–57
John A. Campbell	1853–61
Nathan Clifford	1858–81
Noah H. Swayne	1862–81
Samuel F. Miller	1862–90
David Davis	1862–77
Stephen J. Field	1863–97
Salmon P. Chase	1864–73
William Strong	1870–80
Joseph P. Bradley	1870–92
Ward Hunt	1872–82
Morrison R. Waite	1874–88
John Marshall Harlan	1877–1911
William B. Woods	1880–87
Stanley Matthews	1881–89
Horace Gray	1881–1902
Samuel Blatchford	1882–93
Lucius Q. C. Lamar	1888–93
Melville W. Fuller	1888–1910

David J. Brewer	1889–1910
Henry B. Brown	1890–1906
George Shiras	1892–1903
Howell E. Jackson	1893–95
Edward D. White	1894–1910
Rufus W. Peckham	1895–1909
Joseph McKenna	1898–1925
Oliver Wendell Holmes	1902–32
William R. Day	1903–22
William H. Moody	1906–10
Horace H. Lurton	1909–14
Charles E. Hughes	1910–16
Edward D. White	1910–21
Willis Van Devanter	1910–37
Joseph R. Lamar	1910–16
Mahlon Pitney	1912–22
James C. McReynolds	1914–41
Louis D. Brandeis	1916–39
John H. Clarke	1916–22
William H. Taft	1921–30
George Sutherland	1922–38
Pierce Butler	1922–39
Edward T. Sanford	1923–30
Harlan F. Stone	1925–41
Charles E. Hughes	1930–41
Owen J. Roberts	1930–45
Benjamin N. Cardozo	1932–38
Hugo L. Black	1937–71
Stanley F. Reed	1938–57
Felix Frankfurter	1939–62
William O. Douglas	1939–75
Frank Murphy	1940–49
James F. Byrnes	1941–42
Harlan F. Stone	1941–46
Robert H. Jackson	1941–54
Wiley B. Rutledge	1943–49

Harold H. Burton	1945–58
Fred M. Vinson	1946–53
Tom C. Clark	1949–67
Sherman Minton	1949–56
Earl Warren	1953–69
John Marshall Harlan	1955–71
William J. Brennan, Jr.	1956–
Charles E. Whittaker	1957–62
Potter Stewart	1958–81
Arthur J. Goldberg	1962–65
Byron R. White	1962–
Abe Fortas	1965–69
Thurgood Marshall	1967–
Warren E. Burger	1969–
Harry A. Blackmun	1970–
Lewis F. Powell, Jr.	1972–
William H. Rehnquist	1972–
John Paul Stevens	1975–
Sandra Day O'Connor	1981–

GLOSSARY OF TERMS

amendment, constitutional. Changes in, or additions to, a written constitution. In the United States Constitution, amendments are proposed by a two-thirds majority of both houses of Congress *or* by a convention called by Congress at the request of two-thirds of the state legislatures. Amendments become part of the Constitution if and when they are approved by the legislatures or special conventions of three-fourths of the states.

appellate jurisdiction. The authority of a court to review the decisions of a lower court. See also *jurisdiction* and *original jurisdiction*.

bill of attainder. A law declaring a person guilty of a crime without trial. Forbidden in the United States by Article I, Sections 9 and 10 of the Constitution.

blockade. The use of armed forces, usually naval, to prevent trade with an enemy in wartime. To be recognized under international law, blockades must be proclaimed and enforced according to strict rules.

common law. In England, law based upon custom and tradition as expressed in court decisions, rather than upon acts of Parliament. Portions of English common law have become parts of the law of American states.

concurrent powers. Authority shared by both the state governments and the national government—for example, the power to tax and to maintain courts.

contract. An agreement between two or more persons or parties to do or not do something. To be binding in law, contracts normally must involve a "consideration," or something of value, given and received by all parties to the agreement.

corporation. An artificial being, created by law and having legal existence as a person, independent of the actual person or persons who compose it.

de facto. Existing in fact or in reality, irrespective of whether recognized as existing in law. See also *de Jure.*

de jure. Authorized by law and recognized as legitimate under the law.

due process of law. Procedural rights and other legal rights protecting citizens from arbitrary actions by government. The Fifth and Fourteenth amendments forbid the national and state governments from depriving any person of life, liberty, or property without due process of law.

eminent domain. The power of government to take private property for public use. Under the Constitution, the power must be exercised with due process of law and a just compensation must be paid to the person from whom property is taken.

equity. Court proceedings in cases in which neither common law nor statute law applies, or if applied would lead to injustice. Originally in England, and in some American states, equity cases were heard in special courts. Federal courts have jurisdiction both in equity and in law.

ex parte. Literally, of one side only. Used to refer to proceedings, such as the granting of injunctions or commissions, on behalf of one party without the participation of others.

ex post facto law. A law that makes criminal an action that was legal when it was committed, or that increases the penalty after the action was committed. Prevented by Article I, Sections 9 and 10 of the Constitution.

fiscal policy. Financial policy of a government, particularly in regard to the management of its debts and the money supply.

holding company. A corporation that derives all or part of its revenues from the ownership of other corporations.

impeachment. A formal accusation against a public official, voted by the lower house of a legislature. The impeachment is tried in the upper house of a legislature. Upon conviction, the official may be removed from office.

injunction. A court order forbidding some anticipated action.

interposition. The doctrine that state governments can place their authority between the federal goverment and the state's citizens, thus preventing the enforcement of an unconstitutional act of Congress.

jurisdiction. The authority of a court to hear and rule upon certain kinds of cases.

nullification. The doctrine that state governments have the right to declare acts of the federal government unconstitutional and to prevent their enforcement within the state.

obiter dicta. Any parts of the opinion of a court that are not necessary to the decision and are thus not to be regarded as binding precedent for future decisions.

ordinance. An order or regulation issued by an assembly not having full constitutional status as a legislative body. The Congress under the Articles of Confederation passed ordinances, not laws; city councils, whose authority is derived from state legislatures, also pass ordinances.

original jurisdiction. The authority of a court to hear a case at its beginning. Generally, courts of original jurisdiction are trial courts, and courts of appellate jurisdiction hear cases on appeal from trial courts.

police power. The power of government to regulate the health, safety, welfare, and morals of its citizens. Under the Constitution, the police power was originally held to be reserved exclusively to the states; but in the twentieth century the courts have permitted the development of federal police power.

poll tax. A direct tax on individuals as individuals. In early America poll taxes were commonly used as a source of revenue, every adult male being required to pay a designated sum. In the twentieth century poll taxes were required, in some states, of anyone who wanted to vote. The Twenty-fourth Amendment prevented the requirement of paying a poll tax for voting in federal elections.

sovereignty. The supreme law-making power. In the United States, sovereignty is divided or dual, at least in theory: The federal government is sovereign within the area of its constitutionally authorized functions, and the states are sovereign within their spheres. In case of conflict, federal law prevails.

stare decisis. Literally, "let the decision stand." The practice of basing judicial decisions upon similar cases decided in the past.

statute. A law enacted by a legislature.

subpoena. An order compelling the appearance and testimony of a witness.

substantive due process. The doctrine that "due process of law," under the meaning of the Fifth and Fourteenth amendments, includes tangible rights (such as owning property) as well as procedural rights (such as trial by jury).

tariff. A tax on goods imported from foreign countries. Under the Constitution, Congress may levy tariffs but states may not. Congress may not levy taxes on exports.

veto. The power of the chief executive to kill a piece of legislation by refusing to sign it. Congress can enact laws despite a presidential veto with two-thirds majorities in both houses.

warrant. A document issued by a court that gives someone authority to do something.

writ of habeas corpus. An order directing an official to deliver a prisoner to a court with an explanation of the reasons for the prisoner's detention. If the court finds the reasons inadequate, it may order the prisoner's release.

writ of mandamus. A court order commanding a public official to perform a duty associated with his office.

TABLE
OF
CASES

	Page
Ableman v. Booth (1859)	117–18
Abrams v. U.S. (1919)	190–91
Addystone Pipe and Steel Co. v. U.S. (1899)	165
Adkins v. Children's Hospital (1923)	184, 204
American Communications Association v. Douds (1950)	212–13
Ashton v. Cameron County Water District (1936)	197
Ashwander v. Tennessee Valley Authority (1936)	197, 204
Bailey v. Drexel Furniture Co. (1922)	184
Baker v. Carr (1962)	249–50
Bank of Augusta v. Earle (1839)	86
Barron v. Baltimore (1833)	37n, 68
Bartels v. Iowa (1923)	192
Bartemeyer v. Iowa (1874)	144
Berea College v. Kentucky (1908)	154
Board of Education v. Newbury Area Council (1975)	243

Board of School Commissioners of Indianapolis   243
  v. Buckley (1977)

Bolling v. Sharpe (1954)   220–24

Boyd v. Alabama (1877)   157

Bradwell v. Illinois (1873)   143–44

Briscoe v. Bank of Kentucky (1837)   83–84

Brooks v. U.S. (1925)   184

Brown v. Board of Education of Topeka (1954)   220–24,
    230–31,
    241–42

Brown v. Maryland (1827)   82

Carter v. Carter Coal Co. (1936)   196–97, 204

Champion v. Ames (1903)   169, 184

Champion and Dickason v. Casey (1792)   49

Charles River Bridge v. Warren Bridge (1837)   84–86, 88

Cherokee Nation v. Georgia (1831)   105

Chicago, Milwaukee & St. Paul R.R. Co. v. Min-   159
  nesota (1890)

Chisholm v. Georgia (1793)   49–50

Civil Rights Cases (1883)   151

Cohens v. Virginia (1821)   101–2

Colegrove v. Green (1946)   250

Collector v. Day (1871)   160

Consolidated Edison Corp. v. National Labor Re-   203–4
  lations Board (1938)

Cooley v. Board of Wardens of the Port of Phila-   89
  delphia (1851)

Corn Tassel Case (1830)   104–5

Craig v. Missouri (1830)   84

Cumming v. County Board of Education (1899)   154

Cummings v. Missouri (1867)   138

Dartmouth College v. Woodward (1819)   77–78, 84

Davis v. County School Board of Prince Edward   220–24
  County, Va. (1954)

In re Debs (1895)   165, 169

Dennis v. U.S. (1951)   213, 217

Downes v. Bidwell (1901)   185

Dr. Bonham's Case (1606)   14
Dred Scott v. Sandford (1857)   115–17,
                                                        122, 123,
                                                        142
Duplex Printing Press Co. v. Deering (1921)   184
Employers' Liability Cases, First (1908)   182
Employers' Liability Cases, Second (1912)   182
Ex parte Endo (1944)   212
Engel v. Vitale (1962)   247
Erie v. Tompkins (1938)   53n
Escobedo v. Illinois (1964)   247
Evans v. Buchanan (1975)   243
Fahey v. Malonee (1946)   179
Fairfax's Devisee v. Hunter's Lessee (1813)   100
Federal Power Commission v. Hope Natural Gas   203
    Co. (1944)
Fletcher v. Peck (1810)   75–77, 157
Fullilove v. Klutznick (1980)   246
Ex parte Garland (1867)   138
Georgia v. Stanton (1867)   139
Gibbons v. Ogden (1824)   80–82, 163
Gitlow v. New York (1925)   191–92
Gomillion v. Lightfoot (1960)   249
Granger Cases (1877)   158–59
Green v. Biddle (1823)   77, 102
Green v. County School Board of New Kent   242
    County, Va. (1968)
Grovey v. Townshend (1935)   219
Hammer v. Dagenhart (1918)   184
Hampton v. U.S. (1928)   179
Hayburn's Case (1792)   49
Helvering v. Davis (1937)   199
Henderson v. U.S. (1950)   220
Hipolite Egg Co. v. U.S. (1911)   184
Hirabayashi v. U.S. (1943)   212
Hoke v. U.S. (1913)   184
Holden v. Hardy (1898)   180

Home Building and Loan Association v. Blaisdell (1934) — 194

Humphrey's Executor v. U.S. (1935) — 196

Hylton v. U.S. (1796) — 51

Illinois Central R.R. Co. v. Illinois (1892) — 157–58

Interstate Commerce Commission v. Alabama Midland R.R. Co. (1897) — 161

Interstate Commerce Commission v. Cincinnati, New Orleans, & Texas Pacific R.R. Co. (1897) — 161

Interstate Commerce Commission v. Illinois R.R. Co. (1910) — 178–79

Kaiser Aluminum and United Steelworkers v. Weber (1979) — 245–46

Keyes v. School District No. 1 of Denver (1973) — 243

Kinsella v. Krueger (1957) — 226

Korematsu v. U.S. (1944) — 212

Legal Tender Cases (1870, 1871) — 160–61

License Cases (1847) — 88–89

Loan Office Association v. Topeka (1874) — 156

Lochner v. New York (1905) — 180–81

Loewe v. Lawler (1908) — 169

Louisville Bank v. Radford (1935) — 196

Luther v. Borden (1849) — 110

Marbury v. Madison (1803) — 57–58, 60–61, 139

Martin v. Hunter's Lessee (1816) — 101

Ex parte McCardle (1869) — 140–41

McCray v. U.S. (1904) — 169

M'Culloch v. Maryland (1819) — 73–74, 76, 102

McGrain v. Daugherty (1927) — 215

McLaurin v. Oklahoma State Regents (1950) — 219–20

Ex parte Merryman (1861) — 126–27

Meyer v. Nebraska (1923) — 192

Ex parte Milligan (1866) — 136–37

Milliken v. Bradley (1974) — 243

Minor v. Happersett (1875) — 144
Miranda v. Arizona (1966) — 247
Mississippi v. Johnson (1867) — 139
Missouri ex rel Gaines v. Canada (1938) — 218
Missouri v. Holland (1920) — 186, 224–25
Morehead v. New York (1936) — 197
Muller v. Oregon (1908) — 181, 185
Munn v. Illinois (1877) — 158
National Labor Relations Board v. Jones and Laughlin Steel Corp. (1937) — 199
Neal v. Delaware (1881) — 150
Near v. Minnesota (1931) — 192–93
Nebbia v. New York (1934) — 194
New Jersey v. Wilson (1812) — 156
New York v. Miln (1837) — 83
Norman v. the Baltimore & Ohio R.R. Co. (1935) — 195
Northern Pacific R.R. Co. v. North Dakota (1919) — 190
Northern Securities Case (1904) — 167–68
Nortz v. U.S. (1935) — 195, 204
Ogden v. Saunders (1827) — 80
Olcott v. Supervisors of Fond du Lac County (Wisc.) (1873) — 155
Osborn v. U.S. (1824) — 102–3
Palko v. Connecticut (1937) — 210–11
Panama Refining Co. v. Ryan (1935) — 195
Passenger Cases (1849) — 88
Pennsylvania v. Nelson (1956) — 217
Perry v. U.S. (1935) — 195
Piek v. Chicago and Northwestern R.R. Co. (1877) — 159
Pierce v. Society of Sisters (1925) — 192
Pine Grove Township (Mich.) v. Talcott (1874) — 155
Plessy v. Ferguson (1896) — 153–54, 220–21
Pollock v. Farmers' Loan and Trust Co. (1895) — 161
Prigg v. Pennsylvania (1842) — 113, 151
Prize Cases (1863) — 127

Propeller Genessee Chief v. Fitzhugh 88
(1851)

Providence Bank v. Billings (1830) 79, 85

Pumpelly v. Green Bay and Mississippi Canal Co. 157
(1872)

Quock Walker v. Nathaniel Jennison (1783) 22

Reagan v. Farmer's Loan and Trust Co. (Texas) 159
(1894)

Regents of the University of California v. Bakke 244–45
(1978)

Reid v. Covert (1957) 226

Retirement Board v. Alton R.R. Co. (1935) 196

Reynolds v. Sims (1964) 250

Rice v. Elmore (1947) 219

Roberts v. City of Boston (1849) 153

Roe v. Wade (1973) 247

Rutgers v. Waddington (1784) 48

Santa Clara County v. Southern Pacific R.R. Co. 159
(1886)

Schechter Poultry Corp. v. U.S. (1935) 196

Schenck v. U.S. (1919) 190

Selective Draft Law Cases (1918) 189–90

Ex parte Siebold (1880) 151

Sinclair v. U.S. (1929) 215, 217

Sipuel v. Oklahoma (1948) 219

Slaughterhouse Cases (1870) 142, 151,
191–92

Slochower v. Board of Education (1956) 217

Smith v. Allright (1944) 219

Smyth v. Ames (1898) 159–60,
180, 203

Springer v. U.S. (1881) 160–61

Standard Oil Co. v. U.S. (1911) 182

Stone v. Mississippi (1880) 157

Strader v. Graham (1850) 114, 115,
116

Strauder v. West Virginia (1880)   150
Stromberg v. California (1931)   192
Stuart v. Laird (1803)   56–57
Sturges v. Crowninshield (1819)   79, 81
Swann v. Charlotte-Mecklenburg Board of Edu-   242–43
    cation (1971)
Sweatt v. Painter (1950)   219–20
Swift v. Tyson (1842)   53n, 87
Swift & Co. v. U.S. (1905)   168
Test Oath Cases (1867)   138
Texas v. White (1869)   141
Trevett v. Weeden (1786)   48
U.S. v. American Tobacco Co. (1911)   182
U.S. v. Belmont (1937)   225
U.S. v. Butler (1936)   196
U.S. v. Cruikshank (1876)   144, 151
U.S. v. Curtiss-Wright Export Corp. (1936)   186, 224–25
U.S. v. E. C. Knight Co. (1895)   163, 165,
                                                        168
U. S. v. Grimaud (1911)   179
U.S. v. Hudson and Goodwin (1813)   53n
U.S. v. Jefferson County Board of Education   242
    (1966)
U.S. v. L. Cohen Grocery Co. (1921)   190
U.S. v. Lovett (1946)   205
U.S. v. Nixon (1974)   240–41
U.S. v. Pink (1942)   225
U.S. v. Reese (1876)   144
U.S. v. Trans-Missouri Freight Association (1897)   165
U.S. v. Worrall (1798)   52
Ex parte Vallandigham (1864)   128, 137
Veazie Bank v. Fenno (1869)   160
Virginia v. Rives (1880)   150–51
Wabash, St. Louis, and Pacific R.R. Co. v. Illinois   159, 161
    (1886)
Ware v. Hylton (1796)   51

Watkins v. U.S. (1957)   217
Wesberry v. Sanders (1964)   250
West Coast Hotel Co. v. Parrish (1937)   198
Whitney v. California (1927)   192
Wickard v. Filburn (1942)   204
Willson v. Black Bird Creek Marsh Co. (1829)   82
Worcester v. Georgia (1832)   105–6
Writs of Assistance Case (1761)   12–13
Ex parte Yarbrough (1884)   151
Yates v. U.S. (1957)   217
Ex parte Yerger (1869)   141
Youngstown Sheet and Tube Co. v. Sawyer   205
    (1952)

INDEX

Abolitionism, 22, 24, 112–13, 117, 122–23, 130
Adams, John, 15, 45, 47, 55–56
Adams, John Quincy, 71, 103, 112, 113
Adams, Samuel, 24
Adamson Eight-Hour Act, 184
Addison, William, 59
Affirmative action, 243–46
Agricultural Adjustment Acts, 194 196, 204
Alabama, 86, 108–09
Alien Acts, 54, 96–97
Altgeld, John P., 164
Amendments, constitutional, 19, 35, 36–37, 50, 122, 176–77.
    See also amendment number
American Bar Association, 225

American Federation of Labor, 183
Annapolis Convention, 25
Anti-federalists, 36–37, 45–46, 72
Antitrust suits, 162–69, 182, 183–84, 207
Appointment power, 28, 40
Arkansas, 131, 231
Articles of Confederation, 18–19, 25, 26
Attainder, bills of, 24, 138, 193, 205

Bank of the United States, 41–44, 72–74, 84, 102
Bankruptcy, 79–80
Banks and banking, 79, 84, 85, 160, 178

Baruch, Bernard, 187
Bill of Rights, 36–38, 52–53, 68, 211
Black, Hugo, 202, 211
Blacks, 131, 133, 142–45, 150–55, 191, 218–24, 231–33, 241–46
Blackstone, Sir William, 14–15, 27, 30
Blockades, 125–27
Bolingbroke, Henry St. John, 15
Bradley, Joseph, 143
Brandeis, Louis, 181, 191, 194, 202
Brewer, David, 165, 167
Bricker, John, 225
Bricker Amendment, 224–26
Brown, Henry B., 153
Bureaucracy, 178–79, 194, 199, 206–10, 236, 237–40, 248
Bureau of Forestry, 178
Burger, Warren, 246
Burnside, Ambrose, 128
Burr, Aaron, 47, 60, 98
Business, regulation. *See* Economy, regulation of
Butler, Elizur, 105–06
Butler, Pierce, 194, 202

Calhoun, John C., 106–07
California, 114, 192
Calvert, Charles, 11
Campbell, John A., 126
Cardozo, Benjamin, 194–95
Carter, James E., 237, 239, 241
Cass, Lewis, 109
Central Intelligence Agency, 241
Chase, Salmon P., 127, 139, 141
Chase, Samuel, 52, 59–60

Checks and balances, 32–33, 175, 246–52
Cherokee Indians, 103–05
Chicago Tribune, 193
Children, 20, 184, 224, 243
Citizenship, 116, 117, 133, 134, 142–43, 159
Civil rights, 53–55, 144–45, 188–93, 210–17. *See also* Due process, Equal protection
Civil Rights Acts, 133, 150–51, 233, 241, 244–45
Civil Rights Commission, 231
Civil service, 177–78. *See also* Bureaucracy
Civil War, 127–131
Clay, Henry, 108
Clayton Antitrust Act, 183
Clean Air Act, 234
Clear and present danger doctrine, 190–91, 213
Cleveland, Grover, 164
Clinton, George, 72
Coke, Sir Edward, 14
Commerce clause, 71, 74–83, 197–99
Commerce, international, 23, 80–83, 88, 169–70, 199
Commerce, interstate, 53n., 80–83, 123, 159–60, 163–64, 168–69, 196, 199, 204
Committee on Public Information, 189
Common law, 14, 52–54, 162
Communism, 190–92, 205, 212–16
Communist Control Act, 216
Compact Theory, 10–17, 97, 123–25

Compromise of 1850, 114
Concurrent powers, 87–89,
   93–94
Confederate States of America,
   122–31, 133
Confederation Congress, 22–25,
   40, 69
Confiscation Acts, 129–30
Congress of Racial Equality, 232
Congress, U.S., 27–28, 33,
   70–71, 111, 113, 126–27,
   131–36, 161, 198–99, 217,
   235–36, 249
Conkling, Roscoe, 159
Connecticut, 11, 19, 37, 48,
   98–99
Conscription, 129, 186, 189–90
Conservation, 178–179
Constitutional Convention, 25–31
Continental Congress, 16, 18–19
Contracts and the contract
   clause, 24, 49, 66–67, 74–80,
   155–57, 184, 198
Coolidge, Calvin, 177
Corporations, 43–44, 78–79,
   148, 156, 162, 165–66, 183,
   237
Court-packing plan, 197–98
Crane, Philip, 252
Creek Indians, 103, 108–09
Creel, George, 189
Currency, 41–42, 160–61, 195,
   204–05
Curtis, Benjamin, 115, 117

Davie, William R., 48
Davis, David, 137
Davis, John W., 221–22
Debs, Eugene V., 164–65

Debts, private, 24, 49, 50–51,
   79–80
Debts, public, 23–24, 41–42,
   71–73, 134
Declaration of Independence, 10,
   17–18
Declaratory Act, 13
Delaware, 11, 25, 165
Delegation of powers, 179, 196
Democracy, 20, 24, 175–77, 185,
   199
Democratic party, 219
Department of Commerce and
   Labor, 178
Department of Health, Education,
   and Welfare, 244, 248–49
Desegregation. See Racial
   segregation
Dickinson, John, 13–14, 25
Dirksen, Everett, 251
District of Columbia, 114, 154, 221
Divided sovereignty. See
   Federalism
Dorr, Thomas W., 110
Douglas, William O., 202
Draft. See Conscription
Due process of law, 37, 68, 134,
   143, 155, 158–59, 181, 184,
   191–92, 198, 204, 247

Economy, regulation of, 66–69,
   81, 88–90, 155–71, 179–85,
   186–89, 193–99, 207–10,
   237–39
Education, 154, 218–23, 241–43,
   248–49
Eighteenth Amendment, 176
Eisenhower, Dwight David, 209,
   214, 216, 226, 231, 239

Electoral college, 28–29, 47
Eleventh Amendment, 50, 103
Elkins Act, 170
Ellsworth, Oliver, 38–39, 48, 50, 53
Emancipation Proclamation, 130
Embargo Act, 97–99
Eminent domain, 68, 155–57
Endangered Species Act, 235
English law, 11–13, 32, 38, 48, 52, 75, 88, 162
Environmental Protection Agency, 238
Equal protection clause, 143, 159, 218–23
Espionage Act (1917), 188, 190
Evans, M. Stanton, 238
Excise taxes, 51, 94–95
Executive departments, 39–40, 45, 178
Executive power, 11–16, 18–20, 27–29, 32, 33, 42, 127–28, 135–36, 139, 166, 177, 179, 185, 186, 201–05, 224–26, 237–41
Executive privilege, 46–47, 60, 240–41
Ex post facto laws, 138

Faubus, Orval, 231
Federal Farm Bankruptcy Act, 196
Federalism, 32–33, 60, 65, 93–94, 141, 149, 248. *See also* Federal-state relations
Federalist, The, 31–32, 36, 40, 48, 50, 94
Federalists, 31, 47, 50, 53–54, 56, 74, 97–98

Federal Power Commission, 206, 239
Federal Reserve Board, 183
Federal-state relations, 68, 69, 73, 93–118, 138–41, 201, 248
Federal Tariff Commission, 178
Federal Trade Commission, 178, 183, 196, 206
Field, Stephen J., 138, 143, 157
Fifteenth Amendment, 136, 142, 144, 151, 219, 249
Fifth Amendment, 66, 68, 116, 198, 206, 215
First Amendment, 37, 53, 112, 190–92, 212–13, 215, 247
Florida, 22, 136
Food and Drug Administration, 206, 238
Force Act (1870), 136
Force Bill, 108
Ford, Gerald, 240
Foreign relations, 185–86, 224–26. *See also* Treaties
Fourteenth Amendment, 37n., 134, 142–44, 150, 153, 158, 191–92, 198, 210–11, 218–19, 221–22, 245–47
France, 22, 44–45, 46, 52–53, 98, 129
Frankfurter, Felix, 202, 250
Franklin, Benjamin, 28
Freedmen's Bureau, 132–34, 150
Freedom of speech, 37, 52–53, 190–93, 212–13. *See also* First Amendment
Fugitive Slave Acts, 95, 112–13, 117–18
Fuller, Melville, 163
Fulton, Robert, 80

Gag rule, 112
Gallatin, Albert, 70–71, 72
Garfield, Harry, 187–88
General welfare clause, 43, 70,
    165, 197
Genet, Edmund, 44
Georgia, 20, 24, 50, 75–76, 86,
    103–07, 133, 136, 138
German-Americans, 189
Gompers, Samuel, 183
Grant, Ulysses S., 130, 135, 136,
    139
Great Britain, 9, 12, 16, 22–23,
    40, 46, 51, 98, 129
Great Society, 234–35
Grier, Robert, 127, 140

Habeas corpus, writ of, 126, 127,
    137, 141
Hamilton, Alexander, 25, 32,
    40–46, 48, 50, 55, 70, 72–73,
    76, 94
Hamilton, James, 107
Hand, Learned, 213
Harding, Warren G., 177
Harlan, John M., 167, 185, 217
Hartford Convention, 99–100
Hayne, Robert Y., 108
Helms, Jesse, 252
Henry, Patrick, 13, 48, 75
Hepburn Act, 170–71
Holding companies, 165–66
Holmes, Oliver Wendell, 168,
    180–81, 190
Hoover, Herbert, 177, 187–88
House of Representatives,
    United States, 27–28, 32,
    37, 41, 46–47, 130,
    249–51

House Un-American Activities
    Committee, 205, 215–17
Hughes, Charles Evans, 185,
    192, 195
Humphrey, Hubert, 216
Hutchinson, Thomas, 13, 15

Illinois, 122
Immigrants and immigration,
    82, 83, 88, 147–48, 188–89,
    191
Impeachment, 29, 40, 47, 56,
    59–60, 135, 139
Implied powers, 43–44, 74
Indiana, 112, 122
Indian Removal Act, 104
Indians, 22, 44, 103–06
Inherent powers, 225
Integration. See Racial segregation
Interior Department, 178
Internal improvements, 69–72,
    123
Interposition, doctrine of, 96,
    98–99, 100
Interstate Commerce
    Commission, 161, 170–71,
    188, 206, 237

Jackson, Andrew, 71, 73–74, 83,
    103–09, 239
Jackson, Robert H., 212
Jackson State College, 233
Japanese-Americans, 211–12,
    222
Jay, John, 32, 46, 50
Jay's Treaty, 46–47, 101
Jefferson, Thomas, 16, 18, 24,
    43–47, 55, 57, 59, 60, 96–98,
    203, 240

Johnson, Andrew, 132–35, 137, 138, 140
Johnson, Lyndon B., 225, 234, 239
Johnson, William, 98
Judicial activism, 149, 203, 223, 241–48
Judicial power, 27, 29–30, 37, 39, 44, 103, 149, 185, 202, 246–47, 250
Judicial restraint, 44, 76–77, 102–03, 109–10, 202–03, 223
Judicial review, 14, 48–53, 56–58, 60, 65, 101–02, 128–29, 141
Judiciary, 38–39, 55, 59–60, 197
Judiciary Act of 1789, 39, 57, 58, 87, 100–01, 141
Judiciary Act of 1801, 55–56, 58
Judiciary Act of 1802, 56–57
Judiciary Act of 1867, 140–41
Juries, 36, 150–51
Jurisdiction, 29–30, 39, 50, 56, 58, 88, 103, 105, 117, 140–41, 204, 251, 252

Kansas-Nebraska Act, 114
Kendall, Amos, 112
Kennedy, John F., 216, 232, 239
Kennedy, Robert, 232
Kent, James, 80, 86
Kent State University, 233
Kentucky, 56, 77, 96–97
Kentucky Resolutions, 96–97
King, Martin Luther, 231, 232
Knox, Henry, 44
Knox, Philander, 167
Korean War, 205, 208, 213

Ku Klux Klan Act, 151–52

Labor, 164–65, 168–69, 178, 180–82, 194, 198–99, 203–04, 212
Law enforcement, 52–55, 94–96, 104–06, 164–65, 241–43, 247
Lee, Robert E., 130
Legislative power, 11–12, 19–20, 27–28, 32–33, 134, 140, 179, 215, 217, 223
Legislative reapportionment, 249–51
Lever Act, 187, 190
Lincoln, Abraham, 122–31, 132, 137, 203, 239
Livingston, Edward, 46
Livingston, Robert, 80
Locke, John, 16–17
Loose construction, 43–44, 195
Louisiana, 131, 136
Louisiana Purchase, 55, 72, 97, 111
Loyalists, 21, 24
Loyalty oaths, 212, 214–16
Lynchings, 151, 191

Madison, James, 25, 32, 36–37, 40, 42, 46, 57, 71–72, 74, 94, 96, 99
Maine, 111
Mann-Elkins Act, 184
Marshall, John, 48, 56–60, 73–74, 74–83, 84–85, 100–03
Marshall, Thurgood, 220, 222
Maryland, 11, 20, 24–25, 73
Mason, George, 21

Massachusetts, 11, 12, 15, 19, 21–22, 24–26, 37, 88, 98–99, 113, 153
Mayflower Compact, 10–11
McCarran Internal Security Act, 213–14, 216
McCarthy, Joseph, 214–16
McKinley, John, 86
McLane, Louis, 73, 89
McLean, John, 115, 117
McReynolds, James, 194, 195, 197
Meat Inspection Act, 169–70
Mexican War, 113
Mifflin, Thomas, 95–96
Military Appropriations Act, 135
Militia Act of 1792, 94, 96
Miller, Samuel F., 142
Minimum wages, 181, 194, 197
Mississippi, 22, 138, 152
Missouri Compromise, 111, 116
Mixed government, theory of, 9–12, 15, 20, 32, 175
Monarchy, 11, 19
Monopolies, 37, 78–81, 85–86, 162–63, 179–80
Monroe, James, 58, 71
Montesquieu, 15
Morgan, J.P., 167
Morris, Gouverneur, 93
Motor Vehicle Air Pollution Control Act, 234
Murphy, Frank, 202, 212

Nader, Ralph, 234
National Association for the Advancement of Colored People, 218, 220–21
National Housing Act, 207

National Industrial Recovery Administration, 194, 195–96
National Labor Relations Board, 198–99, 203–04, 206
National Traffic and Motor Vehicle Safety Act, 234
Natural law, 12
Natural rights, 10, 16, 17, 66
Negroes. *See* Blacks
New Deal, 193–99, 202–09
New England, 20, 24, 97–99, 103
New Hampshire, 26, 31, 77–78, 88
New Jersey, 122, 165
New York, 19–21, 24, 25, 31, 49, 78, 79, 88, 98, 122, 129, 180–81, 191, 197
Nineteenth Amendment, 176
Nixon, Richard, 225, 239–41, 251
North Carolina, 24, 31, 48, 94, 132, 136, 248–49
Northwest Ordinance, 23, 110, 114
Nullification, 96–97, 106–09, 118

Ohio, 23, 114, 122, 128
Olney, Richard, 164
One person, one vote doctrine, 250–51
Otis, James, 12–13

Paine, Thomas, 16
Palmer, A. Mitchell, 191
Parliament, Great Britain, 12–13, 14–16
Paterson, William, 26
Penn, William, 11
Pennsylvania, 11, 20–21, 24–26, 31, 49, 74, 89, 94–96

Physical Valuations Act, 184
Pickering, John, 59
Pickering, Timothy, 97–98
Pinckney, Charles, 48
Plymouth Colony, 11
Police power, 82, 155, 157, 169,
   180, 181, 203
Political parties, 45–46, 177,
   219
Political questions, court policy
   toward, 76–77, 109–10,
   249–51
Positive law, 14–15, 48
Powell, Lewis, 245
Privileges and immunities clause,
   86, 142–44
Property, confiscation of, 24, 68,
   100–01, 130
Property rights, 15, 66–69,
   78–79, 89–90, 103–04, 116,
   123, 140, 143. *See also*
   Contracts, due process
Protective tariffs, 69–70, 106–08,
   111, 160
Public lands, 23–24, 71–72,
   75
Public utilities, 158–60, 170–71,
   178, 179–80, 203
Pullman strike, 164–65
Pure Food and Drug
   Administration, 169

Quincy, Josiah, 97

Racial segregation, 150–51,
   153–55, 218–24, 230–33,
   241–43
Railroad Control Act, 184
Railroad Retirement Act, 196

Railroads, 66, 71–72, 155–59,
   161, 167–68, 170–71, 182,
   184, 187, 190, 238
Randolph, Edmund, 26, 43, 49
Randolph, John, 59–60
Reagan, Ronald, 252
Reconstruction, 131–45
Reconstruction Acts, 138–139,
   140–41
Reconstruction Finance
   Corporation, 208
Reed, Stanley, 202
Regulation. *See* Commerce
   clause; Economy, regulation
   of
Religion, 17, 24, 36–37, 247,
   252
Republicanism, 19–20, 30, 110,
   175
Republican party, 46–47, 50,
   52–57, 72, 96–97, 124,
   131–36
Reston, James, 251–52
Reverse discrimination, 243–46
Rhode Island, 11, 19, 23, 26, 31,
   49, 88, 99, 109
Roane, Spencer, 100–02
Roberts, Owen J., 195, 198, 212
Rodney, Caesar, 98
Roosevelt, Franklin, 177, 193,
   197–98, 202, 207, 211, 225
Roosevelt, Theodore, 166–68,
   170, 177, 239
Rule of reason, 167–68
Rural Electrification
   Administration, 207
Rutledge, John, 50

Scott, Winfield, 107, 109

Secession, 97–98, 99–100,
    107–08, 122–25, 127, 141
Sectionalism, 111–18
Securities and Exchange
    Commission, 206
Sedition Act (1798), 53–55,
    96–97
Sedition Act (1918), 188, 190
Segregation. *See* Racial
    segregation
Senate, U.S., 27–28, 32, 37,
    44–45, 50, 130, 176, 240,
    249–51
Separate but equal doctrine,
    153–54, 218–23
Separation of powers, 15–16,
    32–33, 133–35, 240–41,
    246–52
Sergeant, John, 104–05
Seventeenth Amendment, 176
Seward, William H., 130
Shays' Rebellion, 25–26
Sherman Antitrust Act, 162,
    164–65, 166, 167, 182–83
Sinclair, Upton, 170
Sixteenth Amendment, 161, 176
Slavery, 17, 20, 24, 32, 70, 95,
    110–18, 122–25, 129–30,
    132, 222
Small Business Administration,
    207
Smith Act, 213
Smith, William Loughton, 40
Social Security Act, 199
Social welfare legislation, 157,
    180–81, 184, 237–38
South, the, 20, 70, 97, 99, 106,
    111, 123, 129, 131–33, 219,
    231

South Carolina, 24, 48, 106–09,
    112, 124–25, 133, 136, 219
Southern Christian Leadership
    Conference, 232
Sovereignty, 19, 28, 30, 43–44,
    50, 93, 110, 114, 175
Spanish-American War, 185–86
Stamp Act Congress, 13
Stanbery, Henry, 138–39
Standard Oil Company, 162–63,
    182
Stanton, Edwin, 135, 139
State constitutions, 17–22,
    24–25, 30
State Councils of Defense, 189
State powers, 28, 30, 36–37, 43,
    68, 110, 142–43, 156–57, 207
States' rights theory, 43, 50, 54,
    96–97, 113, 122, 145. *See
    also* Federal-state relations;
    Interposition; Nullification;
    Secession
Stevens, John Paul, 246
Stevens, Thaddeus, 133, 137
Stone, Harland, 194
Story, Joseph, 74, 78, 80, 83, 84,
    86, 101, 113
Strict construction, 43
Student Non-Violent Coordinating
    Committee, 232
Subversive Activities Control
    Board, 214
Sumner, Charles, 128, 133
Supreme Court, 29–30, 38–39,
    44, 48, 50, 55, 76–77, 126,
    149, 194–95, 241–52
Supreme law clause, 30, 48–49,
    51, 65, 69, 101
Sutherland, George, 194, 202

Swayne, Noah, 143

Taft, William Howard, 182
Taft-Hartley Act, 212
Taney, Roger Brooke, 82, 83–89,
    109–10, 115–18, 123,
    126–27
Tariff of Abominations, 106–07
Tariffs, 23, 69–70, 82, 106–07,
    108, 111, 123, 179. *See also*
    Protective tariffs
Taxation, 19, 23, 24, 26, 28, 36,
    43, 51, 73, 88, 102, 155–56,
    159, 161, 166, 176, 196, 199,
    207, 237
Technology, 66, 85, 148–49
Tennessee, 131, 136, 153
Tennessee Valley Authority, 194,
    197, 204
Tenth Amendment, 43, 99
Tenure of Office Act, 135
Texas, 153, 215, 219
Thirteenth Amendment, 130–31,
    132, 153, 190
Thompson, Smith, 83
Townshend Duties, 14
Transportation Act (1920), 184,
    188
Treasury Department, 23, 40–41,
    95
Treaties, 24, 29, 37, 39, 44–45,
    46–47, 51, 186, 224–26
Treaty of Paris, 22, 51
Truman, Harry S., 205, 208,
    214
Tuck, William V., 251
Twelfth Amendment, 47
Twentieth Amendment, 176–77
Twenty-second Amendment, 224

United Nations, 225

VanDevanter, Willis, 194, 197,
    202
Vattel, Emmerich de, 12
Vermont, 99, 112
Vested rights, 78–79, 85–86, 89
Veto power, 19, 42, 61, 133, 135
Vietnamese War, 226, 233
Vinson, Fred M., 221–22
Virginia, 10, 13, 23, 24, 25, 31,
    48, 50–52, 56, 77, 96–97,
    131, 136
Virginia Bill of Rights, 21
Virginia Resolutions, 96–97
Virginia Resolves, 13
Voting requirements, 20, 27–28,
    109–10, 131, 134, 136,
    144–45, 151–54, 219,
    249–50

Wade-Davis Bill, 131–32
Wagner Act, 212
Waite, Morrison, 158, 163
War of 1812, 72, 97, 99–100
War Labor Relations Board,
    207
War powers, 29, 71, 125–31,
    186–89
War Powers Resolution, 241
War Production Board, 187,
    207
Warren, Earl, 211, 222–24
War Shipping Board, 186–87
Washington, Bushrod, 80
Washington, George, 28, 39,
    41–47, 49, 50, 95
Watergate, 240–41
Webster, Daniel, 81, 86

Whiskey Rebellion, 94–95
White, Edward D., 185
Wholesome Meat Act, 235
Wilmot, David, 113
Wilson, James, 93
Wilson, Woodrow, 177, 183, 186,
    203, 239
Wirt, William, 104–05
Wisconsin, 122

Women, 20, 143–44, 176, 181,
    184
Worcester, Samuel, 105–06
Workmen's Compensation Act, 182
World War I, 186–90
World War II, 207, 211

Yates, Richard, 122
Yazoo lands, 76